Indira Gandhi's India

Westview Special Studies on South and Southeast Asia

India, credited with the best institutionalized democracy of the Third World, changed in 1975, apparently overnight and at the decision of one individual, to a quasi-dictatorship. A transformation so remarkable prompted eight scholars of Indian politics to reexamine the sectors of the system they know well, seeking explanations. They reappraise the carry-over of colonial institutions and procedures, the distribution of power in the ruling party, business influence, the roles of the divided Communist parties, the position of the administrative corps and of the army, and unrest among the rural poor at its most volatile, in the state of Bihar. An introduction shows just what Mrs. Gandhi changed, the situation that triggered her action, and the justification she advances. A concluding chapter tests the facts of the Indian transformation against four major theories of political change in the developing world: projection into politics of personality conflicts of the leader, agrarian class conflict, social mobilization, and cultural assimilation and institutionalization.

Henry C. Hart is professor of political science and former chairman of the Department of South Asian Studies at the University of Wisconsin, Madison. He is the author of *New India's Rivers* (Orient Longmans, 1956), *Campus India* (Michigan State University Press, 1960), and *Administrative Aspects of River Valley Development* (Asia Publishing House, 1963) and is on the editorial board of *Asian Survey*. His research focuses on water resources policies and Indian administration.

Indira Gandhi's India
A Political System Reappraised

edited by Henry C. Hart

Westview Press
Boulder, Colorado

Copyright 1976 by Westview Press, Inc.

Published 1976 in the United States of America by
    Westview Press, Inc.
    1898 Flatiron Court
    Boulder, Colorado   80301
    Frederick A. Praeger, Publisher and Editorial Director

Library of Congress Cataloging in Publication Data

Main entry under title:

Indira Gandhi's India: A Political System Reappraised

    (Westview special studies on South and Southeast Asia)
    1. India—Politics and government—1947-   —Addresses, essays, lec-
tures. 2. Civil rights—India—Addresses, essays, lectures. 3. Gandhi, Indira
Nehru, 1917-   —Addresses, essays, lectures. I. Hart, Henry Cowles.
JQ215 1976.I53   320.9'54'05   76-5433
    ISBN 0-89158-042-5 (hardbound)
    ISBN 0-89158-109-X (paper)

Printed and bound in the United States of America.

Contents

Acknowledgments   ix

About the Authors   xi

1. Introduction   1
   Henry C. Hart

2. The Last Emergency of the Raj   37
   Robert Eric Frykenberg

3. The Civil Service and the Emergency   67
   Stanley J. Heginbotham

4. Mrs. Gandhi's Pyramid: The New Congress   93
   Stanley A. Kochanek

5. The Industrialists   125
   Howard L. Erdman

6. Communism Further Divided   153
   Bhabani Sen Gupta

7. India's Rural Poor: What Will Mobilize Them Politically?   181
   F. Tomasson Jannuzi

8. The Military   207
   Stephen P. Cohen

9. Indira Gandhi: Determined Not to Be Hurt   241
   Henry C. Hart

10. Explanations   275
    Henry C. Hart

Index   309

Acknowledgments

The authors who collaborated on this book were moved to do so by a sudden major turn in world politics, the particular direction of which was unanticipated. Each sensed that his long-accumulated findings about India could help explain the sudden change. But to make that application or reinterpretation in the fall and winter of 1975-76, each had to set aside other commitments, some academic, some personal. As editor, I want to acknowledge the authors' responsiveness to the challenge as well as their overwork.

Our writing could not have been directed toward a single purpose had we not been able at the early stages to meet, present our ideas to an interested audience, and question one another. The fourth Wisconsin Conference on South Asia provided the occasion. Professor Robert Kidder, a sociologist at Temple University, also contributed to our discussions his knowledge of the Indian legal profession. We thank him.

The decision that this was a scholarly venture worth supporting was made by Professor Manindra K. Verma, chairman of the department of South Asian Studies and director of the language and area center at the University of Wisconsin. I feel the more grateful for his confident support of the work because he did not inquire into its substantive conclusions; in fact, he did not know them until they had been set in type.

Editing this book would have been quite impossible without the varied facilities of a well-established language and area center. Most manifest was my dependence on a library collection containing a full range of newspapers delivered by air. I hope the foresight of many pioneers in Congress and the executive branch, in foundations, and in university administrations, who two decades ago established such centers in American universities and have maintained them since, will gather further vindication from this kind of outcome.

About the Authors

STEPHEN P. COHEN, of the political science faculty at the University of Illinois, Urbana, is the author of *The Indian Army* (California, 1971) and of a number of articles on defense and security matters in South Asia and U.S. policy in the region.

HOWARD L. ERDMAN, government professor at Dartmouth, has published *Swatantra Party and Indian Conservatism* (Cambridge, 1967), *Political Attitudes of Indian Industry: A Case Study of the Baroda Business Elite* (Athlone, and Oxford University Press, 1971), and *Politics and Economic Development in India* (Delhi, 1973). His most recent visit to India was in 1976.

ROBERT ERIC FRYKENBERG, professor of history and former chairman of South Asian Studies at the University of Wisconsin, Madison, is editor of *Land Control and Social Structure in Indian History* (University of Wisconsin Press, 1969), author of *Guntur District, 1837-1848: A History of Local Influence and Central Authority in South India* (Clarendon Press, 1965), and of two forthcoming books. He conducted a faculty-training seminar on South Asian history in Madison during the summer of 1976.

STANLEY J. HEGINBOTHAM is assistant chief of the Foreign Policy and National Defense Division of the Congressional

Research Service in the Library of Congress. He previously taught comparative politics for five years at Columbia University. His book, *Cultures in Conflict: The Four Faces of Indian Bureaucracy* (Columbia, 1975), draws on four years of teaching and research experience in India, including eighteen months of intensive field work in Tamil Nadu development administration.

F. TOMASSON JANNUZI is director, Center for Asian Studies, and member of the faculty, Department of Economics, at the University of Texas at Austin. He is author of *Agrarian Crisis in India: The Case of Bihar* (University of Texas Press, 1974), the product of extensive field research in India in the period 1956-1972. His field of specialization is the political economy of rural development.

STANLEY A. KOCHANEK is a professor of political science at the Pennsylvania State University. He is the author of *The Congress Party* (Princeton, 1971), *Business and Politics in India* (University of California Press, 1974), and numerous journal articles.

BHABANI SEN GUPTA, now returned to India after an appointment at the Research Institute on International Change, Columbia University, had a successful career as a Bengali novelist and journalist before turning to the analysis of international politics and communism in South Asia. In 1972 he published *Communism in Indian Politics.* Earlier books include *The Fulcrum of Asia: Relations among China, India, Pakistan and the USSR* and *The Malacca Straits and the Indian Ocean: Strategic Aspects of an Emerging International Problem.*

1

Introduction
Henry C. Hart

THE DILEMMA

At 3:45 on the afternoon of June 24, 1975, the Supreme Court of India issued its order: an earlier judgment finding Prime Minister Indira Gandhi guilty of corrupt election practices remained in effect. Before dawn on June 26, police parties under Mrs. Gandhi's orders awakened her chief political opponents and locked them away. Within those thirty-six hours, India changed from quasi-democracy to quasi-dictatorship. The democracy had been incomplete in that the government retained a repressive authority, dating from the colonial period, and more basically, in that some hundreds of millions of people had in twenty-eight years acquired the habits of voting, but not yet the sharp-edged convictions of liberty. The dictatorship was incomplete because Mrs. Gandhi continued to govern within the forms of legality, gingerly tested in the courts, and opposition representatives could engage her in censored debate.

Mrs. Gandhi had not staged a coup. She had simply changed usages, operating rules, completely. One day the prime minister was governed by law binding all citizens great and small; next morning she had the power to tailor laws at will, and she used that power to wipe out her own offense. One day opposition politicians threatened her legitimacy by demonstrations in Parliament and in the streets; next morning they were in jail.

1

One day the newspapers featured verbal attacks on her, along with her reponses; next morning's papers, if they appeared at all, carried the prime minister's answers to blank columns.

Three hours after the arrests, but still early in the morning, Mrs. Gandhi met with her cabinet. At 7:00 a.m. the president proclaimed a formal state of emergency, following constitutional procedure. Many subsequent ordinances, laws, and constitutional amendments have followed. What changes these entailed, and what results they achieved, are considered in this chapter. At its close, in counterposition, are Indira Gandhi's interpretations of the reasons for what she did and the rather different perspective of the authors of this book.

In chapters 2 through 8 the authors, each from his knowledge of a phase of Indian politics, respond to the question that intrigues us all: How could the transformation of the operating rules of an elaborate political system come to be an option exercisable at the will of a single individual, a prime minister? In answering, each author will reappraise the segment of politics he deals with, pointing out mutations, perhaps unnoticed, that may have occurred before June 26, 1975, and, for such elements of the political system as are durable, indicating their roles in the immediate future of the new order.

The business of chapter 10, the concluding chapter, is to reassemble from these segmental reappraisals a more general explanation of what has happened in India. What processes at work here are common to partly new and largely vulnerable political systems? That these processes conform strictly to general laws of socio-political transformation only classical Marxists and some ambitious contemporary model builders profess. But in our case there is an additional limit upon predictability. What is happening in India now is in significant part the projection of the character of a single human being.

We can gain initial clues to understanding these issues by observing the triggering event, the initial Supreme Court order of June 24.

The Court Decisions

Since Mrs. Gandhi's appeal arrived during the court's vacation, the one judge on duty, Justice V. R. Krishna Iyer, made the interim decision. Justice Krishna Iyer had been appointed by Mrs. Gandhi two years before, amid some criticism that he was ideologically biased in her direction.[1] There is not the slightest evidence that he intended to confront the prime minister with a dilemma. On the contrary, a close reading of his interim decision sustains his claim to have interpreted the election law and the judicial precedents "walled-off" from the "extralegal tumults."[2] The law and the precedents before him were amazingly clear.

Mrs. Gandhi was appealing her conviction announced only twelve days earlier, for violating the corrupt practices law in her 1971 parliamentary campaign.[3] Certainly the violations were minor. Whether they were merely technical or also moral is less clear. Since she defeated her opponent, Socialist Raj Narain,[4] by over 100,000 votes, it is not likely that her offenses were responsible for Narain's loss. The violations involved using an officer of the government (Mrs. Gandhi's long-time aid, then an administrative asistant, Yashpal Kapoor) to make campaign arrangements, and using other state officers to put up speaker's stands in her constituency, Rae Bareli, and supply electricity to her amplifying equipment. Use of a government officer for the "furtherance" of a candidate's election is, under the strict Indian law, a "corrupt practice."[5] The facts and the law were exhaustively sifted (four years is a long trial, even by Indian standards); on June 12 the trial court judge in Allahabad found Mrs. Gandhi guilty on these two counts.

European and American commentators considered the offenses to be peccadilloes.[6] Indeed, Justice Krishna Iyer remarked in his June 24 decision that Mrs. Gandhi had not been convicted of "any of the graver electoral vices." But we should also note that when a parliamentary committee, reviewing the election law after the 1971 election, proposed to downgrade some "corrupt" practices to the category of merely "illegal," the violation of which Mrs. Gandhi was convicted, using government officers in a campaign, was not among them.[7] With some historical perspective, one can discern here a view of elections as fragile innovations vulnerable to the slightest pressure of a much older administrative establishment.

The arguable morality of what Mrs. Gandhi did was not before the trial court. Once the Allahabad judge found her guilty, the law left him no discretion. He had to void her election and disqualify her from further electoral contests for six years.[8] This harsh penalty would thus cost her the prime ministership— that office can only be occupied by a member of Parliament unless she could get the judgment reversed on appeal.

The trial judge had straightaway given Mrs. Gandhi twenty days to take an appeal to the Supreme Court. At that point, she probably could have handed over the prime ministership to a senior colleague from her cabinet and had very good prospects of reclaiming it after the next parliamentary election, due in eight months.[9] Had she temporarily stepped down, she could have drawn about herself the mantle of selfless morality, at least as potent politically in India as elsewhere. (Earlier, a member of her own cabinet had resigned office pending appeal to the Supreme Court of an election conviction analogous to her own. According to a leading Delhi paper, "Mrs. Gandhi herself persuaded him to resign, though he wished to await the verdict.")[10] If the Supreme Court then decided in her favor, she could have claimed the prime ministership back at once, a claim hard to deny since she would not have lost control of the party. Even after losing in the Supreme Court, there would have been two ways open for her to contest the 1976 elections. She could ask Parliament to pass a retroactive law expunging her offense, or the election commissioner could exercise his statutory authority to remove her disqualification for a future race, as he made clear on several occasions.[11] Certainly, were she to run in 1976, having sacrificed office for a few months on high moral grounds and stolen the opposition's only effective charge—that she was clinging to an office corruptly gained—her popular triumph was assured.

The Legislative Option

By June 24 her options had remarkably narrowed and had hardened, clearly, into two horns of a dilemma. She could not resign now without appearing to have been driven from office; and as prime minister while the Supreme Court heard her appeal, she would need either to convene Parliament and seek retroactive elimination of her offense before the court acted (the legislative option), or risk appearing as a candidate after having actually been removed from office for violation of electoral law (the popular judgment option). Justice Krishna Iyer's decision on June 24 made each of these alternatives perilous for her.

Let us consider the legislative option as it must have appeared to her on June 24. Curiously to non-Indian readers, there was little doubt of the constitutionality of legislation retroactively removing an electoral offense. The Supreme Court had recently validated just such a retroactive law passed by a state legislature.[12] In November 1975 it would again uphold this kind of legislative relief, at it was enacted for Mrs. Gandhi by her emergency Parliament. Justice Krishna Iyer himself, in his order of June 24, went far out of his way to call Parliament's attention to this option: "Draconian laws do not cease to be law in court but must alert a wakeful and quick-acting legislature." The hazard lay, rather, in the likelihood that the opposition parties could stall parliamentary action.

Mrs. Gandhi knew well from experiences earlier during her prime ministership that a band of only 50 to 100 obstructionists could balk parliamentary action for weeks, given three conditions.[13] The opposition must be united and determined; its case must win some resonating approval outside parliament; and it must therefore threaten to divide the Congress party's majority in Parliament. In the fortnight ending June 24, all these conditions seemed to materialize.

Some drawing together of the tiny opposition parties was to be expected before a general election. What convinced their leaders that, united, they had a chance to make large gains was the special state election in Gujarat. Its results, a defeat for Mrs. Gandhi, were announced the very day of her Allahabad conviction. Opposing Mrs. Gandhi's Congress party in that election was the Janata (People's) Front, led by her ranking opponent, Morarji Desai. In fact, Mrs. Gandhi was pressured into holding the election only by Desai's well-publicized fast in March 1975. Chief elements in the front were the Old Congress (the residue from Mrs. Gandhi's capture of the major fraction of the party in 1969), the Jan Sangh (with a Hindu appeal), the Bharatiya Lok Dal (a farmer-based regional coalition), and the Socialist party. The front was able to agree on a common strategy and on one candidate in almost every constituency, though not on a single campaign symbol. Mrs. Gandhi accepted the challenge. She made ninety speeches across the state during the campaign. Visiting newspaper reporters, indeed, gave the Congress party a slight edge in the contest, which had come to turn so crucially upon Gandhi's personal standing with the voters.[14] In the previous general elections, 1971 and 1972, a similar situation had brought her an overwhelming victory. It did not now. The

Congress party, with 140 seats in the state after the 1972 election, this time won only 75. The Janata Front won 86, short of a majority, but enabling it to form a government.[15]

The Gujarat results did not reflect a nationwide swing of voter preferences against Mrs. Gandhi. In fact, the Congress party had first lost, but then more recently won, scattered by-elections in other states.[16]. But the Janata Front's victory in Gujarat did reinforce the tendency of the four main allies to join forces nationally.[17] Moreover, the June 12 court verdict against Mrs. Gandhi gave them a clearly understandable, if highly exaggerated, charge of corruption at the top to take to the people. As they stepped up their propaganda against a "disqualified" prime minister, they were joined by the Akali Dal (a Sikh party) in Punjab. The Dravida Munnetra Kazhagam (DMK), which was in power in Tamil Nadu, teetered toward the alliance (its leader had said it "would have been a good precedent" if "Mrs. Gandhi stepped down on her own."[18] The Communist Party (Marxist) (known as the CPM) agreed to consult, with a view to parallel action, though it refused to join so ideologically heterogeneous a front.[19]

Although newly provided with unity and hope, the opposition had only forty-nine votes in the Lok Sabha (the lower house of Parliament), 10 percent of the total. Justice Krishna Iyer's preliminary order gave them a symbolic weapon exactly suited to their tactics. Mrs. Gandhi's lawyers had urged the justice to suspend outright the verdict against her, lest her political career be "irreparably damaged,"[20] but he did not comply. He did go as far as he could, given the unbroken precedents denying members their parliamentary functions pending appeals. He permitted Mrs. Gandhi to take part in debate, to hold and substantially excercise her prime ministership. But he could not absolutely disregard the trial courts' verdict until it had been disposed of by the full court. So he barred Mrs. Gandhi from voting or drawing her legislator's salary pending her appeal. Thus, every vote in Parliament would proclaim her stigma. And any legislation to remove her offense from the statute books could be dramatized as self-serving.[21]

The June 24 order promptly widened the tiny crack that had opened in Mrs. Gandhi's own party. When she first made it obvious that she intended to remain in office while pressing her judicial appeal, she had quickly drawn the support of almost all of her party members, M.P.s as well as state-level leaders.[22]

Mohan Dharia, of outspoken socialist convictions, was the first Congress dissident; in March 1975 his plea that Mrs. Gandhi engage in open talks with the opposition had cost him his ministership. In May, Mr. Ram Dhan, who differed publicly from Mrs. Gandhi's pro-CPI (Communist Party of India) strategy, won election as secretary of the Congress party. These two, plus three others, were conspicuously absent from the June 18 meeting of Congress M.P.s, who unanimously asked Mrs. Gandhi to continue in office.[23] The number of dissidents swelled to twenty or thirty (press estimates differed) when they met to plan strategy following the June 24 court order.[24] This was not sufficient defection to threaten Indira Gandhi's control of her party. What was dangerous to her was the prospect of further growth of the dissident group should a battle in Parliament over amending the election law coincide with a demonstration in the country against corruption in office. In such a political context, other Congress M.P.s might hesitate to enter a reelection campaign tagged as complaisant toward corruption at the very top.

The Popular Judgment Option

A monsoon session of Parliament thus held grave risks for Mrs. Gandhi. Would she not be better off leaving the legislature in recess through the allowable six-month period? However, this popular appeal option, too, was burdened by the conditions contained in Justice Krishna Iyer's decision. For the allied opposition parties could now go to the country with an additional charge against her, saying that she was afraid to face Parliament in its normal monsoon session because of the stigma of her corrupt election. The opposition parties had begun on June 21 laying their plans for a nationwide agitation. But upon learning of the June 24 Supreme Court order, they escalated their strategy. Now they would seek to bring government to a halt in major centers across the country until Indira Gandhi was forced to step down. At a large mass meeting in Delhi on the night of June 25, two new developments were announced. The opposition agitation would begin with a *satyagraha*—a mass sit-in around the residences of top officials, including Mrs. Gandhi's—on June 29. And Jayaprakash Narayan would head the agitation.[25]

Whether Mrs. Gandhi had objective cause to regard a nationwide agitation against her continuance in office as a serious threat to her regime we can best assess by appraising the fifteen-month-old movement against her in Bihar.[26]

The Bihar Agitation. Though known as "J.P." movement, the Bihar agitation had been in progress for a month before Jayaprakash Narayan took its leadership. On March 18, 1974, students had marched to the state assembly building, intending to occupy it to prevent the opening of the session until their demands were answered. Like students everywhere, they were powerfully stimulated by outside models. The success of a directly analogous agitation in Gujarat—on March 16 it had brought down the state government—steeled their resolve. Their key issues were unemployment, high prices—reflected painfully in their dormitory meal charges—and corruption. Forming a joint-action committee of representatives from sixty-seven colleges across the state, they had remarkably united the student wings of the Hinduist Jan Sangh party, the radical Socialists (SSP), and the altruistic Sarvodaya movement. The familiar spiral of an unresponsive state chief minister, impatient demonstrators, and overreacting police—all in an atmosphere of crowd tension—produced violence. News of that violence triggered uncontrolled rioting in college towns across that state, and police firing killed twenty-seven people in a week.[27]

The most telling consequence of the students' agitation was to bring Jayaprakash Narayan into action. He accepted their request that he head their movement, on condition that it be broadened and they accept his final say on strategy. Narayan's reentry into active opposition politics after twenty years of withdrawal into Gandhian social work in Bihar villages was a significant change in the all-India political scene. He had been the romantic underground hero of the 1942 Quit India movement, blowing up railway lines while Gandhi and the Congress party elders were immobilized in jail.[28] Recognizing his nerve and his national reputation, Jawaharlal Nehru had held much-publicized conversations with him in 1952-53 about his rejoining the Congress party with his Socialist party followers. Narayan's refusal was widely interpreted as a renunciation of succession to the prime ministership in favor of the pinciples of socialism, which he had insisted the Congress party adopt as a condition of his reentry. His public persona also included a quality Hindi-speakers call *tyag*—renunciation of ambition. In 1955 he had quit the presidency of the Socialist party, less a forlorn hope then than now, to give himself primarily to Vinoba

Bhave's Bhoodan movement, and episodically to "noble causes." He had stood almost alone in the defense of Muslims against Hindu violence.[29] In old age—he was seventy-two in 1974—with chronic kidney disease and other physical ailments, he remained as fearless as in 1942.

Jayaprakash's charismatic appeal carried its price. In the end he refused to harness his leadership to any political party through which his mass following might have been institutionalized. And with all his gifts for rallying great numbers of people to broad public purposes, even difficult ones, he would not persevere to translate purposes into governmental programs capable of legislation and implementation.

A key criterion of the political potential of agitation is its cumulative capability. Student uprisings are notoriously ephemeral; anti-government uprisings in agrarian countries are more so. The Bihar agitation seems to fall midway between the one-time outbreaks that have been characteristic in the past and the cumulative movement that might be necessary to displace a national government.[30] There were six peaks of antigovernment action in Bihar between March and November 1974, at an average interval of six weeks.[31] Further outbreaks occurred in 1975. Through these dramatic episodes, what cumulated was the tiny organization of activists, mostly students and Bhoodan workers; the image of J.P. as leader; and press sensitivity. The issue of governmental corruption may also have grown more salient. But the early sense that the agitation might topple the government, as in Gujarat, that it was spreading steadily from the center to periphery, and that it represented an alternative to the present government—these perceptions did not build. They had, by the end of 1974, dissappeared. The general impression conveyed in the press in 1975 was that the Bihar agitation was a spent force.[32]

The movement failed primarily because it did not enlist the villagers who make up 90 percent of Bihar's population and provide the Congress party's electoral resource, and whose alienation from the party could have brought the government down. It is not hard to understand the lack of rural support. Unemployment, high prices, and state government corruption are urban issues. Villagers are concerned with land, debts, and water supplies. Narayan did have a solution for village problems: the creation of a hierarchy of rural self-governing institutions; but this was not very different from the existing *panchayati raj* institutions, save that Narayan's workers would act as midwives to the establishment of the new institutions. Without directly engaging and harnessing to local government the deepening cleavage in many villages between landed surplus-producing families at the top and marginal owners, insecure *bataidars* ("sharecroppers"), and laborers on the bottom, it would take an army of ingenious and authoritative field workers to nurse into being a government duly representing the village have-nots. The dedicated and quickly trained students could not fill that role, nor could the consensus-oriented Bhoodan workers.[33] There were dramatic cases of absentee landlords of great estates being pressured by "squat-ins" of laborers rejecting their traditional peonage. There were model villages under *Janata Sarkar* ("people's government"). But these were, in the words of a very sympathetic account, "either embryonic or just conceptual."[34]

That does not mean that the movement lacked durable consequences. It had its impact, first, on the opposition political parties, drawing them into an unaccustomed concert of strategy and leadership. The radical SSP, the conservative Old Congress, the Hinduist Jan Sangh, and the regional coalition Bharatiya Lok Dal (BLD) maintained a working alliance in support of the movement. The strong CPM of neighboring West Bengal (it has almost no organization in Bihar) agreed to ad hoc collaboration. The alliance could be projected onto the stage of national agitation in June 1975; opposition politics was no longer a zero-sum game of enticing away another party's following.

But Narayan's leadership, while projecting an appeal beyond party loyalties, also disrupted party organizations in his own state. He saw no need to build a vigorous national leadership structure that could promise alternative government in Delhi, as Morarji Desai's leadership promised it in Gujarat. In November 1974 he flatly rejected the bid of the assembled leaders of the four principal supporting opposition parties to form and head a national party ready to contest the expected national election. Instead he insisted that

> the struggle is not for the capture of power . . . for replacing the Congress government with the opposition, but for the purification of government and politics, including those of the opposition.[35]

Narayan thus not merely renounced a role only he could fill, but also demonstrated once again that he cared little for institutionalized power. Soon after he had taken direction of the movement in Bihar and escalated its demands to include the dissolution of the state legislature along with the cabinet, he called on all legislators of supporting parties to manifest their commitment to principle by resigning their seats. Ultimately forty-two did, out of a total of eighty-eight in the cooperating parties.[36] The cost was disruption of the three strongest supporting parties. The Jan Sangh and Old Congress expelled their members who did not comply. The SSP, which offered the most appropriate party to channel Narayan's potential rural following into legislative action, withdrew from the movement, charging that his call for resignation sabotaged the common effort.

The Bihar agitation also left its mark on the Congress party. Successive protest marches were met with increasingly more ruthless police action. The Central Reserve Police and the Border Security Force took charge. They succeeded fairly completely in blocking and scattering the last mass march upon government headquarters in Bihar on November 5, 1974, but the price was to spread an image of the Congress government as a fairly distant and high-handed power. The newspaper picture of venerable Jayaprakash Narayan felled, being shielded from police *lathis* by the arms and heads of his companions, was not one favorable to the popularity of the governing Congress.

Lest its counterstrategy be solely one of repression, the Congress party set about mobilizing mass demonstrations in support of the elected government. But though the issue would seem to be a clear one, and though the opposition had been unable, as we observed, to enlist the villagers, the party discovered itself powerless to rally an impressive showing. To enlist thousands of people to march on behalf of the government in power it had to turn to its junior ally, the Communist Party of India. The CPI fielded a demonstration of perhaps 100,000 in Patna on June 3, championing the elected legislature, but mixing in slogans denouncing hoarding and black marketeers.[37] To counter a mass agitation like that in Bihar Mrs. Gandhi had no option: the CPI's members were the only disciplined party activists available to her. Her own party's field men were contented office holders, often mistrusted by those hungry enough to march.

The new threat of agitation. The meaning of this analysis for Mrs. Gandhi's calculations in June 1975 is clear. Jayaprakash Narayan had shown he could not form an alternative government. His movement could not find programs or policies any more likely to deliver results than those of the tried and disappointing Congress government. When his agitation challenged an elected legislature, therefore, the legislature retained its superior legitimacy. But Mrs. Gandhi, formally convicted of corruption, not convening the elected legislature while clinging to office: this was a target to maximize J.P.'s strengths and obscure his crucial failings. He could direct a national campaign strictly *against* something. That something was the supreme incumbent power. And, quite contrary to the situation in an election campaign, no issues of policy need divide the divergent supporting parties until after the government had been toppled.

There was one more threat to Mrs. Gandhi's power as a result of the Bihar agitation. Her dismissal of a fairly well-known minister, Mohan Dharia, in March had been occasioned by his advocacy of a dialogue with Narayan.[38] Would a nationwide struggle multiply such defections from her own party?

PREEMPTIVE STRIKE

Mrs. Gandhi's decision, confronting a seemingly hopeless dilemma, took a characteristic form. She cut the Gordian knot, launching a preemptive strike against the threat to her authority.

Jail

It is not possible to report with certainty the number of opposition politicians picked up by the police before dawn on June 26: the official press statement said 676.[39] Correspondents of foreign newspapers reported higher figures, but they cannot have had hard data.[40] The timing of some of the arrests is significant. Since they occurred before the president's proclamation of an emergency state, which would fully legalize them, the opposition, which might have been heard against the proclamation at the moment it was issued, was thus silenced. It is also clear, from a breakdown of arrests by states,[41] that enough arrests were made in the volatile states to paralyze the leadership of the planned agitation.

By arresting the two national leaders of the agitation, Mrs. Gandhi also removed from political life two implacable

opponents.[42] Morarji Desai, senior among the well-known sur-
viving Gandhians, had been her competitor for the prime ministership in 1966. She beat him then, and again in 1969 when
she maneuvered him onto the unpopular side of the bank nationalization issue she raised, which split the party. But in 1976
his hunger strike had forced her to proceed with the Gujarat
state election, which his coalition then won. J. P. Narayan, midway in age between Mrs. Gandhi and her father, had been
Nehru's protege in the left wing of the Gandhian Congress party. During those years he addressed Nehru as *Bhai*, "brother";
the wives of the two men were even closer comrades.[43] But after Narayan escalated his cause in the Bihar agitation to include
Mrs. Gandhi's ouster, deep personal bitterness reinforced political antagonism.[44]

Other well-known political leaders arrested included the leading figures of the parties forming the core of the activist opposition: Jan Sangh, Old Congress, BLD, and SSP. Top leaders of
two supporting parties, the CPM and the DMK, were not arrested. So far, the list warrants the justification that the arrests
were a preemptive strike against the impending agitation. But
there is a significant addition. Mrs. Gandhi also arrested a few
among the tiny band of dissidents within her own party in Parliament, some of those who had been absent when she was
being congratulated for continuing in office.[45] Preemption of
extraconstitutional agitation could hardly have been the motivation for these arrests.

Once arrested, detainees disappeared completely from public
notice. Since no trials were scheduled there was no forum in
which to argue the justification for the arrests. Since places of
detention were kept secret, there could be no symbol of repression—no Bastille, no Yeravda. Even the list of the jailed was hidden, and the total number included among the number of black
marketeers and evaders of income tax. The unknown limits of
detention, of course, spread wider the circle of fear.

President as Tool

The constitution placed the emergency powers, which as we
shall see are extraordinarily sweeping, into the hands of the
president, who the constitution contemplated would be advised
by the cabinet, led, of course, by the prime minister.[46] The

logic of accountability to Parliament argues that the president take that advice on political matters. But he is sworn to uphold the constitution, and is subject to impeachment if he does not.[47] During the fortnight between Mrs. Gandhi's original conviction and her takeover, the opposition M.P.s showed some hope that the president might act independently of her.[48] Why that was a forlorn hope Stanley Kochanek will explain in Chapter 4. President Fakhruddin Ali Ahmed did not even shorten his visit to Kashmir during the crisis.

Once the emergency was in effect the president could legislate by signing ordinances. This became the regular process for making national policy from June 26, 1975. The constitution also provides, however, that presidential ordinances lapse, once Parliament has reconvened, unless Parliament approves them.[49] Mrs. Gandhi's will could, therefore, have been checked by Parliament. It was not.

Compliant Parliament

The monsoon session of Parliament, in doubt when the Supreme Court delivered its preliminary order, was reconvened on July 21. In forty-eight hours both houses had approved emergency rule. The vote in the Rajya Sabha (the upper house) was 136 to 33; in the Lok Sabha 336 to 59. The total is well short of the membership in both cases, but the ratios are close to the proportions of Congress party plus CPI members relative to opposition M.P.s. The question is, therefore, why Parliament disposed of so profound an alteration of the rules of the political game as though it were a party matter. Three reasons are plausible. Fear is the first. Despite the censorship, correspondents were able to comment that seven well-known M.P.s from the opposition coalition were missing from the Rajya Sabha.[50] One can deduce that one or two of Mrs. Gandhi's opponents in her own party, too, were in jail.[51] The British Parliament, of course, had fought the battle against intimidation of its members by arrest some centuries earlier, specifically against James I.[52] But by the time the Lok Sabha's committee on privileges had need to search British precedents, those had been narrowed and did not protect against criminal arrests or preventive detention.[53] Even so, the preventive detention of a single M.P. in 1952, upon quite plausible grounds that he was inciting Hindu-Muslim passions, stirred the Lok Sabha to an enquiry, and a strong minority of the privileges committee held that the arrest had been a breach of privilege.[54] An enquiry, of course, requires majority assent. Mrs. Gandhi showed her determination not to permit Parliament to question her emergency decisions by introducing a resolution suspending the rules, and with them all opportunities to question ministers or introduce nonofficial resolutions. Behind the success of this tactic, however, lay her ability and determination to discipline her own party. Stanley Kochanek explains in his chapter how she made the party her instrument.

There was another reason Parliament did not resist. By imposing prior press censorship, Mrs. Gandhi had cut the channel through which the minority opposition in Parliament could project an issue to the attentive public outside the house. For example, on July 23, when Parliament had passed the resolution approving the proclamation of an emergency, the entire opposition, save for the CPI and some splinter parties, walked out. Socialist N. G. Goray declared that participation had no more meaning since the majority had deprived the legislative body of the right to question ministers and had completely halted radio and newspaper reporting of the opposition's criticisms of the government. But there was no word of Goray's speech, or of the opposition walkout, in Indian newspapers next day. The sharp-eyed reader may have noticed that the count of votes against government measures has dropped to zero in the upper house and one in the lower, but he had to guess at the reason.[55]

Multiple Exoneration

After the emergency had been proclaimed, Mrs. Gandhi's lawyers pursued her appeal in the Supreme Court. Simultaneously, she sought exoneration in the Parliament. First, the election law itself was amended to wipe out the offenses of which she had been convicted, and some others of which she had been cleared by the trial court. The amended law took effect retroactively—this is not so uncommon to Indian legislation as it would be to American. Further, in what would seem to be overkill, the amendment provided that any person already disqualified for an electoral violation could petition the president for removal of that disqualification.

That was not enough. The constitution was simultaneously amended (the Thirty-ninth Amendment, approved August 10) to authorize Parliament to create a new electoral authority to deal exclusively with the election of the president, vice-president, prime minister, and speaker of the Lok Sabha, to bar challenges to the constitutionality of this new authority in any court, and to void all present proceedings under exitsing law against the election of the four named officers. Thus Mrs. Gandhi obtained from her tamed Parliament not only the retroactive removal of her offense, but the retroactive invalidation of her trial for it.[56]

The Supreme Court, however, would not be so readily pre-empted, and it carried through the hearing on her appeal to its conclusion. Unanimously, it upheld the constitutionality of the electoral law amendment that wiped out her offense, thus granting her appeal. But as to the attempt of the Thirty-ninth Amendment to wipe out the constitutional basis for the pending legal action against her, a majority found that invalid as a derogation of the rule of law.[57]

In any event, Mrs. Gandhi had been vindicated. She needed no emergency rule to enjoy the full authority of a duly elected M.P., one who was the choice of her majority party to lead the government.

THE NEW RULES

Looking back six months later, an opposition M.P. described his feelings on the morning of June 26 as "shock and surprise—the feeling you would have if your 6-year-old son suddenly slapped you in the face. . . . But nobody is shocked any more. We have all learned what the new rules are, and adjusted our own behavior accordingly."[58] The rules by which the political game had been played in India for twenty-eight years had indeed been changed. What were the new ones?

The Dual Constitution

Aside from three or four hours of prematurity, Mrs. Gandhi's preemptive strike was, strange as it may appear, consonant with the words of the Indian constitution. So are the continuing repressive rules. Acting upon the cabinet's advice, the president is empowered by Article 352 of the constitution to proclaim a state of emergency when the nation's security is threatened by war or "internal disturbance."[59] Under such a proclamation, he may suspend the basic civil rights of individuals and their resort to the courts to enforce those rights.[60] Further, while such a proclamation is in effect, officers of state governments are subject to national government orders;[61] Mrs. Gandhi has all police forces in the country at her disposal. There was nothing inadvertent about this gaping hole in the constitutional checks upon executive power. The constituent assembly quite deliberately continued in independent India these prerogatives of colonial rule.[62] Even more than their American counterparts in 1787, the authors of the Indian constitution worked in an atmosphere of genuine threat to public order from unruly masses: the savagery of partition, the war over Kashmir, the Communist seizure of villages in Telengana, the assassination of Mahatma Gandhi, all seemed to warrant the carry-over of repressive powers.[63] Whether there was warrant to exercise these powers in 1975 is, of course, a different question.

Some of the authors of the constitution knew the risks they were imposing on democracy when they wrote in the emergency provisions. In effect, they were creating two sets of government powers. One, limited, would subject the government to the people. The other, unrestricted, put the government in control of the people, based on the assumption that the people could not always be trusted. But the authors included in the constitution a new safeguard by which the second set of powers would be checked by the first. Emergency powers lapse in two months unless they are approved by Parliament.[64] Mrs. Gandhi, however, had by her preemptive strike, turned that dependency around: several prominent members of Parliament were in jail under the second set of powers when Parliament convened in July 1975 to exercise the first set.

One other possible restraint of the democratic portion of the constitution on the imperial portion remained. Indeed, it was given institutional stature by the creation of an independent Supreme Court. That was the process of judicial review.

Prisons and Courts

What is new in India is not the jailing of people without trial. It is the nationwide jailing of people whose opposition to the regime was within the bounds of the democratic constitution, and it is the attempt to deprive those detained from any test at all of the legality of their imprisonment.

Under Mrs. Gandhi's prime ministership India had, well before 1975, taken on some of the attributes of a police state. Central police forces had grown rapidly to a combined strength of about 800,000 men, about three-quarters are large as the army.[65] Amnesty International estimated in September 1974 that Indian jails held between 15,000 and 20,000 persons not accused of specific criminal acts.[66] Most of these were in West Bengal, where in 1971 a tough Congress government demonstrated the efficacy of rooting out Communist followers in the villages by wholesale jailings.

Arrests of persons not charged with committing criminal acts were legal in India from British times. Like emergency rule, preventive detention was specifically considered and authorized in the 1950 constitution, subject only to minimal restrictions.[67] Prior to June 1975, Mrs. Gandhi had two legal instruments for preventive detention. One was the Maintenance of Internal Security Act (M.I.S.A.), the other the Defense of India Act and the rules implementing it (D.I.R.). Both were enacted during the war with Pakistan over Bangladesh. Both had been retained and used against political opponents, but only in strife-torn states or border areas.[68]

We have no reliable current estimates of the number of persons jailed without trial since Mrs. Gandhi imposed the emergency, but the change in type of arrest is obvious. She had placed behind bars the officers of the majority party governing Tamil Nadu, and many of its elected legislators, state and national, as well.[69] She has jailed the national leadership of the political parties that threatened her directly. Most recently she arrested a former minister of her own cabinet, Mohan Dharia, in the midst of his speaking tour on civil liberties.[70] The atmosphere for those inclined to criticize their national or state government is, quite simply fear.

Both M.I.S.A. and the D.I.R. contained modest safeguards against mistaken or personally motivated arrests and those out of line with top government policies. Moreover, these safeguards had been adjudicated and upheld in the courts. The most important was the mandatory review of each preventive detention by partly independent review panels.[71] Up to June 1975 prisoners could be freed by these panels. The president, by ordinance of October 17, 1975, amended M.I.S.A. to make the ground for imprisonment under the act a government secret, not available to the detainee or anyone else.[72] This eliminated the victim's basis for arguing his case before the review panel; it also left him little on which to base a court case.

Nonetheless, a strange, shifting struggle goes on between Mrs. Gandhi, her government lawyers and legislative apparatus, and the Indian courts. On the one hand, Mrs. Gandhi has been able to legislate at will either through presidential ordinance or her subservient Parliament. Since she has the requisite two-thirds of both houses of Parliament and can count on ratification by at least half the state legislatures, she can also amend the constitution as she desires. With these resources, M.I.S.A. was quickly amended to deny detainees the right to appeal to the courts.[73] The constitution was amended (the Thirty-ninth Amendment) to bar the charge in the courts that M.I.S.A. violated civil rights provisions of the constitution.[74] Finally, in January 1976, using his emergency power, the president issued an order suspending the rights of all persons to petition the courts for the enforcement of the basic individual rights in the constitution: free speech, freedom of assembly, freedom to form associations or unions, freedom to move to any part of the country, the right to hold property, and the right to enter a profession, occupation, or business.[75]

Still, a few landmark cases are being heard by the courts. A Delhi high court judge declared illegal the imprisonment of the prominent journalist Kuldip Nayar on the reasoning that personal liberty was a right antedating the constitution, and enforceable in the courts by writ of habeus corpus, despite the emergency.[76]

In January 1976 the struggle went on.[126] The position of Mrs. Gandhi's government was delineated before the Supreme Court, which had taken for review the fundamental question of the existence of justiciable civil rights independent of government authority, in the following exchange:

> *Mr. Justice Chandrachud*: Suppose a man has nothing to do with politics and he goes morning and evening to a temple but he is detained on some false information. How can he get his right to personal liberty enforced under the rule of law?
>
> *Mr. Raman* (Additional Solicitor General): He has no right to know the grounds or any information or material regarding his detention. His rights are suspended with the suspension of Articles 21 and 22.[77]

Guided Press

After she had consolidated her grip on all national power, Indira Gandhi gave the reconvened Rajya Sabha a pithy justification of her censorship of the press. In a battle, she said, the enemy's supply line is cut off. This is what censorship had done.[78] How a press, which until 1975 served well to nourish a variety of political perspectives and initiatives, has been harnessed to a single regime is an enlightening story.

Mrs. Gandhi's government again began with preemptive tactics. Electric-power failures along the street where the powerful daily papers are published stopped their presses while the June 26 arrests were taking place. Then a government censor was stationed in every metropolitan editorial room. As correspondents tried to outwit him, the hand of government fell heavily upon them. Six foreign correspondents were expelled. As we noted, one of the most prominent Delhi journalists, editor of the *Indian Express* and correspondent for the *London Times*, was summarily arrested. Then subtler methods of manipulation began. The government announced plans to merge the large, partly independent news agency the Press Trust of India, with a rival agency and to reorganize control of both.[79]

In December the government was ready to fit formal regulations upon a cowed press. A presidential ordinance barred publication of any materials that "bring into hatred or contempt or excite disaffection towards the Government established by law," or anything defamatory of the president, vice-president, prime minister, or any member of the Council of Ministers, the speaker of the Lok Sabha, or the governor of a state. A year in jail and closure of the printing press are among the penalties. A second ordinance repealed the statute extending immunity from prosecution to newspapers for the publishing of anything said in Parliament. Mrs. Gandhi's late husband, Feroze, had authored that statute twenty years ago. A third ordinance replaced the watchdog Press Council with a government committee.[80] Censorship now appears permanent.

Radio in India is a government monopoly, doing the bidding of the government in power. So is the infant television industry. The press is now unavailable to transmit to the people any criticism their representatives may make of the regime, or any critical reactions of constituents to the programs, or lack of programs, of the government. Mrs. Gandhi's claim that she had cut the supply line of the enemy seems apt.

Political Competition

The other standard criterion, besides certain basic personal liberties, of a democratic constitution is the selection of rulers by the governed, subject to some measure of competition for office. Mrs. Gandhi's strategy on this front is not fully revealed. On July 4, 1975, she banned twenty-six political organizations. Police raided their headquarters, arrested their officers, suppressed their publications. These ranged from a fairly fanatical Muslim organization (Jamaat-i-Islami) and two secret, probably violent Hindu groups (Anada Marg and Rashtriya Swayam Sevak Sangh), to nine splinters of the originally Maoist agrarian terrorist movement loosely called Naxalite.[81] We must in fairness recognize here that most democracies, even those less hard-pressed than India, have also had occasion to deny the legality of such extremist groups.

Extremist groups have not, in any case, generally, run candidates for elective office. The parties that have offered Mrs. Gandhi elective competition in the past are still free, formally, to do so. But *Motherland*, the organ of the Jan Sangh, has been banned.[82] Censorship has pulled the teeth of other opposition papers. Most damaging to the electoral prospects of the national parties is the blackout in the censored press of the speeches their spokesmen make in Parliament. One main function of Parliament, to legitimize criticism of the regime, is thus cut off from another function, vital in India: to rouse a fragmented, latent public reaction to government measures that might eventually (were communications not cut) emerge as campaign issues. It is possible, too, though there is no way of ascertaining this, that enough opposition legislators have been incarcerated that parties other than the Congress party would have serious difficulties fielding strong slates in any forthcoming general election.

The weight of these constraints upon the opposition has become a moot question, however, as a result of Mrs. Gandhi's decision not to hold the parliamentary election due in 1976.[83] The constitution calls for Lok Sabha elections every five years, and these have been held faithfully in India since the constitution took effect. But the dual constitution also permits Parliament to extend its life one year at a time while a state of emergency is in effect. Mrs. Gandhi has availed herself of this provision. It is not easy to understand why. To outside observers, her prospects of electoral victory are at least as bright as they were in 1971 and 1972 when she won an overwhelming popular endorsement. The opposition is hamstrung, and described unceasingly in the media and by Congress workers as saboteurs and underminers of the state. Mrs. Gandhi's economic program has wide appeal. If it fails of implementation, that will not appear until later. Perhaps most important, the monsoon and winter crops are India's largest, and food prices have fallen.

It may be, as the *London Economist* speculated, that Mrs. Gandhi, though confident of winning a simple majority in a fresh election, has doubts about holding her present two-thirds majority, which she requires to amend the constitution. A draft of an altered constitution with a Gaullist presidency and an appointed council taking over judicial review from the Supreme Court has been circulated in India.[84] There is another hypothesis. Mrs. Gandhi began late in 1975 to deny the legitimacy of the two opposition governments still remaining among India's twenty-two states. In January 1976 she referred to them as "two islands" in India where efforts are being made to destroy the discipline of the emergency.[85] Shortly after that, using another constitutional emergency power, she deposed the elected DMK government in Tamil Nadu, arrested many hundreds of its political leaders, and instituted rule of the state from Delhi. It is possible that she will feel India is ready for elections when the other opposition state government has undergone *Gleichschaltung*.[127] As we shall see, her own recent words leave that dubious.

ECONOMIC PROGRAM

A main reason for the political changes she imposed, Mrs. Gandhi has said, was to achieve economic gains, especially for the poor. In a radio broadcast on July 1, she told the country what those gains were to be. Her list of economic and social measures have since come to be known as the twenty points;[86] they preoccupy the media, government policy discussions, and the talk of Congress party politicians in India.

The meaningful test of the twenty points is not the value of the declared aims, but their realization. Some of the points are objectives of all contemporary governments, e.g., lowering consumer prices. The cutting edge of the program is not new, but was, in fact, decided at a meeting of Congress party leaders called by Mrs. Gandhi at Narora more than six months earlier. It is hard to think of any reasons Mrs. Gandhi did not announce the Narora decisions save that she felt she could not secure their implementation without emergency powers. I will attempt here a summary evaluation of the twenty points, leaving details on the industrial policies to chapter 5, and on the agrarian programs to chapter 7. My judgments as to their success, current and potential, in overcoming intrinsic obstacles are based on clues suggested by parallel efforts in the past.

Consumers

Five of the economic points would benefit consumers. Prices of necessities are to be brought down, with special attention given to making more available the fixed-price cotton *dhotis* and *saris* and making cheap food and school supplies available to students in dormitories. Toward this general end, progress had been enviable. Throughout India, in fact, consumer prices went down 10 percent from their peak in September 1974 to the end of 1975; food prices fell 20 percent.[87] Half the drop occurred during the July-December period, while the emergency was in effect. Did emergency measures cause prices to drop? Inflation was mainly checked by a severe slowdown in the expansion of the money supply, which had been effected earlier (expansion in the year ending March 1975 was 6.3 percent, compared to 15.2 percent in the previous year),[88] coinciding with good wheat crops in both 1975 and 1976, with a good rice crop in between. The remarkable change in harvests after three semifailures was due to excellent rains. Mrs. Gandhi's program can, however, be credited with reversing the minor upturn (about 1 percent per month) in consumer prices during the three months just preceding the emergency,[89] and in holding prices down despite a subsequent expansion of bank credit to fuel the economy. Her success was probably due to pressures on retailers (all prices of essential commodities had to be posted) coupled with the disincentives to hoarding implicit in the police raids on black marketeers. Coming after three years in which the rupee had lost half its buying power,[90] the downturn in prices was an enormous relief not only to urban consumers but to agricultural laborers who have to buy grain. To students the benefits were signaled by the opening of cooperatives serving almost 4,000 dormitories.[91] What are called in India "middle classes"—the tiny stratum next to the top, earning 5,000 to 15,000 rupees—were given a modest reduction in income taxes.

Industry

In chapter 5, Howard Erdman will appraise the impact of Mrs. Gandhi's program on industry. Statistics in two areas will, in the meantime, suggest that the impact was immediately positive. First, man-days lost on account of labor disputes during July to December 1975 (2.3 million) were a mere quarter of the volume of a year before;[92] labor peace was chiefly responsible for the 15 percent increase in the physical output of the chronically strife-torn public sector plants.[93] Second, the stock market, after falling steadily in 1975 to a low of 111 points on June 28, climbed equally sharply and held, at the end of 1975, at 123.[94]

Corruption

The agitation against Congress rule in 1974 and early 1975 had focused increasingly upon alleged corruption. Mrs. Gandhi proposed three measures related to this. The oft-promised ceiling on ownership of urban real estate (land speculation is seen in agrarian India, and especially in the Gandhian tradition, as corrupt) is now being legislated. Tax evasion has been dramatically attacked. Surprise raids on some of the luxury flats of Bombay and Delhi turned up large inventories of expensive furnishings, jewelry, and currency; the owners have had to explain how they came by these hoards within their declared incomes. While this was going on, the income tax authorities designated the final eleven weeks of 1975 as a grace period within which unreported income and wealth could be disclosed without criminal penalties. Nothing is more bitterly resented among newspaper readers in India than "black money," concealed wealth that not only escapes the tax assessors, but is available (not being on the ledgers) for use in bribing administrators and making huge hidden campaign contributions to the party in power. Popular estimates ran at the level of 30,000 million rupees ($3,333 million). Unlike all previous campaigns to get black money onto the account books, the 1975 drive produced results. Over $1,600 million worth of previously concealed assets were disclosed; the added income tax receipts alone amounted to $270 million.[95]

Rural Poor

It would be fair to regard Mrs. Gandhi's efforts on behalf of the rural poor as the acid test of her success. For five years, since she fought and won the 1971 election upon the *garibi hatao* (abolition of poverty) issue, she had done more than any Indian to create the expectation that poverty could be wiped out. The impact of her 1975 emergency program on the villages is analyzed by F. Thomasson Jannuzi in chapter 7; his study of Bihar provides a basis for understanding the likelihood of implementation.

In the meantime, we can indicate the status, after six months of emergency effort, of two of Mrs. Gandhi's five programs for the rural poor: (1) enforcement of existing ceilings on land holdings; and (2) a moratorium on legal action by private moneylenders to collect debts from small farmers (under two hectares), and the extension of alternative sources of credit to them.

In the first six months of the emergency, the period fixed originally for substantial achievement toward the first goal, 653,000 acres have been declared in excess of the maximum permissable farm size, 323,000 acres have been taken over by state governments, and 136,000 acres have been redistributed to the landless.[96] That is not much—less than 10 percent of the acreage redistributed in the previous twenty years of an ineffectual redistribution program. If we assume that 10 hectares (24 acres) is the average limit throughout India for a legally permissible farm, 24 percent of India's agricultural land was in surplus holdings in 1961-62. But the acreage held in excess of that ceiling had risen by the time of the 1970-71 agricultural census to 31 percent of the total. More than 25 million acres would have to be redistributed merely to deconcentrate ownership to the level of a decade earlier.[97]

As to the relief of the rural poor from their crushing debts, progress is going to be equally difficult. By the year's end, twelve of the twenty-two states had legislated moratoriums on debt-repayment obligations of the poor. One on-the-spot study of two villages in Rajasthan casts a pinpoint of light on the knotted problem of making redistributive statutes work in the inequalitarian world of the village. Three-fifths of the village households continued, two months after passage of the moratorium legislation, to depend on private moneylenders for loans; among other reasons, 40 percent of the debtors in the more developed village, 53 percent in the rest, depended for employment on the land owner-creditor. Since the net effect of the moratorium was that the creditor would no longer advance them money, they were worse off than before.[98]

But while Mrs. Gandhi has not solved the problem of redistributing rural resources, she has gone farther toward identifying as enemies the forces opposing redistribution. In other words, there may be some political returns for her amid economic difficulties. In Gujarat, where the opposition Janata Front has been in power since the June 1975 election, Mrs. Gandhi has drawn political battle lines in the countryside between the substantial farmers, championed by the front, and the have-nots, who in south Gujarat, at least, back her. The Front government's response to Mrs. Gandhi's redistributive program was to appoint a state land reforms commission headed by a prominant legislative spokesman for the rural rich. The state has not, since July 1975, declared a single acre surplus.[99] In the meantime, Gujarat held rural self-government (*panchayat*) elections in December. Mrs. Gandhi's Congress party defeated the Front almost two to one, though the Front keeps control of the major cities. Mrs. Gandhi continues to be the tribune of the rural poor.

Another development also helps her to identify for some of the rural landless a set of common enemies. The principal immediate obstacle to land redistribution that has emerged in the states is an epidemic of lawsuits in local courts to block enforcement of the land ceilings laws. The cases are, of course, brought by those who can afford lawyers. Late in 1975, 800,000 such cases were pending,[100] amounting to more than one lawsuit per acre earmarked for redistribution. The rule of law has a different meaning in the villages than among the college-educated in the cities. Mrs. Gandhi is well aware of the numbers of those who see it each way.

At the end of this consideration of Mrs. Gandhi's economic aims and the initial results of the emergency regime we are left with a conundrum. Why does Mrs. Gandhi's opposition, weak as it may be, arise in the cities, among the educated, where her programs continue to achieve some results? Why does her staunchest support come from among the rural poor, for whom her promises have yet to be fulfilled?

MRS. GANDHI'S CASE

The authors of this book are not agreed on a single interpretation of what Mrs. Gandhi did. Our arguments are not over. We join, however, in skepticism that the emergency was necessary. We are not convinced that it will, over a period of five or ten years, contribute to the achievement of the social and economic goals Mrs. Gandhi has set forth. To each of us, the loss by close Indian associates of their accustomed spontaneity to say what is on their minds, to associate publicly with their comrades, and to act out their beliefs brings a renewed appreciation of a value now diminished in India—liberty.

We would not close any arena of dissent. Especially would we hear out Indira Gandhi. As prime minister she has had access to the most complete information, born the burden of decision, and will ultimately be judged by history. Fortunately, Mrs. Gandhi is one of the most articulate of world leaders. She has said what she was doing, and why, and we feel it appropriate that she speak for herself here. In selecting the material below, we have not intended to display her inconsistencies. Rather, we have chosen her words from her years as prime minister, especially from the stifling days of June and July 1975, which seem most cogently to express her present rationale.

Long-Term Goals

"India has the privilege of being the world's largest composite society, the home of many . . . ancient faiths.[101] India has more major languages than any other country . . .[102] and next to religion, language arouses the strongest loyalties and emotions.[103] As we survey the national scene, we feel there is indeed cause for anxiety and also cause for shame that lives of Indian nationals should be threatened in their own homes and in their places of business because of their community or religion. . . . In all periods of India's true greatness she has stood for tolerance . . . But this . . . cannot mean tolerance for those who strike at the very root of our unity.[104]

"I want to give you the talisman which Gandhi gave us. He said that if you are assailed by doubts you should always think of the lowest and the weakest of our countrymen. If an action

is going to improve their lot, then it is the right action.105
When we use the word socialism, we use it to mean primarily the
welfare of the entire Indian people, of the vast masses who live
in the villages and who bear the heaviest brunt of poverty.106

"Some people talk of revolution. Our government has already
begun one. One of its biggest achievements has been creating a
tremendous awakening among the people.107

"The question is not who is Prime Minister. It is in which direction the nation will be led.108 What they have been opposing all along are the radical programs for the uplift of the
people.109

The Need to Act

"The 'Indira Hatao' [Indira Must Go] campaign was not initiated after the Allahabad judgment. It began because of the
radical socio-economic measures we introduced in 1969 after
the Congress split. The attempt has been sustained by vested interests ever since.110 A climate of violence and hatred has been
created which resulted in the assassination of a Cabinet Minister
and an attempt on the life of the Chief Justice. The Opposition
parties had chalked out a program of countrywide *bundhs*
[shutdowns], *gheraos* [sit-ins], agitations, disruption and incitement to industrial workers, police, and defense forces in an
attempt wholly to paralyze the Central Government. One of
them went to the extent of saying that Armed Forces should
not carry out orders which they considered wrong. . . . This had
to be prevented.111

"In the name of democracy it has been sought to negate the
very functioning of democracy. Duly elected governments have
not been allowed to function and in some cases force has been
used to compel members to resign in order to dissolve lawfully
elected Assemblies."112

The Emergency Is Constitutional

"Preserving the integrity of the fabric is a major challenge in
the early years of any new nation. Our Constitution makers
were fully aware of the problems involved and knew . . . the
center should hold at all times. . . . Every country arms itself
with powers to meet external threats and internal disorder.

Making use of such provisions cannot be termed unconstitutional or anti-democratic. The action we took was warranted by a specific provision (Article 352) of our Constitution and was therefore within the constitutional framework."113

Only When We Have Set Things Right

"Emergency has set a new wave of discipline in the country, an atmosphere in which the nation's strength is the prime consideration. Personal difficulties and hardships take second place.114 The emergency came as a boon to people engaged in the task of building the country. The record of the last few months shows that.115

"[However], the country has never been in such grave danger before. Some powers which had tasted success in their destabilization game in Chile nurtured similar designs against India.116 In Bangladesh they succeeded. Not in India.117 But now the situation is that the antagonists of socialism have started joining forces. The persons who oppose us from within the country derive their inspiration from without.118

"Difficulties in implementing the 20-point program continue. Powerful classes and interests are against implementation. . . . They are sabotaging the 20-point program. . . . These forces must be combatted with all the strength at our command. That is what we are trying to do.119

"Today one of the greatest obstacles is the cynicism of our intelligentsia, because no matter what is done they always look at it as of no account. And this opinion is reflected in our press and it does have an influence on the people.120 Unlike in the affluent countries, it does matter in India [if the press should again] spread alarm and despondency.121

"The kind of opposition we are facing today is not conducive to unity, to the strength and stability of the country. It can well harm us all. Where they [opposition party leaders] control government, violence continues. These forces are also trying to create hatred. They are fanning the flames of communalism.122 [Some opposition parties] talk about separatism and greater autonomy.123

"The painful necessity of the emergency is, therefore, going to be used to usher in a new era for realizing the common aspirations of the people. What prevailed before the emergency was not normalcy. There will be no return to the total license and political permissiveness which was assiduously used by the opposition for eroding the democratic structure and challenging the political legitimacy of the government. That situation will never be allowed to return.[124]

[Announcing her decision to continue the emergency, postpone the general election due early in 1976, and extend the life of the Parliament for another year,] "I don't want to go in for elections because that will put the 20-point program in jeopardy. After it is implemented and the people benefitted we would certainly hold elections."[125]

NOTES

[1] Justice Krishna Iyer had been minister of law, home, and irrigation in the initial Communist party government of Kerala (1957-59). Since the emergency, he has been outspoken in advocating reform of the constitution and the legal system to make them less obstructive of land reform and other measures on behalf of the poor. On his appointment, see *Thought* (New Delhi), April 5, 1975, p.5.

[2] The text of the order was printed in the *Hindu* (Madras), June 25, 1975.

[3] Lengthy summaries of the 258-page opinion of the Allahabad trial court were printed in the *Hindustan Times* (Delhi) and the *Hindu*, both on June 13, 1975.

[4] Then a Socialist, he has since been elected to the Rajya Sabha (National upper house) as a member of the Bharatiya Lok Dal, a regional peasant-based opposition party.

[5] India, Ministry of Law and Justice, *Manual of Election Law* (Delhi: Manager of Publications, 1972), sec. 123 (7) (a), p. 152.

[6] *Newsweek*, July 7, 1975, p. 23 ("to foreigners trivial enough . . ."); *Economist* (London), June 21, 1975 ("a peccadillo"); *Guardian* (Manchester), June 27, 1975 ("trifling malpractice").

[7] India, Lok Sabha, Joint Committee on Amendments to Election Law, *Report* (New Delhi: Lok Sabha Secretariat, 1972). Part I, pp. 50, 20.

[8] Representation of the People Act of 1951, Secs. 99, 100, and 8A. *Manual of Election Law* (cited in note 5 above), pp. 142-43, 115.

[9] "Most educated Indians" believe this: *Guardian Weekly* (Manchester) July 5, 1975.

10 *Hindustan Times*, June 18, 1975. The leader of the D.M.K. party governing the South Indian state of Tamil Hadu, who had been Mrs. Gandhi's ally in many national affairs, said it would have been better had she resigned. See note 19, below.

11 *Economic Times* (Bombay), June 13, 1975; *Hindu*, June 18, 1975.

12 Smt. Kanta Kathuria v. Manak Chand Surana (C.A. No. 1869/68, Dt. 16.10.69; 1969 (3) SCC 268).

13 This had occurred in 1966. *New York Times*, July 26, 1966.

14 The most informative account of the election is Marcus F. Franda, "The Gujarat Election, 1975," *Field Staff Reports* (American Universities Field Staff), South Asia Series 19, no. 9 (Sept. 1975). See also the *Hindu*, June 4 and 5, 1975.

15 *Hindu*, June 17, 1975.

16 *Hindustan Times*, May 7 and 14, 1975; *Hindu*, June 17, 1975.

17 *Hindu*, June 7, 16, and 20, 1975.

18 *Hindu*, June 14, 1975.

19 Ibid., June 18, 1975; *Hindustan Times*, June 22, 1975. The CPM split leftward from the parent, pro-Soviet CPI in 1964.

20 Ibid., June 24, 1975.

21 *Hindustan Times* reported, June 22, 1975, "According to informed sources" the chances of a monsoon (July) session being called depended on the Supreme Court giving an absolute stay, i.e., temporarily lifting all disqualifications imposed by the trial court.

22 *Hindustan Times*, June 19, 1975.

23 *Hindu*, June 19, 1975.

24 Ibid., June 25, 1975; *Hindustan Times*, June 25, 1975.

25 *Hindustan Times*, June 26, 1975.

26 A review of the Bihar agitation can be found in Rakshat Puri, "India's Opposition Parties Find a Leader," *South Asian Review* 8, no. 2 (Jan. 1975): 91-96. An entirely sympathetic account is Vasant Sadashiv Nargolkar, on J. P.'s *Crusade for Revolution* (New Delhi: S. Chand, 1975).

27 *Keesing's Contemporary Archives* (London), April 22-28, 1975, p. 26481.

28 For a short critical sketch of Narayan, see Welles Hangen, *After Nehru Who?* (London: Rupert Hart-Davis, 1963).

29 Jayprakash Narayan, *Nation Building in India*, ed. Brahmanand (Banares: Navachetna Prakashan, n.d.) pp. 170-84.

30 For two studies of a previous episode, see T.J.S. George, *Revolt in Bihar, a Study of the August 1965 Uprising* (New Delhi: Perspective Publications, 1965); and Herbert Heidenreich, "Anatomy of a Riot: A Case Study from Bihar 1965," *Journal of Commonwealth Political Studies* 6 (July 1968): 107-24.

31 Tabulated from *Keesing's Contemporary Archives*, Feb. 17-23, 1975, pp. 26977-78, and Nargolkar, *Crusade for Revolution*.

32 *Guardian*, July 12, 1975.

33 But see the account of such linkage working in one village in Amiya Rao, "Mirage or Reality in Bihar," *Hindustan Times*, June 4, 1975.

34 Nargolkar, *Crusade for Revolution*, p. 141.

35 Ibid., p. 168.

36 *Keesing's Contemporary Archives*, Feb. 17-23, 1975, p. 26977.

37 Ibid.

38 Details are in *Keesing's Contemporary Archives*, Oct. 6-12, 1975, pp. 27365-66.

39 *Economic Times*, June 27, 1975.

40 See, e.g., the *New York Times*, June 29, 1975, and July 8, 1975.

41 *Economic Times*, June 27, 1975.

42 A biographical appraisal of Desai was included in Hangen, *After Nehru Who?* Desai's contempt for Mrs. Gandhi comes out in Oriana Fallaci, "Mrs. Gandhi's Opposition: Morarji Desai," *New Republic* 173, nos. 5-6 (Aug. 2 and 9, 1975): 12-138.

43 Jawaharlal Nehru, *A Bunch of Older Letters* (New Delhi: Asia Publishing House, 1958), pp. 296, 436, 458. For the relation between Kamala Nehru and Prabhavati, J.P.'s wife, see Promilla Kalhan, *Kamala Nehru, An Intimate Biography* (Delhi: Vikas Publishing House, 1973), pp. 24, 50.

44 In June 1973, when relations between Indira Gandhi and Jayaprakash were still civil, she referred to "your friendship over the years" (Nargolkar, *Crusade for Revolution*, pp. 193-94). He later accused her of "harboring corrupt ministers" (ibid., pp. 157-58). A November 1, 1974, meeting to seek accommodation was apparently pressed upon them both by followers and crystallized the distrust and antagonism between them. J.P.'s perspective is suggested by Nargolkar, pp. 144-45. Mrs. Gandhi's bitter reaction dominated an interview she gave a visiting foreigner (he told us) in the late summer of 1975.

45 Prominent Congress M.P.s Chandra Sekhar and Ram Dhan are reported by a number of recent visitors to India to have been arrested in the first wave. Reports in the British press that Jyoti Basu, CPM leader of West Bengal, was arrested proved false.

[46] Article 74. References to the constitution are to India, Ministry of Law and Justice, *The Constitution of India as Modified up to the 1st of January, 1973* (New Delhi: Ministry of Information and Broadcasting, 1973).

[47] Articles 60, 61. On the constitutional issue contrast Zaheer M. Quraishi, *Struggle for Rashtrapati Bhawan* (Delhi: Vikas, 1973), with H.N. Pandit, *The P.M.'s President* (New Delhi: S. Chand, 1974).

[48] *Hindu*, June 14, 1975.

[49] Article 123.

[50] *Hindustan Times*, July 22, 1975.

[51] The method used, a shaky one, is to look for mentions of the best-known of the Congress dissidents in the press accounts. Mohan Dharia and Lakshmi Kanthamma are there, Chandra Sekhar and Ram Dhan are not. Six months later the number of jailed M.P.s was reported as thirty-two. *Guardian*, January 6, 1976.

[52] Robert Zoller, *The Parliament of 1621: A Study of Constitutional Conflict* (Berkeley: University of California Press, 1971), pp. 2-4 and passim.

[53] Thomas Erskine May, *A Treatise on the Law, Privileges, Procedures and Usage of Parliament*, 14th ed., ed. Gilberg Campion (London: Butterworth, 1947), chap. 5; S. C. Hawtrey and H. M. Barclay, *Parliamentary Dictionary* (London: Butterworth, 1970), p. 164.

[54] House of the People, Committee of Privileges, *The Deshpande Case* (New Delhi: Parliament Secretariat, 1952).

[55] From a reading of the *Hindustan Times, Hindu*, and the *Indian Express* (Delhi) of July 24, 1975.

[56] For the legislation, see the *Hindu*, Aug. 5 and 7, 1975; for the amendment, ibid., Aug. 11, 1975.

[57] Long summaries of the opinions of the five judges are in the *Hindu*, Nov. 8, 1975.

[58] *New York Times*, Dec. 28, 1975.

[59] Article 352. An emergency arising from an external threat had already been in effect since 1971.

[60] Articles 358, 359.

[61] Article 353.

[62] Granville Austin, *The Indian Constitution: Cornerstone of a Nation* (Oxford: Clarendon Press, 1966), pp. 70-71, 74-75, 108, 111-113, 174.

[63] Ibid., pp. 44-45.

[64] Article 352. There is a minor exception: if only the Rajya Sabha is in session and approves, the emergency may survive until thirty days after the Lok Sabha reconvenes, which must be within six months.

65 *Economic and Political Weekly* (Bombay) 9 (June 1, 1974): 846-47. See also a summary of a Public Accounts Committee report to Parliament on growth of police expenditures, *New York Times*, Oct. 24, 1974.

66 *Hindustan Times*, Sept. 17, 1974.

67 Austin, *The Indian Constitution*, pp. 106-13. See also David H. Bayley, *Preventive Detention in India* (Berkeley: University of California Press, 1962).

68 In Tripura, for instance in May 1975, the chief minister said he had no alternative but to arrest eleven CPM members of the state legislative assembly to prevent them "from using hungry people as tools to serve their political interests." He jailed them under M.I.S.A. *Hindustan Times*, May 8 and 24, 1975.

69 *New York Times*, Feb. 3, 1976.

70 *Far Eastern Economic Review* (Hong Kong), Jan. 16, 1976. pp. 29-31.

71 B. P. Srivastava, "Right Against Arbitrary Arrest and Detention under Article 9 of the Covenant as Recognized and Protected under the Indian Law," *Journal of the Indian Law Institute* 11, no. 1 (1969): 29-56.

72 *Hindu*, Oct. 18, 1975; *Economist*, Oct. 25, 1975, pp. 46-47.

73 *Hindu*, July 16, 1975.

74 Ibid., Aug. 8 and 11, 1975.

75 *Indian Express* (New Delhi), Jan. 9, 1976.

76 *Keesing's Contemporary Archives*, Oct. 6-12, 1975, pp. 27372-73.

77 *Hindustan Times*, Jan. 10, 1976.

78 Verbatim from the *Indian Express*, Jan. 8, 1976, which did not use quotation marks.

79 From the interesting account by John Grigg, "India's Clampdown," in *Index on Censorship* (London) 4, no. 4 (Winter 1975): 5-11.

80 *Hindu*, Dec. 9, 1975. Parliament converted all three ordinances to legislation in January 1976.

81 *Hindu*, July 5, 1975.

82 *Keesing's Contemporary Archives*, Oct. 6-12, 1975, p. 27369.

83 *Deccan Herald* (Bangalore), Dec. 30, 1975, reporting the decision of the Congress party to this effect.

84 *Economist*, Jan. 3, 1976, p. 9.

85 *Indian Express* (New Delhi), Jan. 8, 1976.

86 As presented in her talk, the points were not numbered and were a little discursive. They were originally counted as twenty-one. A convenient list of them is in *Keesing's Contemporary Archives*, Oct. 6-12, 1975, pp. 27369-70.

[87] President's address opening the Parliament, *Economic Times*, Jan. 6, 1976.

[88] Economic report, Minister of Finance, *Economic Times*, July 31, 1975.

[89] Editorial, *Economic Times*, July 28, 1975.

[90] *Economic Times*, Jan. 4, 1976.

[91] Ibid., July 31, 1975.

[92] According to the Union Minister of Labor. *Statesman* (Delhi), Jan. 12, 1976.

[93] April to December 1975, compared to the corresponding nine months of 1974. *Economic Times*, Dec. 29, 1975.

[94] Ibid., Dec. 22, 1975.

[95] Ibid., Jan. 1 and 7, 1976; *Hindu*, Jan. 3 and 7, 1976.

[96] *Economic Times*, Dec. 26, 1975.

[97] Ibid., Dec. 27, 1975.

[98] G. L. Gadhich, "Case Study of Two Villages in Rajasthan," *Economic Times*, Dec. 28, 1975.

[99] *Economic Times*, Dec. 12, 1975.

[100] Ibid., Dec. 26, 1975.

[101] Statement in Parliament, Dec. 22, 1967. Indira Gandhi, *Selected Speeches* (New Delhi: Government of India, Ministry of Information and Broadcasting, 1971), p. 78.

[102] Speech on November 17, 1970, quoted in N. B. Sen, *The Wit and Wisdom of Indira Gandhi* (New Delhi: New Book Society, 1971), p. 152.

[103] Lok Sabha debate, Dec. 12, 1967, in Gandhi, *Selected Speeches*, p. 73.

[104] Speech on June 20, 1968, ibid., pp. 80 and 82.

[105] Translation of Hindi speech from the Red Fort, Aug. 15, 1969, in ibid., p. 62.

[106] Speech, March 12, 1967, quoted in Sen, *The Wit and Wisdom*, p. 280.

[107] Speech to crowd on her lawn, *Hindu*, June 26, 1975.

[108] Similar speech, ibid., June 25, 1975.

[109] Similar speech, ibid., June 20, 1975.

[110] Ibid., June 21, 1975.

[111] Radio talk, ibid., June 28, 1975.

[112] Nationwide radio talk on proclamation of emergency, ibid., June 27, 1975. Detailed allegations of the long-standing plot against her was provided to the Lok Sabha by the Home Ministry on July 21 (*Economic Times*, July 22, 1975).

113 "Prime Minister Indira Gandhi Responds to Charges that Democracy in India is Dead," *Saturday Review*, Aug. 9, 1975, p. 10.

114 From an interview distributed to delegates at the 1975 Congress party conference. Text in *Times of India*, Dec. 28, 1975.

115 *Hindustan Times*, Dec. 30, 1975.

116 Associated Press dispatch from New Delhi, *Milwaukee Journal*, Jan. 2, 1976.

117 Address to party conference, *Economic Times*, January 1, 1976.

118 *Times of India*, Dec. 28, 1975.

119 *Economic Times*, Jan. 10, 1976.

120 This criticism was made in a 1969 speech in New Delhi titled "Can India Survive?" in Indira Gandhi, *Indira Gandhi, Speeches and Writings* (New York: Harper and Row, 1975), p. 84.

121 *Times of India*, Jan. 10, 1976.

122 Lok Sabha debate, *Economic Times*, Jan. 10, 1976. A sentence has been interpolated from Mrs. Gandhi's speech at the party conference, reported in the *Hindustan Times*, Dec. 31, 1975.

123 *Times of India*, Dec. 28, 1975.

124 In Parliament, July 22. *Economic Times*, July 23, 1975.

125 *Hindustan Times*, Jan. 1, 1976.

126 An April Supreme Court decision settled the issue in the government's favor, denying the writ of haebeus corpus to 43 citizens, four of them M.P.s, who had been jailed without charges or trials. *New York Times*, April 29, 1976.

127 The last remaining opposition government, Gujarat state's, fell on March 12, 1976. *New York Times*, March 13, 1976.

2

The Last Emergency of the Raj
Robert Eric Frykenberg

The Committee resolves, therefore, to sanction, for the vindication of India's inalienable right to freedom and independence, the starting of a mass struggle on non-violent lines on the widest possible scale. . . . The Committee appeals to the people of India to face the dangers and hardships that will fall to their lot with courage and endurance (2:624).[1]

* * *

[The Government of India] has been aware, too, for some days past of dangerous preparations . . . for unlawful, and in some cases violent, activities, directed among other things to the interruption of communications and public utility services, the organization of strikes, tampering with the loyalty of Government servants, and interference with defense measures, including recruitment. To a challenge such as the present there can be only one answer. The Government of India would regard it as wholly incompatible with their responsibilities to the people of India . . . that a demand should be discussed the acceptance of which would plunge India into confusion and anarchy . . . and would paralyze her effort in the common cause of human freedom (2:611-01).

These statements are expressions, not of Jayaprakash Narayan's mass action committees to force Indira Gandhi to vacate her office, nor of Mrs. Gandhi's firm response, but of the All-

India Congress Committee (A.I.C.C.), demanding that Britain quit India, and of the imperial government, maintaining its authority. The year was 1942.

The familiarity of tone and of phrase is more than coincidental. The government of India is not newly modeled. Mrs. Gandhi assumed control of a set of institutions, reoriented to be sure, that had taken mature shape by 1942 and that have retained that shape to the present: army, police, bureaucracy, courts, laws and precedents of their interpretation, and the relations of all this to the humble villages on the periphery. The imperial role models live in the minds of those who fill the roles now.

The antigovernment side, too, has its memories. Its institutions are less structured, and the principal institution that opposed government in 1942, the Indian National Congress, is now in government. Nevertheless, methods of evoking in the minds of semipolitical people scattered across a diverse subcontinent a consciousness of shared grievances, methods of holding followers to a strategic line, the hazards of the suddenly politicized young enthusiasts *not* following the strategic line, the moral claims, the counterploys to standard government control methods, the propaganda appeals—all these are partly inherited in the persons of Morarji Desai, and above all Jayaprakash Narayan.

Let us reexamine the familiar encounter of the empire against the nationalists, then, from a 1975 perspective. We will wish to look at 1942 through the eyes of the government in power, for the analog we seek is to the measures taken by the government of 1975. We are examining what a government feels it must and can do to retain its authority under conditions of critical stress. Specifically, as we review the record, we wish to learn:

1. What threat was perceived by government officers?
2. What control measures did they employ?
3. What effects did those measures have upon the threatening groups or forces?
4. What effects did they have upon larger constituencies to whom officers felt in some way accountable?

THE CRISIS

By January of 1942, British leaders knew that they were in desperate straits. Their backs were to the wall in Europe, where their survival as a people seemed at stake. They had suffered defeat after defeat from the Japanese. Their political situation in India looked precarious. Gandhi's "nonviolent resistance" campaigns (*satyagraha*) and demands for *swaraj* ("self-rule"), as parts of a long and complex struggle over succession to imperial power, were beset by communal crosscurrents. Gandhi and other Congress leaders had concluded that the time had come for one last knockout blow, their takeover of the raj. With Hitler's *Wehrmacht* about to cross the Channel and the Battle of Britain darkening the sky, Congress felt confident. India's "entry" into war in 1939 had provided a pretext. After some hot words from their high command, Congress leaders had dramatically resigned from all governments and taken their appeals to the streets.

Such direct action, with its quickening implications, had not been lost upon Mohammad Ali Jinnah and his Muslims. Muslim leaders, deeply bitter over the aftermath of the 1937 elections and their exclusion from any share in government, had staked out their demand for Pakistan in the Lahore Resolution (1940).

With alarm, the British watched as these events diminished their room for maneuver. The situation as seen in London was succinctly summarized on January 28:

> The political deadlock in India today is concerned, ostensibly, with the transfer of power from British to Indian hands. In reality it is mainly concerned with the far more difficult issue of what Indian hands, what Indian Government or Governments are capable of taking over without bringing general anarchy and civil war. The former issue has been settled . . . by pledge after pledge. . . . What would be equally necessary . . . is some measure of agreement as to who constitute the people or peoples whose freedom of choice as to their form of government is to be respected (1:81).

Such urgency led to the Cripps Mission. The mission's purpose was to reach a workable accommodation with Indian leaders and to shore up support enough to enable the raj to play its part in the war. To this end, the British promised India a full place among the "fellowship of independent and freedom-loving nations" and a "constitutional structure of Indian devising" which would "correspond to Indian social, economic, and political conceptions and to the peculiar conditions of her complex structure." As for procedure, the Cripps Declaration made clear that this would "be decided by agreement among Indians themselves." Cripps hoped that Indians would "find agreement upon some constitutional scheme" which would preserve "that essential unity of India as a whole which the course of history has shown to be of such vital importance" (1:258, 256-66).

But the Cripps Declaration was foredoomed. Cripps immediately revealed to his Congress friends the whole plan—a new central government, immediate control (responsibility) for major parties, and full independence right after the war, all in return for India's full support in the war effort—which left him with nothing more to offer in bargaining. Worse, his hastiness conveyed the impression of imminent British collapse. Mistakenly, as it turned out, Gandhi and his party thought they sensed panic. Gandhi, while he sought to "bargain for a better position," also scorned the offer as a "post-dated cheque on a failing bank." Nor was Jinnah any longer listening. His mind was already implacably set on Pakistan. Except for Rajagopalacharia, who saw rejection of the Cripps offer as the final expression of disdain for the Muslim cause by Congress and the deathblow for Indian unity, there was no support for the Cripps offer. Other groups, such as that of Ambedkar and Rajah, opposed it out of fear for what it gave the Congress. The Congress itself (through Azad) formally demanded an immediate transfer of power to "a National Government responsible to no one but itself" and constituting "an absolute dictatorship of the majority"; and then it scored the British for their "wrecking policy" of "promoting discord and disruption" (1:733-45).

With such words the gauntlet was thrown down. Without agreement on the rightful succession (by "free choice" to "representative" Indians), there could be no abdication. As long as war threatened them and the Japanese might, even by remote chance, come to use India's resources against them, the British would hold on.

The government had no doubt that Gandhi intended an all-out campaign, and watched his every move. Having already infiltrated the Congress, it was able to monitor preparations for the Quit India rebellion and to note the discussions (and dissensions) within the Congress high command. By May 5, it judged that Congress could "now definitely be regarded as irreconcilable." The failure of the Cripps negotiations had dramatized that point "for the edification of the world at large, and in particular, of the United States and of certain circles at home" (2:33). The reports of a secret agent (transmitted from Bombay on May 15) gave an alarming glimpse of Gandhi's intentions:

The British make us fight, although I don't hide for a moment that we too want to fight. Else, we would never fight. But the only way to achieve unity is by getting India to ourselves and achieving it. . . . Anarchy is the only way. Someone asked me if there would be anarchy if the British go. Yes, it will be there. But I tell the British to give us chaos. I say, in other words, leave India to God. . . . So to those of you to whom nonviolence is not a belief but only a weapon, I say you needn't desist from helping Japan. Nay, to be true to yourselves, you should help it by every means, by even violent means if possible (2: 129-32).

With the certainty of imminent insurrection in hand, therefore, the government weighted its options. Its decisions were constrained by political realities, by constitutional "givens" within existing structures, and by available legal (or extralegal) sanctions. As the viceroy remarked, the government was "faced with a political problem, the solution of which and the control of which [did] not rest entirely in our own hands" (2: 33). Resources and constraints consisted also of men—men who must decide, and others who must carry out the orders. Finally, different concentric and overlapping circles of opinion—in India, in Britain, in the United States, and in the world at large—responding to each decision created another set of constraints which obsessed the imperial authorities. During the time from April 11 to August 8, 1942, as detailed intelligence called for specific decisions day after day, the potency of these resources and the constraints upon their use emerged in the two control strategies we have chosen to examine: the censorship of the press and the detention of the nationalist leaders. These are, of course, the control strategies whose use in 1975 has evoked corresponding reverberations of public opinion.

PRESS CENSORSHIP

Authority to control the press descended from two lines of precedent. The first, going back to 1767 and having continued to remain in standing laws since 1867 allowed simple remedies for an objectionable press: censorship or deportation. The battle for a free press was long and uneven, suffering defeats with every national emergency. Remedies for civil disturbances were sought in laws. These laws, requiring registration of presses and printed materials, gave district magistrates the power to refuse or to cancel registration for publication of objectionable matter. Later, more flexible controls enabled the government to require deposits of variable sums (up to 10,000 rupees, by 1931), subject to forfeit if objectionable matter were printed. More severe sanctions also enabled seizure of printing presses, seizure of issues of papers, and fines and imprisonment for editors and publishers.[2] The other precedent was the Defense of India Act and Rules of 1915, and of 1939. Called the D.I.R., this was a very general wartime grant of emergency powers to discipline society, including the press. As might be expected, the D.I.R. permitted the banning of publication of any document or class of documents that might interfere with "the maintenance of public order or the efficient prosecution of the war."[3]

Just such a document came to the attention of the government on May 1, 1942. The Congress Working Committee had passed resolutions on April 28 which, among other things considered objectionable, alleged molestations of women by soldiers. The government saw these resolutions as calculated attempts to arouse hostility to the military forces. A ban on their publication, therefore, was ordered, under the D.I.R. But before the ban could be enforced throughout India, summaries of the resolutions had already appeared. Moreover, even this ineffective attempt was costly. The press was provoked to hostility (2:6).

Meanwhile, in the United Provinces (now Uttar Pradesh), two clashes that had occurred between Indians and British troops were attributed to inflammatory news. The governor, Sir M. Hallett, felt sure that the mere censoring of specific documents was not enough. Certain newspapers, as he saw it, were chronic instruments for stirring popular disaffection. Gandhi, in the April 28 issue of *Harijan*, had published the report of alleged molestation of women under the headline "Foreign Soldiers in India." This item had been picked up by vernacular newspapers. Worse, the story had been promptly broadcast to the world by Berlin radio. Clearly, censorship was woefully inefficient. Or worse, from Hallett's viewpoint, the Axis powers had informants in India, possibly in the Congress itself (2:23-25). The worst offender in the United Provinces (U.P.), according to Hallett, was the *National Herald* of Lucknow, of which Nehru was board chairman. At the end of May its security deposit of 6,000 rupees was forfeited. Hallett charged it with publishing "objectionable matter" earlier in the year, and so took action under the 1931 Press Act (2:148, 193).

At about the same time, the government intercepted a text of the War Resolution of the Congress Working Committee. This resolution, approved in final form on April 27, was passed by the A.I.C.C. at Allahabad on May 1, and then published. Drafts of the document, enclosed with a letter from Sadiq Ali to Rajendra Prasad, were caught in the ordinary mails. The normal Congress practice had always been to send its important documents by courier. Why now by ordinary mail? Intelligence officers reasoned that someone in the Congress high command wanted these drafts intercepted because of the "pro-Japanese" wording of the original draft. Whether Sadiq Ali himself or someone of the "Communist group" was responsible for this leak, the government was soon convinced that it was Gandhi who had drawn up the most bellicose first draft and that he was either "a fifth columnist or a Quisling." But the viceroy, Lord Linlithgow, did not take this too seriously (2:122). After all, first Rajendra Prasad and then Nehru had successively watered down the draft sent by Gandhi from Wardha (2:63-70). Clearly there were broader considerations than censorship alone. It was important for the government to identify its core opponents and its possible allies within the broad spectrum of the Congress.

Curiously, the very virulence of Gandhi's writings in *Harijan* during the months between April and August were a chief reason for the government's withholding of censorship. Such phrases as "Leave India to God!," "Get Britain Out!," and "Better Anarchy Than the Present State!" were felt to be doing Gandhi harm by discrediting him with moderates (2:611). Such hopes were not entirely vain. As already shown, C. Rajagopalacharia considered that Congress had made a fatal mistake in not responding to the Cripps offer of seeking an accommodation with Muslim aspirations. He had resigned from the Working Committee before the end of April, and soon broke with Congress (2:45, 88, 115). Outside the Congress, Ambedkar was one of several important leaders to rally to the British standard. Although still bitter over the attempted Cripps "sell-out" of Untouchables and other minorities, he urged all Indians, as their patriotic duty, "to resist with all the power and resources at their command any attempt on the part of Congress to launch civil disobedience." Such efforts during a time of war, he declared, were "treachery to India" and "playing the enemy's game" (2:436). M. N. Roy, once a Communist and then Radical Humanist leader, had already come out in support of the government during the Cripps Mission. In his view, "To defend India against imminent Japanese invasion and also possible invasion from the west [was] the supreme task of the moment" (1:606).

At the end of May, police raided the Congress offices in Anand Bhawan, Allahabad. This brought them a sizable haul of papers which were felt to show up the differences between Gandhi and other leaders in the Working Committee and which could be used "for getting across" in America and Britain Gandhi's pro-Japanese attitude (2:148). Gandhi reacted with his June 7 *Harijan* note entitled "A Triple Tragedy": "What do Governments expect from repressive policy? Triple act of forfeiture of *National Herald* security, arrest of Rafi Ahmad Kidwai, ex-Minister, and wanton and almost indecent search of A.I.C.C. office is in my opinion a great hindrance to national war effort. . . . Let the British take risk of abdication and it will be their greatest war effort" (2:193).

In June the U.P. governor urged that the strategy of punishing the hostile core of opponents and cultivating friends be stepped up a notch. It was not enough to crack down on a few local spokesmen for sedition, like Kidwai, Paliwal, or the *National Herald*, while Gandhi and other top leaders were left alone. Hallett quoted a senior Indian officer: "Why should an Indian help whole-heartedly in the war when Congress obstructs and is certain to control the destinies of this land, whatever the outcome of the present struggle?" (2:221). Hallett was convinced the Cripps Mission had furthered this attitude by dealing with the Congress, first and last. Now it was time to look to the Communists, to lift the ban on their party and release those still in detention. He suggested an antidote for the untempered support of Congress in the Indian press: give more prominence among the Indian intelligentsia to "Communists" like M. N. Roy who published "spirited anti-Congress articles" in his paper *Independent India* (2:222).

The Wider Constituency

One of the curious ironies of the government's efforts to control public opinion lies in the fact that some of its worst troubles came from Britain. At the end of June it was possible to report progress in controlling opinion in India. Both Gandhi and the Congress position appeared to have been weakened—Gandhi's War Resolution had brought him some defeat and loss of face at Allahabad, and Congress leaders were seen as implicated in the breakdown of the Cripps proposals, or so official strategists thought. But now the British media became an embarrassment. Linlithgow made it plain to Leo S. Amery (secretary of state for India) that a much tougher line would have to be taken with the BBC, with Reuters, and with the British press generally. Without this, all the efforts of government in India might be undone (2:273-75).

Very soon after this, the viceroy let loose one of his strongest blasts on British failures to control propaganda. The government of India was particularly disturbed by the prominence given to Nehru's and Gandhi's utterances in the overseas broadcasts of the BBC. Nehru's press interview in Bombay on June 17 had been quoted at considerable length; moreover, extracts had been selected in such a way as to put Nehru's views in the most favorable light. Linlithgow voiced his outrage in his June 27 telegram to Amery:

> You are as well aware as I am that the whole object of Congress propaganda is to present the Congress demands in a reasonable light so as to discredit British policy in the eyes of the world and particularly America and under pressure of world sympathy to make things go the Congress way, which is the Axis way. Why our sole national broadcasting organization, which is presumably under the control of His Majesty's Government at least in war, should lend itself to this propaganda passes my comprehension. In doing so not only does it help the Congress case but it creates a worldwide impression that Nehru and Gandhi are entitled to speak for all India and are our natural and only successors in the event of the transfer of power which they demand.

Recognizing that in dealing with the BBC the British government had to cope with a delicate question of home politics, the viceroy nevertheless suggested that, if it was not possible to debar the BBC from giving publicity to Gandhi and Nehru, the matter ought still to be investigated as if the news came from an enemy source. And Reuters could be prevented from carrying material (2:276-77).

The secretary of state's response to the BBC problem was to exert some influence by the back door. He went to see Sir Cecil Graves (BBC's director-general) and Cyril Radcliffe (director-general, Ministry of Information). He got both to agree that the BBC had "a very special responsibility in this matter" and that they should do all possible to keep a proper balance in the news, so as not to embarrass the government of India. Amery then concluded that "no absolutely hard and fast line in the treatment of political news from India [was] desirable." It would indeed have been nice if more prominence could have been given to the "hollowness" of Gandhi's policy and his constant change of tactics. But the solution to the problem, as pointed out by Amery, was through informal cooperation and persuasion, rather than legal control (2:350-51).

As early as November of 1940, a parallel strategy in Delhi had resulted in a "gentlemen's agreement" with representatives of the press. "In return for an assurance that the Press would not impede the war effort, the Government of India had rescinded an order under the D.I.R. prohibiting publication of any matter calculated to foment opposition to the successful prosecution of the war" (2:381). But on July 10, 1942, the agreement broke down. A full summary of a resolution passed by the Congress Working Committee at Wardha was published in the *Hindustan Times*. In effect, this resolution was seen as the action of a countergovernment:

> 1. Whereas various complaints have been received regarding Government orders for evacuation of villages, lands and buildings without due notice and proper compensation, seizure and destruction of country-boats, even where life is impossible without them . . . the Working Committee issue the following instructions for guidance of people concerned . . . provided that in all cases before final decision to disobey an order or resist any measure taken, all avenues of negotiations shall be thoroughly explored.
> 2. . . . full compensation should be demanded and until question of compensation is settled they [i.e., landed property, crops, houses, boats, vehicles, etc.] should not be parted with.
> 3. In view of the scarcity of salt and apprehended famine of it due to war . . . people may manufacture salt for their own and their cattle's consumption.
> 4. [The] Committee consider it inherent right of all to protect their own and their neighbors' life and property, so all restrictions on organization for self-protection should be disregarded (2:362-63).

(One must recall the context of the resolution: the Japanese were on the threshold of Assam; indeed, the reason for confiscation of country boats in Bengal was to deny them to the Japanese, in case they broke through.)

This action was immediately interpreted by the British as a setting up of "parallel authority in defiance of established Government" (2:362-65, 374-75). Upon learning of it on July 12, Amery quickly decided to put the matter before the War Cabinet. At the same time he wired Linlithgow that if, before a cabinet decision could reach India, he should think it necessary "to take drastic action with Gandhi and the Working Committee [such as immediate arrest pending prosecution] and with the Press" (at the very least, impounding all copies of papers carrying the resolution), the viceroy was not to hesitate to act "on your own responsibility and mine. You know the story of the telegram from the station clerk to Calcutta. 'Tiger on platform eating stationmaster. Please wire instructions'" (2:375). Of course, since prompt measures had to be taken with the press to prevent circulation of the resolution, this ended the "gentleman's agreement" (2:380).

Publicity was recognized by the government to be Gandhi's chief weapon. Because, as a result of the Congress move of July 10, the situation had become much more dangerous, and because more direct and positive steps would soon become unavoidable, two further measures were considered on July 15. Sir B. Clancy (Punjab governor) proposed (1) imposing precensorship on Congress pronouncements, on *Harijan*, and on other publications and (2) a campaign of "intensive counter propaganda at home and abroad." Among the suggested ways of casting doubt upon Gandhi's credibility was a plea to publicize Gandhi's admission that one of his earlier fasts (1939) had been sinful. On that occasion he had used a fast to put pressure upon the government and a princely ruler (2:388).

On July 14, the Congress Working Committee at Wardha approved a resolution calling for the British to "Quit India" forthwith or face the consequences:

> The events happening from day to day and the experience that the people of India are passing through confirm the opinion of Congressmen that British rule in India must end immediately. . . . India in bondage can play no effective part in defending itself. . . . Ever since the outbreak of the world war, the Congress has studiedly pursued a policy of non-embarrassment. . . . These hopes have, however, been dashed to pieces. The abortive Cripps' proposals showed in the

clearest possible manner that there was no change in the British Government's attitude towards India and that the British hold on India was in no way to be relaxed. . . . This frustration has resulted in a rapid and widespread increase of ill-will against Britain and a growing satisfaction at the success of Japanese arms. . . . Should [our] appeal [to the British] fail . . . the Congress will then be reluctantly compelled to utilize all the non-violent strength it might have gathered since 1920. . . . Such a widespread struggle would inevitably be under the leadership of Mahatma Gandhi (2:385-87).[4]

Despite what it saw as "objectionable passages," "blatantly hypocritical" tone, and a continuing "threat of civil disobedience," the government found no "good ground for immediate action against Congress at any rate until [the resolution was] ratified by the A.I.C.C." Moreover, "it would do us more harm than good to attempt to suppress it or even prohibit its publication pending ratification." Accordingly, publication in India and transmission abroad was allowed. But the government determined to use the interval before the scheduled A.I.C.C. ratification of the resolution to disseminate its own propaganda and plan its own action. Through individual American correspondents the government's interpretation was to be directed to Washington and also to Chungking. Assuming that Congress would allow a decent interval before launching its civil disobedience campaign, the government planned "to strike before they are ready and the best moment for doing so may well be immediately after ratification." Since the tactics of the agitation were not yet known, it was "difficult to decide upon the appropriate instrument to use against it." One possibility was to use the resolution as a basis for proclaiming Congress an unlawful association under the Criminal Law Amendment Act. Meanwhile, provincial governments were told "to have their plans in complete readiness by August 7th [meeting date of the A.I.C.C.] and in the interval to confine action to enforcing the law against those individuals who clearly [broke] it and especially those who [instigated] others to offer defiance in pursuance of first Working Committee resolution" (2:394-95).

Finally, instead of attempting precensorship, which was seen as neither practicable nor wise, the government decided to ask the All-India Newspaper Editors Conference, meeting in Bombay that week, publicly to declare its attitude toward the coming civil disobedience and to do so "in light of their previously expressed intention not to support any obstruction to the war effort" (2:394-95).

On July 24, the machinery of the empire began to move. Sir G. Laithwaite wrote to the provincial governors outlining actions to be taken when the A.I.C.C. ratified the Quit India Resolution. The viceroy was most anxious that government "intentions should be kept wholly secret." Three days later W. G. Lacey (governor of Bihar) asked Laithwaite whether, once the government's counteraction had reached the stage of arresting the Congress leadership, each provincial government would have the option of suppressing, without prior reference to the government of India, individual newspapers which persisted in opposing the government and in advocating rebellion (2:468). His only answer was that separate instructions would be issued on the question of controlling the press (2:537). After three more days, Sir Arthur Hope (governor of Madras) suggested that the time for being gentle with the press was over. In particular, he felt that *Harijan* should be suppressed immediately; so should all vernacular papers. These were publicizing protest meetings, alleged police brutality, and so on (2:501). But Linlithgow objected on August 2. Suppression of *Harijan* would tip the government's hand prematurely. Besides, much of what Gandhi was writing provided material for counterpropaganda, and did Congress as much harm as good. In any case, only another issue or two would be run (2:529).

As plans advanced, tortuous discussions over precise tactics were held. Convinced that most of the country was in sympathy with them, the British were anxious to avoid any action which might swing sympathy to Gandhi. However they were also unanimously agreed that when the mass movement did begin, it had to be quickly and completely quashed. Those convicted should be treated as criminals and (except for Gandhi) not as political prisoners. Most important of all, "the villain of the piece, Gandhi," had to be entirely removed from public view. Thus, whatever happened to him and whether he fasted or not should not be known. Here, one worry nagged the British: what if Gandhi should die while in detention? The chance had to be taken. As August 7 approached, on the night of which the All-India Congress Committee would make its seditious decision, final approval of the government's plan was received from the War Cabinet. According to the plan:

1. Congress leaders, including Gandhi, were to be arrested immediately on ratification of the resolution.
2. Provincial and All-India committees were to be declared unlawful, offices and funds seized, and all potential organizers arrested.
3. If these measures failed to stultify civil disobedience, Congress as a whole was to be declared an unlawful association and an emergency powers ordinance promulgated, giving fullest powers to the government for dealing with all forms of Congress activity (2:618).

The fateful day came, and its fateful action. The Quit India Resolution as adopted by the A.I.C.C. on August 8, 1942, included these words:

> The immediate ending of British rule in India is an urgent necessity.
> . . . The continuation of that rule is degrading and enfeebling to India. The possession of Empire, instead of adding to the strength of the ruling power, has become a burden and a curse. India, the classic land of modern Imperialism, has become the crux of the question, for by the freedom of India will Britain and the United Nations be judged (2:621-24).[5]

Within hours, before Gandhi and the Congress leaders could disperse or disappear underground, the long-prepared trap snapped shut. All of the highest echelon of the Congress (300 or more of them) were swiftly arrested and interned; moreover, with the imposition of strict press censorship, they vanished from public view.

During the next three years, as the documents plainly show, many matters of grave consequence, including famine as well as the conduct of the war, held the attention of local authorities in India. The firm clampdown upon the Quit India movement, while it put off any immediate chaos or climateric and effectively restored tranquility in most places, left a larger question unanswered in the aftermath. It was the question of the legitimacy of the raj, a question in the minds not only of Indians, but of some Englishmen as well.

Even with almost all high leaders of the Congress in detention, an armed insurrection did occur. But this was confined to Bihar and the eastern (Oudhi) United Provinces, where much of its impetus came from Jayaprakash Narayan, and within three weeks government control had been restored (with but minor and sporadic exceptions). Masses of people remained largely indifferent, as did most minorities and the bulk of official, professional, and commercial classes. Thereafter, for the next five years until its end, no serious challenge was made to the power of the raj. In fact, there are grounds for presuming that, but for its own will, it might have continued much longer. "But the will to stay had gone," concluded one highly placed British officer, "and after the Cripps Mission it could not be revived."[6]

Immediately after the arrest of the Congress leadership, the viceroy had decided against tightening press controls. Publicity of the violent acts perpetrated in a supposedly nonviolent movement, he thought, might discredit it. But three weeks later, the War Cabinet in London met to consider "the sensational character of the news reports regarding the state of public order in India. Though the extent of disorder was relatively small," as far as the cabinet knew, "it was being reported in such a way as to give the impression that there was widespread rioting throughout the whole of India." One report given prominence suggested that public whipping was widespread in Bombay. The secretary of state for India was asked by the cabinet to: (1) find out how extensive whipping was; (2) urge the government of India to find some way of getting press representatives in India to use more discretion (checking to see what was done); and (3) influence newspaper editors in Britain to use greater discretion in the handling of reports from India (2:680-81). Of course, news of whipping made headlines in Britain and America, influencing public opinion against the raj. Amery wired Linlithgow about the unabated "flood of Reuters and other Press tripe" and asked for more information (2:385).

British editors soon seemed to comply with suggestions of the Secretary of State for India for more temperate handling of news from India. Consequently, a more formal address to newspaper editors in Britain became "hardly necessary." But on the mishandling of news by Reuters, the British government decided to exercise "a measure of Government control." Henceforth, representatives of Reuters were to receive directions "as to the form of their messages from India, in order to avoid further misrepresentation of the position" (2:668).

On August 15, Linlithgow reported major sabotage around Patna. There were organized, large-scale attempts to tear up railway lines and to interrupt communications across northern India. It was known that Bihar had an "evil reputation" for wrecking trains, even in time of peace. Floods made it impossible to move troops to the area in time to stop the destruction. In light of such circumstances, it was deemed necessary to order machine-gunning from the air. Resort to this weapon in other areas seemed likely. The viceroy was anxious to keep information on this matter out of the press (2:708).

Two days later, the government acknowledged that the press had been "a great nuisance" in the Patna affair and that not enough was being done to "curb the flood of news." Yet, fourteen Calcutta newspapers, in protest against strict restrictions, had closed down. It was feared that such pressures might be brought to bear, if the restrictions were not called off, that rumors would gain more circulation and credibility than the press had (2:743).

In this connection, a reflection of how opponents of the raj perceived news blackouts and press censorship appeared on September 10. M. L. Saksena, a Congress member who remained at liberty, wrote to protest the violent government repression of protest. He demanded justifications for repressive actions and refused to accept the withholding of information— on the grounds of "public interest"—from the forthcoming session of the Central Legislative Assembly, of which he was a member. Specifically, he wanted the assembly to be informed as to the number of times and places where the military had been called to control a situation; the total number of times firing had been resorted to; the total amount of ammunition consumed; and the total number of casualties. In addition, with respect to consequences for the war effort, he wanted to know the total number of working hours lost from strikes and sabotage since August 9; the total losses sustained by the railways (he had heard of 10 million rupees lost for the Luckow division alone); and the total amount of damage to government property. Finally, Saksena warned the viceroy against false, misleading, and complacent communiqués: "The Government is no doubt taking extra care to suppress report of the black doings of its underling, but it forgets that thereby *it has made the whole country a sort of whispering gallery, where all sorts of news—true, false or exaggerated—gets currency without any check*" (2:938-42, italics added).

Shortly after this, on August 19, Sir C. P. Ramaswamy Aiyar (the ex-diwan of Travancore, now a member of the enlarged Viceroy's Executive Council) wrote to Linlithgow, expressing his deep concern over the state of affairs in the country. He had heard a provincial governor talk of "crushing" the Congress organization. "What is needed," wrote C. P., "is to arouse the people to realize the futility and terrible danger not only to the present Government but to all future Governments of the Sabotage that is threatening to assume the dimensions of a civil war." C. P. felt that the only person who could check the sabotage movement was Gandhi. If Gandhi refused, the fact that he refused could be published. Gandhi would be under a moral duty, however, to denounce the campaign of antigovernment violence or to give up his professed doctrines. Whichever way Gandhi went, C. P. felt that the government could not lose. Beyond that, he advocated use of the press as the best way of combating terrorism and sabotage. He was wholly against any policy which might set the press against the government or set the government to suppressing the press. Frank talks and discussions held with various newspaper editors had convinced C. P. that some sort of accommodations could be made with the newspapers. He felt that the government had more to gain by trying to conciliate the press than trying to use coercion. As he saw it, "The big stick [had] been too freely used by local authorities against the press" (2:750-51). (Such excesses by local authorities, whether in 1942 or 1975, have been notable features of authoritarian clampdowns on civil liberties.)

On September 1, Amery supported Linlithgow's imposition of precensorship. Sir M. Hallett, after complaining about Reuters telegrams on such matters as whipping and negotiations with Congress, had already taken measures to control the flow of news. In his words, "If such messages cannot be held up in England, surely they can be stopped in India." He had then arranged that press messages reporting views of people or groups like the India League or Hewlett Johnson should be submitted for censorship before they were freed for transmission abroad. He had proposed to do the same for "left-wing" papers like the *Manchester Guardian* and the *News Chronicle*. For these actions, Amery warned there would be criticism in the British press and in Parliament, especially when British papers were censored. Even on the question of censorship, he reminded the viceroy, the tide of public opinion would be a determining factor (2:865-67).

PREVENTIVE DETENTION AND DEPORTATION

The Defence of India Act of 1939 (and the Rules thereunder) had precedents dating back to a similar act in 1915 and, before that, at least to Bengal Regulation III of 1818. Rule 26 under this act conferred powers on the central or provincial governments to restrict the movements or activities of, or to detain, any particular person if it was necessary to do so "with a view to preventing him from acting in any manner prejudicial to the defence of British India, the public safety, the maintenance of public order; relations with foreign or Indian States, or the efficient prosecution of the war." Rule 129 enabled the police or other officers to arrest without warrant persons who were suspected of acting (past, present, or future) with intent to assist an enemy state "or in a manner prejudicial to the public safety or to the efficient prosecution of war." No person could be detained for longer than fifteen days without order of the provincial government; and no person could be detained for longer than two months.[7]

In applying these powers to Gandhi, Nehru, and a few other top Congress leaders, the first control measure considered was deportation. The War Cabinet wanted quick and decisive action "once it [became] clear that Gandhi's activities [should] be repressed." In June and July there was incessant discussion on the remotest and tiniest details connected with how and where and when Gandhi should be dealt with (2:210-16, 224). Amery wrote privately to Linlithgow on June 22: "But he still means mischief, I imagine, and once his action becomes overt you may be forced to take uncompromising measures, including, I dare say, the declaration of Congress as an illegal organization and the deportation of Gandhi and other leaders. It is difficult for me at this distance to judge what would happen in that case, but my instinct tells me that there would be very little trouble, and that India as a whole would be immensely relieved" (2:250). A month later (July 21) it was possible for Linlithgow to report that he had ordered his "people to get on with working out detailed plans for deportation of up to 15 people by air to Uganda" (2:424). It was urgent that all proceedings should be secret. As for the legal side, there was a precedent. The India and Colonial Offices had recently (April worked out such a procedure for the case of the Pir Pagaro. This leader of a Muslim sect, arrested in October 1941 for incitement to unrest, had been permanently cut off from his followers by deportation. A reasonable construction of the Government of India Act of 1935 (7th Schedule, List 1, No. 17) had extended the governor-general's ordinance-making powers to deportation, though some doubted whether this extended to detention while in transit (2:438-39). The basic assumptions underlying the strategic thinking of high officials in India were well put by the Governor of Madras. Sir Arthur Hope wrote that "the villain of the piece, Gandhi," still had such great influence among "the ignorant masses" that, until he was absolutely removed from politics (Hope wanted deportation to Mauritius), non-Congress politicians could have no confidence. But, for the same reason, action against Gandhi would have to be kept entirely secret. Any reference to him in the press would have to be prohibited. In Hope's words: "If he fasts let it not be known; and if he dies announce it six months later" (2:443).

By late July, with texts of the Working Committee's resolutions (of July 10 and 14) in hand, the government finalized its plan. The Congress resolutions clearly fell within the scope of "prejudicial reports," as defined in the D.I.R. (2:419). Whether true or false, they incited to a "prejudicial act," which is to say, any act "intended or likely" to bring into contempt any duly constituted authority in India or in any of His Majesty's dominions, to cause fear or alarm, to impede transport, or "otherwise to prejudice the efficient prosecution of the war and the defence of British India, or the public safety or interest."[8] "Any person who [attempted] to contravene, or [abetted, or attempted to abet, or committed] any act preparatory to, a contravention of any of the provisions of Rules, [was] deemed to have contravened that provision" (2:393).[9] By its first resolution Congress could be declared an unlawful association. Because it instructed people to interfere with the administration of government (and law), the words of Congress fell under the Criminal Law (Emergency Powers) Amendment Act. But, by its second resolution, Congress could not be declared unlawful *until after* its demand was formally rejected by His Majesty's government in Britain since *only then* was it committed to implementing its threat of a mass movement. Such being the case, the British planned to take no action before the A.I.C.C. meeting in Bombay on August 7.

Until then, nothing provocative was to be done. Rather, propaganda was to be employed to undermine or weaken the effectiveness of the Congress resolutions. As soon as the Quit India Resolution was ratified, however, the second stage of the government's plan would instantly take effect. Then, simultaneously: (1) Gandhi and Working Committee members would be arrested; (2) the A.I.C.C. and province-level committees would be proclaimed unlawful by all governments; (3) all Congress offices and funds, together with all leaders and organizers of importance, would be seized; and (4) statements denouncing in strongest terms the actions of Congress leaders would be issued (2:448-49).

The government counted on the likelihood that Gandhi might reasonably expect an interval to elapse after ratification before launching his campaign. It hoped that he would not yet have circulated detailed instructions to his followers; moreover, it hoped that swift action would prevent Gandhi's campaign from ever taking shape. But to be successful, it would be necessary for the British government to reject the Congress demand *in advance*. In fact, this rejection, garbed in suitable language, would have to be in India so that it could be neatly fitted into the government of India's draft of denunciation, which would be sent later to London. The purpose of the operation was not to discredit the Congress membership as a whole, but severely to discredit the Congress leadership. Some widespread protest meetings and possibly even some disorder would have to be anticipated. Yet, to delay or postpone arrests would court disaster. All arrests execpt that of Gandhi himself would be under D.I.R. Rule 26(1)(b), relating directly to the circumstances of war, and would avoid unnecessary publicity and the excitement of trials.

Gandhi, on the other hand, would be a state prisoner; furthermore, it was considered that he would probably be taken to a house reserved for him in Poona. The possibility of even interning him in his own ashram at Sevagram was not beyond consideration. The main point was to keep him strictly separated from all outside contacts.

Stage three of the plan would take effect if stage two failed. Only then would it become necessary to proclaim the whole Congress unlawful and to promulgate the Emergency Powers Ordinance. It was still uncertain whether the situation would come to that. Yet Gandhi's idea of allowing local individuals to use wide discretion to select any line of action they might wish, whether legal or otherwise, to foment a maximum amount of embarrassment and to obstruct the administration could produce a situation in which stage three would have to be implemented. Sir M. Hallett's telegraph of July 24 urgred that at zero hour all Congress committees, all volunteer organizations, and all supporting elements should be proscribed under the Criminal Law Amendment Act; and all offices, buildings, and presses of the Congress should be seized (2:451).

After examining these plans, Amery entirely approved. But he was not sure why the government of India proposed to arrest and detain the Working Committee under the Defence of India Rules while its action against Gandhi was under the old preventive detention law of 1818.[10] After all, D.I.R. Rule 26(1)(b) seemed to apply equally to Gandhi. The 1818 law provided for arrest without trial upon "reasons of State" including preservation of "the security of the British dominions from foreign hostility and from internal commotion." The central government could act, in such cases, in all provinces of British India, especially in matters of defence, external affairs, and relations with princely states.[11] The catch in Rule 26 was a clause that prohibited the removal of a person from British India if that person was a "British Indian subject of His Majesty." Thus, in the case of Pir Pagaro, deportation had been under power conferred by the Government of India Act of 1935. Amery, already leery of the kinds of criticism that the authorities would face, especially in Britain and America, wrote: "We must face the fact that whatever may be possible as to keeping place of detention secret, the fact of arrest cannot be kept dark." Moreover, the dramatic value of sudden arrest might be weakened if Gandhi and others then had to be kept in India on medical grounds. Already the fact of Gandhi's high blood pressure and what high altitude flying might do had begun to undermine the deportation scheme (2:452-3).

Linlithgow's reply in support of the 1818 authority was twofold: (1) that public opinion in India would see it as appropriate to Gandhi's age and position; and (2) that under D.I.R. a "Security prisoner" was entitled to a certain number of interviews, letters, etc., while for a "State prisoner" ad hoc rules could be made to suit each case. Neither the viceroy nor his advisers wanted Gandhi to have any interviews or communications (2:461). On July 27 Linlithgow asked for opinions from the governors on his main alternatives: (1) deportation of all or some of the Working Committee and certain other troublesome characters, or (2) imprisonment of them in India, (perhaps divided between Yeravda Jaul and Attock Fort (2:466-67). From the replies received, it became clear that there was no unanimity. Sir R. Lumley (Bombay), Hallet (U.P.), and Sir T. Steward (Bihar) were against deportation. Its doubtful deterrant effect, its possible arousing of outpourings of sympathy, and the difficulty of knowing where to draw the line were but a few of their objections (2:475, 476, 478). The decision of the viceroy against deportation was finally made on August 1. He informed Amery that most of his advisers were against it. While his own inclination had been toward deportation, he respected the experience of those around him too much to insist. Only two things were important regarding those detained: (1) that "they [be] completely cut off from the outside world"; and (2) that "they be treated with utmost consideration" (2:517).

In Britain, meanwhile, the War Cabinet had other ideas. They wanted Gandhi sent to Aden by sea and the others to East Africa. It was considered important to avoid words like "arrest" and "detention in jails," and their connotations of criminality. The persons in question would be interned and treated as "*détenus*." As for the dangers of a "fast-to-death" action by Gandhi, a "cat-and-mouse" strategy was not agreeable, and should be avoided (2: 586-88). In the end, after all the palaver, Gandhi went not to Aden, nor Uganda, but to the Aga Khan's palace, while many of his colleagues went to Ahmednager Fort.

Perhaps the one possibility which most concerned everyone and over which there was a flood of communication and consultation, from long before the Quit India Resolution until long after, was the prospect and then the reality of Gandhi's fast-to-death. This was an event of compulsive human concern as well as an episode of high moment in Anglo-Indian relations. Gandhi, housed in the palace of the Aga Khan, was provided with all possible attention and comfort. But the resolute refusal of the government to make any concessions to end his fast, or to allow it that kind of publicity so necessary for its effective impact upon public opinion, brought the matter to a conclusion which "more than satisfied" the viceroy. The record of this fast, together with its immediate aftermath, forms a gripping documentary narrative not dealt with here. In the face of strong disagreements, severe strains upon Indian members of government, and heavy pressures from the United States and China, as well as from moderates who pushed for Gandhi's release and for "avenues of reconciliation," the viceroy remained adamant.

Gandhi was kept "strictly incommunicado." And all the while the Muslim League gathered strength, forming ministries in Bengal and the North-West Frontier Province, in preparation for the fire-storm that it knew was coming.

CONCLUSION

The old raj is gone, and a new one is now in place. A "corporate dynasty"—if one can use that term to describe an organized elite community of rulers whose sustaining powers of succession and constraint gave them sway over a continent for over two centuries—has been replaced by another, newer model. And yet, despite many changes during a quarter-century, the constitutional foundations of the raj remain much the same.

The precedents described in this study have served to emphasize continuities between constitutional crises of the present and similar episodes of over thirty years ago. The capacity of a huge political machine to sustain and to strengthen itself can be truly phenomenal. Its bureaucratic and legal "memory" and its mechanisms for withstanding shock and stress in times of emergency—whether from war or famine or insurrection—are among the wonders of human culture and technology. India was not buried under an avalanche of protest and civil disobedience—neither in 1975 nor in 1942.

But two questions can still be asked about the old raj and its rulers.

First, in what way were decisions really made? That is: in the broadest sense of decision making and high policy, how many or how few were involved in making really hard choices? Actually, on the basis of documentary evidence found in this study, one would think that only two men, or perhaps half a dozen at most, made the real decisions. There is certainly no question but that they thought that they did. The viceroy, Lord Linlithgow, and the secretary of state, Leo Amery, surely made the outward signs of deciding what to do with Gandhi and the Congress. Yet, this upper pinnacle of action hides a multitude of other factors. Aside from the emergency wartime situation and the world threat to Britain that encouraged Gandhi to think that his moment of destiny had arrived, and aside from the personality of Gandhi and his command over a well-organized party machine, there were also institutional legacies on which the top rulers could count. Among these were: (1) an already existing and highly developed body of law and precedent for questions like press censorship and preventive detention; and (2) an efficient imperial bureaucracy that not only reached all the way down—through provinces and districts to the villages—but that also fed information upward to the seats of power. Through a network of hierarchies, the rulers had the means to gain the data by which they could make decisions and then see decisions implemented.

One must remember in this regard that it was not the British who literally carried out the operations of August 7-8, 1942. British soldiers were on the frontiers. So were most of the Indian Army. Rather, it was the efficient and faithful work of an *Indian* administration that put Gandhi and Congress leaders into detention and that supervised the day-to-day working of press censorship.

Second, is it possible to find limits beyond which the British rulers were not prepared to go in order to maintain their control of the imperial raj? Or, were the constraints so weak that, whatever they might be, the British would dispense with them in order to keep the Union Jack flying at the Raj Bhavan?

The answer to this question can be either complex and long, or short and simple. If one judges just by the documents used for this study, one has to conclude that it was the constraints that determined the situation, not the situation the constraints. The great lengths to which the government of India was prepared to go in order to observe even the smallest niceties of the law, in order to guard the prestige of the raj abroad, and in order to guard it from dangers, internal or external, are manifold.

The data seem to say that opinion and legitimacy and principle mattered more than personal power. Indeed, the fairly candid correspondence in the records reveals almost no attempts at personal aggrandizement. It seems clear that by this time none of the British rulers, either as individuals or as members of any particular class, had any large personal stake in the longevity of British power in India. And yet they also seem to have been caught up in the internal logic of the system. They thought as members of a corporation whose task was to preserve that corporation and its structure from disruption. They involved themselves in the efforts we have sampled not for themselves or their continued positions as rulers as much as for the raj. This is a tradition which they left behind. It is a legacy which India can ill afford to lose.

Perhaps the ultimate rule of a constitution, in its capacity to balance and check and limit the destructive excesses of power, is its ability to serve as the institutional referee, the ultimate umpire of a political battle. In the crunch, therefore, the legitimacy of a system of power would be found in the authentication of its constitution; and this authentication occurs in the resolution of conflicts and crises. Constitutions, as formal instruments, really have no other function.

As applied to India, one must ask: Where did this capacity to serve as referee lie? Was it only in an external parliament residing in Britain? If one sees an external parliament as the ultimate authority, then all of the internal structures of India are discounted as having minor roles in its constitutional system. But then one is referring only to an *imposed* frame. This indeed is what is meant by "imperialism"—the denying of the authority of the internal institutional structures of a society (or group of societies). But if the locus of ultimate authority is imbedded within the very framework of all the structures and processses of power, that whole framework *is* the constitutional system and it *is* the ultimate authority. This is the "common law" perception. By it, *mamool* ("custom") and precedent are enshrined. They become the ultimate umpire. Thus, what the British hoped to leave was an authority by which conflicts and crises could be met inside India and within its own institutions. The hope was that the constitution, through instruments of judicial review, would serve this function.

On the very day of the Quit India Resolution (August 8, 1942), when Gandhi and the Congress declared all-out and total rebellion against the raj and when the raj snapped shut its long-prepared trap, locking up the highest-echelon leaders of the Congress, Amery wrote to Linlithgow:

> The more I think of the whole business, the more clear it is to me that what we are confronted with and have been confronted with all along is a direct conflict between two different conceptions of the Indian problem. The one is the constructive democratic conception that India can only live in freedom under a constitution arrived at by agreement and acceptable to the various elements which make up India; the other, that a single highly-organized and highly-centralized party is entitled, in the name of Indian nationalism, to take over the whole country. One or other of these conceptions has got to win (2:631).

Was it then (and is it now) as simple as all that? This study of events in 1942 would indicate that it was not.

That is to say, what one sees are two sets of "double" constitutions simultaneously at work within the larger framework of the Indian political (then imperial and now national) system. By this I mean that the distinctions Amery made applied to both parties. Both the British and the Congress—albeit at different times, under different conditions, and in different styles—partook of both models.

Except in times of critical stress, the raj itself functioned as a conglomerate of compacts, contracts, and consultative arrangements. It was far from a Weberian rational-legal order. Over much of the countryside it functioned through traditional institutions—through agrarian villages, *zamindars*, princes, and plantation proprietors. To its urban elite constituencies it was avowedly different, more progressive and democratic. The very conception of a strong and united India that the British intended to leave behind them was of a consultative unity that took minority feelings systematically into account. We have seen the pains they took over the constituencies of Jinnah, Ambedkar, Tara Singh, M. N. Roy, and C. P. Ramaswamy Aiyar, over the princes, and over the potential influences of dissident Congressmen like C. Rajagopalicharia. The reconstituted Viceroy's Council, in which eleven of fifteen cabinet portfolios were in Indian (albeit non-Congress) hands, is evidence. But, whenever the crunch of an emergency came, the government of India was not without means nor will to fall back upon the authoritarian instruments and precedents which, built into the constitution of its old hierarchical structure, harked back to Mughal times. Here, while the British remained openly consultative among themselves (more than in the past) and while they continually strove to conciliate public opinion (in India, in Britain, and beyond) through propaganda, they ultimately relied upon the main force of their administrative machinery. The "logic" of the raj demanded no less. For, as Benoy Kumar Sarkar put it: "A swordless state is a contradiction in terms."[12]

For their part, the Congress was no less dualistic. Normally led by consultation—often deadlock—among brokers of provincial or even district and town followings, among crusaders of localized charisma, the Congress would tighten every ten years or so into an ad hoc monolith. These were the times of confrontation with the raj, of mass civil disobedience and *satyagraha*. In these episodes, the high command, claiming to represent *the* people of India, would brook no opposition. At such times there was small quarter for its foes—whether for Jinnah or Ambedkar, whether for dissidents within its own ranks (e.g., Subhas Chandra Bose in 1939 or Rajaji in 1942) or for anyone else who dared to differ with Gandhi. (Such traits, under Nehru, were felt by Tandon and Kripalani, and under Indira Gandhi, by Kamaraj, Moraji, and Jayaprakash.) It was for Congress in this phase (or guise) that Benoy Kumar Sarkar could coin the term "despotocracy" and could see an *"imperium in imperio"*: "The Congress High Command," he wrote, "has during the entire course of its history comprised from time to time just a few individuals or families. . . . These individuals or families are . . . the sinews of war, i.e., its bullion."[13] The antipathy of Sarker for the Gandhian system and for a despotic Congress machine, one lubricated and powered by the *"dal-roti"* of a patronage system tying the voters to the privileged few, seems almost prophetic.

Yet, after each crisis phase, Congress leaders would revert to a more loose and open phase of conciliation. Then, in the role of a brokerage, it would arbitrate between contending interests, speak sweet reason to fearful communities, and draw new and wider circles of political support and consensus beneath its umbrella.[14] (After independence, during much of the fifties and sixties, the "democratic" face was more often in evidence; but the other face, the "despotic" one, was never completely hidden.) In each decade this process brought further strength to the Congress. Whether through reorganization into linguistic regions, through the Khilafat movement, through appeals to ideologically left-wing or communally right-wing groups, or through the "discovery" and elevation of Harijans to Hindu status (with rights to temple entry), the Congress gains during times of conciliatory dialogue were as great as those of its other phase.

In this real, functioning, sense the duality within the constitutional legacy of the raj is double. Both the British rulers and the Congress counterrulers developed instruments and precedents for despotic action and authoritarian control of their respective constituencies within India which could supplant their more liberal, democratic propensities. In times of emergency (and "war") we can see how each could match the other's escalation of provocation and threat. What could be done quite constitutionally through instruments of censorship illustrates the government's powers to tighten controls: (1) news could be declared "objectionable"; (2) news media security deposits could be increased, and forfeited; (3) copies of newspapers could be seized and impounded; (4) a "gentlemen's agreement" could be negotiated, and superseded; (5) precensorship could be imposed upon hostile presses; (6) Congress could be pronounced an "unlawful" association; (7) wire services could be "instructed"; (8) overseas dispatches could be controlled; and (9) the BBC could be influenced. Only the British and foreign presses were beyond reach. Reaching farther: (10) mail could be intercepted; (11) Congress offices could be searched and their files seized and used in propaganda; and, finally, (12) parties hostile to Congress (e.g., the CPI) could be selectively legalized. Against such instruments, the Congress capacity for countergovernment through manipulation of the public communication media was progressively curtailed. In the end, relatively little more could be done by Congress than to inspire the shutting down of sympathetic newspapers and the circulating of clandestine rumors (with risks of such efforts backfiring).

The blunt instrument of preventive detention provided much less scope for delicate surgery. Detention is a final resort, for in the face of a total threat, its effect would have to be total. The threat was identified when Congress was seen as setting up a parallel government. At this stage the government saw no more room for half-way measures. It tried to make sure that (1) no Congress leaders would escape its net; (2) no contacts with *détenus* would occur; (3) no funds remained available; and (4) no part of the Congress organization remained lawful or functioning.

What remains for us is some relative calculation of costs. As each measure of government sanction was set to match each countergovernment threat, was such action necessary? In short, did the government of India go too far? Quite obviously, from official records, the British did not think so. What Congress leaders thought is equally obvious. It seems clear from the words of both sides that, had the government not acted as it did, Gandhi's revolution might have succeeded. Rulership succession, or the "transfer of power," might well have occurred in 1942 instead of 1947. Whether there might have been less or more bloodshed, less or more communal strife, less or more unity in the subcontinent are questions for which answers can never be certain. Differing opinions cannot be reconciled as long as so much data and so many variables remain beyond our grasp.[15] But of one thing there can be no doubt: the legacy of the present raj is of a double sort and, therefore, its despotic potential is derived both from the imperial structure and from the now loose-jointed, now monolithic party which rules that structure.

Finally, something must be said about the "one-eyed" character of this study. Our approach to the last emergency of the raj has been based almost exclusively on the official documents of the government of India. This limitation has been deliberate. Its consequence is an obvious bias. We have wanted to know how the emergency looked from the official point of view. Much has been written on the Congress point of view, or on the points of view of individual politicians. One of the best attempts to put the whole within a balanced, constrained, and detached framework is Francis G. Hutchins's *India's Revolution: Gandhi and the Quit India Movement*.[16] Fortunately, if Hutchins betrays any unwitting bias, it is in Gandhi's favor, and thus serves to balance this paper.

NOTES

[1] Documents from which this narrative is taken have only in recent years (following the "twenty-five year" rule) been released from the confidential sections of the government archives and records. The records are fascinating as much for what they do not tell us as for what they do tell us. The process of their release and publication has been slow and arduous. Under the scholarly editing of Professor Nicholas Mansergh and Penderel Moon, who, upon the recent death of E. W. R. Lumby, has taken up the assistant editorship, the work is only half done. Another five volumes are still to appear. This narrative draws upon the first two volumes: *Constitutional Relations Between Britain and India: The Transfer of Power, 1942-7*, vol. 1, *The Cripps Mission, January-April 1942* (London: HMSO, 1970); vol 2, *'Quit India,' 30 April-21 September 1942* (London: HMSO, 1971). References to these volumes are indicated in the text simply by volume and page number.

[2] Press and Registration of Books Act (XXV of 1867); Press (Emergency Powers) Act (XXIII of 1931).

[3] India, Legislative Department, *Legislation and Orders Relating to the War*, 3rd ed., 3 vols. (Delhi: Manager of Publications, 1942), vol. 2, p. 83.

[4] Text of the Quit India resolution was published earlier in Great Britain, Parliament, *Statement Published by the Government of India on . . .*

Disturbances in India, 1942-43, Session 1942-43. Cmd. 6430 (London: HMS, 1974), pp. 827ff. Note that twenty-two years earlier in 1920, the Congress creed had been changed to eliminate the declared adherence of that body to the British connection and to the constitutional methods of agiation.

5 Also Cmd. 6430, noted above.

6 H. V. Hodson, *The Great Divide* (London: Hutchinson, 1969), p. 107.

7 India, Laws, Statutes, etc., *Defense of India Act, 1939 and Rules Made Thereunder up to 30th November 1942* (Delhi: Manager of Publications, 1944), pp. 51ff.

8 Ibid., Rule 34(1)(c), and Rule 34(7).

9 Ibid., Rule 38(1)(b), and Rule 34(6)(e), (g), (h), (k), and (p).

10 Bengal State Prisoners Regulation III of 1818, extended to other parts of India by 1929. See Granville Austin, *The Indian Constitution: Cornerstone of a Nation* (Oxford: Clarendon Press, 1966).

11 Bengal Code, 5th ed., vol. 1 (Calcutta: Government Press, 1939), pp. 157-61.

12 Benoy Kumar Sarkar, *The Politics of Boundaries* (Calcutta: N. M. Ray Chowdhury, 1926), p. 1.

13 Subodh Krishna Goshal, *Sarkarism* (Calcutta: Chuckertty Chatterjee, 1940), p. 36.

14 Survival of the brokered structure of the Congress through the first mass confrontation is a major theme of Judith M. Brown, *Gandhi's Rise to Power: Indian Politics 1915-1922* (Cambridge: Cambridge University Press, 1972).

15 A most valuable contribution to preserving the perspectives and recollections of scholars and eyewitnesses is C. H. Philips and M. D. Wainwright, eds., *The Partition of India: Policies and Perspectives 1935-1947* (Cambridge: M.I.T. Press, 1970).

16 Cambridge: Harvard University Press, 1973.

3

The Civil Service and the Emergency
Stanley J. Heginbotham

Political regimes conventionally depend on public bureaucracies to make their will felt on the societies over which they pre-
side. The civil service is a key instrument not only for the repressive and extractive activities of governments but also for
their efforts to transform and develop societies. When a change
in the character of a regime becomes the focus of social science
analysis, it is of special importance to examine the response of
the civil service to the change. This seems especially important
in the case of the recent transition to an emergency regime in
India, where the public services are generally considered to be
among the society's more progressive and modernized forces.
How did this sector respond to the declaration of the emergency and the governmental decisions that followed it? To what
extent did it oppose, resist, or interfere with the restrictions on
political freedoms and civil liberties that were ordered by Mrs.
Gandhi and her associates? How does one interpret the responses of the civil service? Against what standards does one
measure them?

These questions give shape and direction to the first section
of this chapter, which explores the character of changes brought
about by the emergency and the activities the civil service was
instructed to carry out. The response of the public bureaucracies
is then discussed and interpreted from three perspectives: the

bureaucrats as modernizers, the bureaucrats as civil servants, and the bureaucrats as members of an Indian administrative tradition.

The emergency also raises broader questions about the role of public administration in India. The record of the country's government bureaucracies in stimulating economic development and social justice has been disappointing. Many observers—particularly those who support the emergency regime—have pointed to the demoralizing and debilitating effects that self-interested intervention of politicians into administrative matters has had on the civil service. Others argue that there are more fundamental problems responsible for the ineffectiveness of Indian public bureaucracies. In order to place this issue in perspective, the second section of this chapter examines the character of political influence on administrative practice in the post-independence period. The subsequent section projects the likely consequences for administrative performance of the political and economic directions followed by the emergency regime in its initial months.

ADMINISTRATIVE RESPONSE

The initial manifestations of the changes in Indian political processes after the declaration of the emergency status were the arrests of thousands of politicians and others who were thought or alleged to be opponents of the regime, instigators of civil disorder, or perpetrators of such antisocial or illegal economic behavior as smuggling, hoarding, or trading on the black market. In addition, very severe restrictions were placed upon press coverage of politics.

However much these restrictions of civil liberties and political discourse violated notions of democratic process, they were all legal. The Indian constitution specifically provides for the declaration of states of emergency, and press censorship and preventive detention are explicitly authorized when such states are in effect. Mrs. Gandhi retained the loyalty of her Congress party majority in Parliament, and that group, with the support of the Communist Party of India (CPI), willingly—indeed enthusiastically—ratified her decision to declare the emergency and passed the retroactive legislation that led to the Supreme Court of India overturning her conviction for violation of the election code.

Members of the Indian bureaucratic institutions carried out these policies, and the wide range of continuing policies and programs of the emergency regime, without question. Extensive inquiries among both civil servants and observers of the administrative apparatus of the government at the time of transition have not uncovered any examples of resistance to the restrictions placed on civil liberties—emergency measures were implemented fully and properly, and there were apparently no resignations or other acts designed to indicate displeasure or disapproval.[1] Whether reservations were expressed more discreetly is difficult to determine, though it seems quite possible that some of the thousands of officers forced into early retirement because of "inefficiency" and dubious "integrity" were singled out because of their lack of enthusiasm for the emergency regime.[2] For the most part, however, where members of administrative services expressed any feeling about the transition, it was generally one of approval and even enthusiasm.

In subsequent weeks, manifestations of the new regime struck more directly at the interests of the civil service. First there was the forced early retirement of the administrators whose work was reputed to be substandard or whose loyalty to Mrs. Gandhi seemed in doubt. Then, for the vast majority who remained, a swift end was brought to the casual routines whereby employees in many offices conventionally arrived at work as much as two or three hours after the official working day had begun and took extended breaks for coffee and lunch. Public employees were told to show up on time and to work their full day. Reports from many parts of the country confirm that these orders were generally obeyed and that, in the first months following the declaration of the emergency at least, a noticeably more serious and industrious atmosphere pervaded the halls and offices of the state and national governments. Even these challenges to the traditional routines and job security of members of the public service seem not to have mobilized significant opposition to Mrs. Gandhi's new order.

Is it cause for surprise that the members of the country's administrative establishment did nothing significant to oppose or interfere with the transformation in India? Does it suggest a weakness of character, value commitments, or institutional differentiation in the bureaucracy? Or is it simply an accurate reflection of how bureaucrats in most societies might be expected to respond to similar events?

The expectation that elements in the Indian administration would have done something to oppose or interfere with the transition to an emergency regime seems to be rooted in the view of Indian administrators as leaders in the process of modernization and Westernization. It is generally recognized that forces for change in Indian society are predominantly located in a narrow range of occupational sectors. The agricultural sector is thought of as basically conservative and oriented toward the status quo. In the business community, though there are clearly individuals and institutions who operate technologically and managerially sophisticated enterprises, much of India's entrepreneurial activity is still directed by particularistic family concerns that see the maximization of short-term profit margins as the key to business success. And in the political sector, despite the dynamic character of Indian party politics, the more successful Indian parties have drawn their support from the generally traditional and conservative agricultural and business sectors, which makes them unlikely sources of support for modernizing change.

Thus, the major thrust of translating ideas of modernity into significant patterns of social and economic change is generally seen to be taking place not in the private sector of the economy, nor in the competitive political sector of the government, but rather in the public sector of the economy and the administrative sector of government. For most advocates of modernization in India, it is the higher levels of the public administration that hold the key to social and economic modernization. The Indian Administrative Service (IAS) is seen as having inherited the norms and standards of British elite education: personal integrity and dedication combined with a finely honed intelligence and problem-solving ability. The best and brightest of the Indian colonial society strove mightily for admission into the progenitor Indian Civil Service (ICS). Their presence as a critical mass shaping the expansion and extension of the Indian administrative establishment in independent India seemed to be an important cause for optimism that significant modernization could be brought about in the postcolonial era. The continued power of the IAS to draw India's most highly educated and intelligent young people into its ranks further focused attention on the upper-echelon civil service as the leading sector in the country's modernization. Of those recruited during the years 1966-67 and 1968-69, for example, over three-quarters had postgraduate degrees.[3]

Western investment in the future of India over the past twenty-five years has focused heavily on the elites of the public sector bureaucracies. Project-oriented assistance has been channeled primarily into government bureaucracies designed to play innovational roles in stimulating rural economic and social change. Investments in human talent have been heavily concentrated on individuals whose careers are in the public sector.

Much of the analysis of the process of modernization has seen it as a constellation of interrelated phenomena linking together greater rationalization and increased levels of communication, participation, and equity. As a result, it has often been assumed that the chief proponents of modernization in India— among them the public sector elites—would also be among the chief defenders of democratic processes. Since many observers recognize the preservation of civil liberties—and especially unfettered press and political opposition—as essential features of competitive political systems, they have looked instinctively to the modernized, Westernized, and educated leaders of the civil service for some measure of opposition or resistance to the restraints that were placed on civil liberties in the wake of Mrs. Gandhi's declaration of the emergency.

A realistic assessment of the values and goals that underlie the behavior of these agents of modernization must, however, take into account that they are also civil servants and share the pervasive values of that occupational sector. A fundamental feature of the civil service ethos is that the bureaucracy provides continuity and stability in the face of political change and uncertainty. Whatever issues may be at large in the political arena, the implementation of a vast range of programs and policies must continue uninterrupted. Dependability in implementation is the hallmark of the civil service. N. Raghavan Pillai, an ICS officer from 1921 until 1960, clearly summarized the tradition that pervades Indian public administration:

> In a parliamentary democracy, such as ours, the permanent services form a vital part of the apparatus of government. Governments may change, and with them national policies, but the varied, continuing tasks of administration are carried on uninterruptedly by the vast complex machine that the public services are today.[4]

This concern for continuity and proper performance must naturally be a matter of primary importance to the higher-level public servant, for his work has real meaning only if the quality of policy implementation—as apart from the quality of policy-making—makes a significant difference.

We should remember that the commitment of elite members of the civil service to administrative continuity and performance, even in contest with the highest loyalties of nationalism, was tested during the period of Indian nationalist agitations, and most intensely during the Quit India movement of 1942. G. D. Khosla, a contemporary of Pillai who served in the ICS from 1925 through 1960, rejected the notion that not to resign from the ICS would be to "compromise with my conscience and disregard my real duty by harnessing myself to a foreign yoke." He argued:

> If I resigned, somebody else would be appointed in my place. He might be a hard-boiled imperialist, unsympathetic and hostile to Indian aspirations or an Indian who was prepared to toe the line all the way with bureaucrats of the ruthless school.[5]

The issue was clearly not so much one of whether or not to resign from the civil service or to disregard or subvert orders, but one of whether or not implementation was carried out as humanely as possible.

Of special significance are Khosla's extensions of this general argument after he joined the judicial branch and eventually became Chief Justice of Punjab state from 1959 to 1961. The first draws parallels between the executive and judicial services, and the second between the status of civil liberties in the preindependence and postindependence periods:

> It would be wrong to suggest that no Indian should have remained a member of the judiciary because in discharging his duties he was perpetuating foreign rule by punishing all those who were engaged in the struggle for freedom. . . . The judge (or for that matter, the civil servant on the executive side) was upholding the law of the land. He had developed an attitude of mind that abhors chaos, criminal violence and disruptive tendencies. This same attitude of mind was maintained by him in free India and served him as an efficient weapon for fighting the forces of disruption whenever they were in evidence.[6]

> The Preventive Detention Act is a repressive measure, and since it enables the government to imprison any number of its opponents without proper trial, it is a most dangerous instrument and liable to be abused. Indeed, there is no doubt at all that it is frequently abused and its drastic provisions are employed not for the purpose of pre-

venting crime or by way of a security measure but to silence honest and often justified criticism of the Government. But judges do not decline to enforce its provisions nor do they resign and leave the Bench on the ground that in their view the law is unjust, undemocratic and therefore, to an extent, unpatriotic. I need scarcely add that human and liberty-loving judges do . . . [not] hesitate to grant a writ of Habeas Corpus if it can be shown that the governmental order of detention is an abuse of the process of law.[7]

It might, of course, be argued that this attitude reflects only Indian, rather than more general, civil service views, but the bureaucratic imperative of allegiance to any legal order is clearly established in British parliamentary government and accurately reflected in its Indian offshoot. As recently as 1959, Herbert Morrison wrote, in his *Government and Parliament: A Survey from the Inside*, that "the civil service should at all times know that the lawful orders of ministers must be carried out."[8] The boundary between the minister and the civil servant is clearly drawn, and, as the then home secretary noted, "The position of the civil servant is that he is wholly and directly responsible to his minister." It is within the ranks of ministers that responsibility to the public lies. It is they who are accountable to the public for the wisdom, appropriateness, and uprightness of policies implemented by the civil service. This includes, certainly, policies balancing civil liberties against government stability and law enforcement. Morrison continued:

> There may, however, be an occasion on which so serious a mistake has been made that the Minister must explain the circumstances and processes which resulted in the mistake, particularly if it involves an issue of civil liberty or individual rights. Now and again the House demands to know the name of the officer responsible for the occurrence. The proper answer of the Minister is that if the House wants anybody's head it must be his head as the responsible minister, and that it must leave him to deal with the officer concerned in the Department.[9]

Historical experience further reinforces the predominance of the civil service devotion to the separation of responsibility for policy and for policy implementation. Though it clearly would be erroneous to suggest that there have been no cases of members of well-defined civil service cadres acting to oppose, interfere with, or express disapproval of authoritative and legal politically ordered measures to restrict civil liberties, the incidents of such behavior are certainly very rare.[10] In Japan, Germany, and Italy during the 1930s, in the United States during the 1920s and under the influence of Joseph McCarthy, and in the Philippines in 1974, to cite examples that constitute partial parallels to the Indian regime transition of 1975, the civil service remained firm in its dedication to policy implementation duties.

The American image of public servants resigning in protest rather than carrying out policies with which they have fundamental disagreements is probably exaggerated. But there are three special characteristics of American bureaucracy which make this image more realistic in the United States than in British and Indian tradition.

1. Foremost among these is the lack of clear boundaries between American civil and political service. The proper anallogue to many American resignations by appointed administrators is the resignation of the minister in the parliamentary system.

2. There is frequent personnel movement between civil service and private sector positions. Mobility lessens the cost of resignation and diversifies the sensitivities and loyalties which may prompt it.

3. Many top American bureaucrats are lawyers. These men can leave a top bureaucratic post without quitting their profession or career. Moreover, with reference to the specific question before us, lawyers probably have a greater awareness of and sensitivity to civil liberties issues within the civil service.

Indian public service, in comparison, is characterized by very clear boundaries between political and civil service, very limited personal interpenetration with the public sector, and almost no tradition of training in the law as appropriate preparation for the civil service. Indeed, B. S. Khanna's data on the 116 entrants into the Indian Administrative Service and Indian Foreign Service during 1961-62 indicate that not a single one of them had a law degree.[11]

Thus, given the character of civil service in general, and the structural characteristics of the Indian civil service in particular, there is little reason to expect that its members would be active in opposing or impeding the implementation of policies established under Mrs. Gandhi's emergency regime.

Examination of the Indian civil service in its historical dimension reinforces the revised expectations produced by this comparative view. The traditions of civil service implementation of the sometimes repressive policies of government that evolved during the colonial era were not significantly modified after independence. The government was now one of Indian rather than foreign leadership, and heavy social and economic tasks were added, but the old goals had not been abandoned. Law and order remained a preeminent concern of the public bureaucracies. David Potter, in analyzing the transition from colonial to independent government, writes:

> The maintenance of order in a district enjoyed absolute priority during I.C.S. days; it is so today. The training of I.A.S. officers both at the National Academy and later in the states, as well as the influence of more seasoned officers under whom young recruits work, stresses this priority; although at the same time his training broadens the orientation to include the importance of development work as well.[12]

Within organizations generally, the primary concern of participants is often diverted from policy and program goals to the bureaucratic mechanisms designed to meet those goals. This phenomenon, which Merton has identified as one of goal displacement,[13] is especially powerful in the Indian context and has important implications for understanding the responses of civil servants to the emergency.

Generalized bureaucratic tendencies to goal displacement are strongly reinforced by two aspects of organizational tradition that are central to Indian administrative experience. The first is the culturally distinctive notion of duty that characterizes Indian society and is frequently transposed into bureaucratic settings; the second is the historically embedded notion of unquestioning acceptance of legal orders that has been transmitted from British colonial bureaucracy.[14]

Prevalent Indian notions of duty are closely linked to the concept of *dharma*. This is at once a highly abstract and very practical and specific guide to behavior deriving from Hindu tradition. At the abstract level, *dharma* is the cosmic ordering of the universe that ought to be replicated as far as possible in discrete social entities of the world. Operationally this is achieved through the definition of an elaborate complex of rights and duties of individuals. If appropriately formulated and performed, these rights and duties will bind members of the social organism together into an ordered, balanced, and harmonious community. For the individual, *dharma* has the much more explicit and concrete meaning of those specific acts which he must perform in order to make his or her personal contribution to the maintenance of societal harmony. One's *dharma*, or duty, then, is defined very explicitly and its proper performance is a matter of great seriousness since an individual's failure to do his duty in a proper way not only reflects adversely on him, but also threatens to generate disorder and conflict in the community as patterns of rights and duty are thrown out of balance.[15] Traditional patterns of behavior are the major source of understanding about *dharma* and individual duty. Where these patterns are for any reason called into question, reference is made to community authority figures who are recognized as especially skilled in perceiving and restoring the character of *dharmic* order.

The unquestioning character of a proper sense of duty is quite explicit in the *dharmic* tradition. The pattern of interrelations between individuals is seen to be so complex, and any one interaction to have so many ramifications, that it is impossible to anticipate by any ends-means calculations the results of a specific action that is not an element of one's duty as ratified by traditional experience. The imperatives of *dharma* are such that one should not calculate the consequences of one's performance of duty; indeed, the highest praise for duty-consciousness is reserved for the individual who sees that the proper performance of his traditionally defined duty will produce overwhelmingly negative results, but persists nevertheless in performing those duties. This notion of duty, of course, corresponds to, reinforces and legitimizes the tendencies of bureaucrats under pressure to focus on the specific procedures they are ordered to carry out, and to ignore the goals those procedures were designed to achieve. It contributes to the unquestioning performance of specific duties that might, from the perspective of ends-means calculations, be difficult or impossible to reconcile with personal goals or the goals of a bureaucracy.

This tendency toward unquestioning acceptance of bureaucratic authority was incorporated and built upon in the molding of the British colonial bureaucracy. As a regularized administrative apparatus evolved as the central mechanism of British management in the subcontinent, it became essential that large numbers of indigenous employees, whose loyalties to the crown were suspect, contribute to orderly administration. A bureaucratic system evolved that incorporated extraordinarily elaborate checks and crosschecks on the vast numbers of subordinate authorities whose duties were to carry out routine tasks according to thoroughly elaborated procedures, and to prepare files on nonroutine issues so that they could be disposed of by the British officials concerned. Again, the unquestioning performance of specific procedures was an essential feature of the orderly operation of the apparatus, both in terms of the services it performed for the crown and in terms of its own internal control mechanisms, which depended on indigenous employees constantly reporting on each other's work.

Though the Indian public administration is a complex and highly differentiated phenomenon whose specific elements incorporate widely varying traditions of authority and duty, the *dharmic* and British colonial traditions were clearly present and important in the Tamil Nadu development bureaucracy that I studied. The predominance of Hindu tradition throughout much of the subcontinent, and the extensive penetration of well-elaborated British colonial bureaucracies within the boundaries of what is now India, suggest that these same traditions are likely to have a similar effect on bureaucrats throughout much of India.

This is not to suggest, of course, that Indian bureaucrats differ in fundamental respects from their counterparts in other societies, but rather to argue only that common tendencies among bureaucrats to fix their perceptions of their own responsibilities on procedures rather than goals have a special force in India. That Indian civil servants should have effectively and efficiently performed the procedures assigned to them in the implementation of the emergency regulations should, therefore, come as no surprise.

THE COMPETITIVE POLITICAL ENVIRONMENT

As the character of the new Indian political system becomes more clearly established and institutionalized in the wake of the emergency, one naturally begins to ask how the changes of 1975 will affect the country's administrative processes. The public bureaucracies of state and central governments have been the dominant institutions exercising influence over the lives of citizens since independence, just as they were during most of the era of British raj. The key questions, however, revolve around (1) the roles that have been played by other institutions in directing, informing, and constraining that influence, and (2) how the ending of those roles will affect the bureaucratic order. The first of these questions is the subject of this section and the second will be dealt with in the subsequent section.

During the postindependence period, direction of public bureaucracies came from the leadership of elected parties at the center and in the states. The vitality of state party units, the importance to most rural citizens of the powers controlled by state administrations, and the need for electoral strength to control those administrations made this division of political direction between state and national party leadership groups a very real and important feature of the Indian political process. At the state level, policy decisions were generally centralized in the hands of relatively small numbers of party leaders trusted by their chief ministers. The expertise of senior civil servants was broadly recognized, however, and much of the initiative for policy development came from within the career services. Since the Congress party at the center was dependent for its continued existence upon the capabilities of the state party organizations, central cabinet positions with potential for bureaucratic policy authority were frequently distributed among leaders with independent power bases of their own. Leadership powers were thus diffused among state and national party organizations and were broadly shared by both politicians and senior civil servants.

During this period, despite the diffusion of operational powers, general direction, coherence, and continuity were maintained as a result of the remarkable dominance of the Congress party during most of the period both at the center and in most of the states. Even where that dominance was broken, a broad national consensus on the legitimacy of a succession of five-year plans as general statements of economic direction, and the extensive role of career civil servants in policymaking decisions, provided surprising coherence.

The most distinctive characteristic of Indian public bureaucracy within an open political process was not, however, in the character of the forces directing it, but rather in the kinds of constraints imposed upon it. To a very great degree, the Indian political process focused not on the making of specific policies to be implemented by the administrative machinery, but on intervening within that machinery to influence policy implementation in individual cases. One of the ubiquitous themes of empirically grounded research on the political process during this period was the susceptibility of governmental bureaucracies to the influence of politicians representing the interests of individual constituents. To a degree that is inconsistent with normative Western theories of parliamentary democracy and that far exceeds practice in Western countries, Indian legislators—and especially those in state assemblies—were so involved with arranging for special treatment of constituents under the laws that they were generally quite prepared to leave the functions of formulating those laws to civil servants and the narrow circle of party officials who specialized in such matters.[16] Indeed, one study in the 1960s showed that most party leaders strove for positions as ministers not so that they could provide executive leadership for agencies, but so that they would be in strong positions to penetrate those agencies' lower levels on behalf of constituents.[17]

In addition to national and state legislatures, in the late 1950s the Indian political system added a set of local legislative institutions concerned specifically with developmental issues. Two-tier—and in a few states three-tier—structures of elected council members that were set up to make local development policy decisions in nonpartisan settings, these *panchayat* institutions have in practice added new layers of elected party activists whose primary concerns are penetrating the remote outposts of state bureaucracies in behalf of their local supporters.[18]

Indian democracy of the postindependence period was extraordinarily responsive to the interests of a broad range of its citizens. That responsiveness was not, however, based on the aggregation of interests of individuals who shared distinctive socioeconomic, regional, and ideological concerns. Instead, individuals sought—and frequently received—particularistic attention to personal concerns. Frequently, of course, this responsiveness took the form of corruption: bureaucrats were persuaded to violate the law in behalf of a petitioner or to acquiesce to the petitioner's wishes in return for a bribe. Such behavior was not a product of competitive politics; it long antedated independence in India, is widespread in neighboring countries that lack democratic institutions, and will undoubtedly persist as an important pattern within postemergency India.

The institutionalization of corruption within an open and competitive political system does, however, have important consequences. On the positive side, it may constrain bribery by substituting political pressure for financial profit as the motivating force behind bureaucratic decisions to depart from the universalistic norms they are instructed to follow. On the other hand, the scope of corruption and the seeming inability of the system to cleanse itself have powerfully disillusioning effects on the middle-class supporters of the democratic ideal.[19] Because elected leaders of legislative bodies—whether from the government or the opposition parties—have generally built their careers through such servicing activities, they are often reluctant to press enquiries into most forms of political intrusion on bureaucratic processes.

Such intrusions are by no means always illegal or designed to produce benefit for one's constituents at the expense of some broader public interest. Frequently the local political activist simply "expedites" bureaucratic action, achieving promptly an end that would eventually have been forthcoming as a result of normal bureaucratic processing.[20] In other cases, the motivation for intervention is the legitimate one of simply helping unsophisticated constituents negotiate the intricate bureaucratic requirements that must be fulfilled before they can qualify for government programs designed to benefit them. Local politicians also intervene frequently to extricate their constituents from situations in which the requirements of universalistic laws and regulations do not seem to fit the idiosyncratic circumstances of a particular family or individual.

However one views the legitimacy of such forms of responsiveness in a political system of parliamentary structure, it is clear that they generate extraordinary strains both within the ruling parties and within the bureaucracies. For the ruling parties, the pressures have been acutely divisive. Their executive leaders, dedicated to the definition and implementation of rational and effective general policies that would achieve publicly articulated goals, continually found their efforts being undercut by their party colleagues in servicing positions, who were systematically extracting concessions from the bureaucracies charged with implementing those policies.

Nehru, though dedicated to social and economic reform, was convinced that the Congress party was dependent on its servicing wing for the mobilization and maintenance of its electoral base. As a result, he assiduously mediated between contending forces in the party. Mrs. Gandhi was selected by leaders of the servicing organization to succeed Lal Bahadur Shastri as party leader and prime minister because of her presumed malleability. However, she challenged—and overwhelmed—their attempts to constrain her executive leadership: she forced a split in the party, separated by a period of a year national parliamentary elections from the more salient and servicing-oriented state assembly ones, and won the 1971 parliamentary elections convincingly on the issue of who could provide the most effective national leadership.[21] This resolution of the conflict within the Congress led to the progressive deterioration of its servicing organization and the gradual replacement of its constituency-based leaders by loyalists to Mrs. Gandhi's concept of executive dominance.

Within the public bureaucracies, of course, political efforts to assure "responsiveness" were seen as blatant and unwarranted interference with appropriate bureaucratic procedure and routine. Repeatedly placed in uncomfortable binds between legal mandates and powerful political pressures, bureaucrats learned to make difficult and often dangerous compromises, but the insecure and arbitrary character of their positions gave them good reason for holding ambivalent attitudes about the values of competitive politics.

In addition to directing and constraining public bureaucracies, the institutions of open and competitive political processes played important roles in informing the executives of these bureaucracies about what was going on both inside and outside their own institutions. Every bureaucracy needs extensive feedback from its lower levels so that it can respond to changing environments. The accuracy of information received through its own chain of command is likely to be seriously flawed, however, when—as in the Indian case—that information is also widely used as the basis for evaluating the performance of the individuals who collected it. The difficulty of obtaining accurrate feedback from the field in postindependence India has been alleviated by the competitive and pluralistic character of the system. In their interventionist roles, politicians provided middle and higher level civil servants with alternative sources of information about the performance of their subordinates and the impact of their programs. This flow of information was supplemented by the extraordinarily open character of the professional bureaucracy while it operated under diffused centers of political control. Continuing dialogues between central and state agencies, between planning and operational institutions, and among counterparts in various states added both knowledge and ideas to the resources of the bureaucracies. An openness to an enquiring and critical press as well as to a broad range of foreign analysts and advisers further contributed to the continual infusion of new information and knowledge into the administration.

THE POSTEMERGENCY ENVIRONMENT

In order to anticipate the kinds of changes that are likely to take place in the Indian administration during the transition to a much more centralized and closed political system, one must be sensitive to the specific tasks performed by its public bureaucracies. A prior need, however, is to understand how these tasks are perceived within India. It is useful in this context to consider some of the historically and culturally based attitudes that shape expectations of bureaucratic performance. The concern for the maintenance of law and order that is so central to perceptions of the bureaucratic role is part of a broader vision of government as an institution that both defines and regulates appropriate behavior in society. Political, social, economic, and religious thinking within the Hindu cultural tradition reflects a view of the community as an organic entity whose continued well-being is dependent on the carefully specified cooperative actions of its component parts. Maintenance of harmony and order in the community is the goal, but it is achievable only if its members are restrained from pursuing their own self-interest, since such pursuits are satisfied only through the loss by others of benefits due them.[22] The clear and authoritative definition of duties and rights, a strong sense of duty on the part of the citizenry, and powerful enforcement bodies are thus necessary components of an effective polity.

This model differs fundamentally from many Western notions of governmental roles in that it accords no real place to the perception that individual advancement can also be achieved by generating new resources, and indeed, that social betterment is achieved precisely through government's encouragement of such pursuits in a competitive environment. Much of the Indian political and economic debate of the postindependence period has centered around disagreements about the extent to which government encouragement of self-interested behavior would produce growth and the extent to which it would produce socioeconomic injustice and political disintegration. Though some compromises have been made with those who argue for governmental manipulation of incentives in a market environment, the dominant tone of Indian administration since 1947 has been that of defining duties and rights for components of the society and then attempting to enforce compliance with those norms through intricate, elaborate, and costly bureaucratic control mechanisms.

Thus, in addition to the maintenance of law and order, the Indian administration has been heavily involved in formulating and enforcing a broad range of measures designed to prevent economic exploitation by traders, speculators, and self-interested entrepreneurs, in addition to the smugglers, black marketeers, and traffickers in permits and licenses who proliferate when administered prices are systematically disassociated from market values. The heavy load on the society's administrative apparatus resulting from the need to implement and enforce these highly restrictive control measures, then, reflects a conscious pursuit of time-honored values and a deeply engrained suspicion of entrepreneurial intentions.

These comments indicate the importance, in suggesting the likely character of administrative performance in postemergency India, of considering not only likely changes in the political environment of administration, but also possibilities of changes in perceptions of appropriate bureaucratic tasks. Mrs. Gandhi's actions in implementing and institutionalizing the political changes associated with the emergency, combined with her declaration of a twenty-point economic program, provide a preliminary basis on which to suggest likely trends along both dimensions.[23] Such a discussion can appropriately be organized around four salient bureaucratic tasks: maintaining law and order, controlling economic exploitation, managing redistributive programs, and fostering economic growth.

Law and Order

There seems to be little doubt but that the task of maintaining law and order became an increasingly difficult one in the several years preceding the declaration of the emergency. There are numerous explanations for this change, but they all generally reflect increasing levels of political and economic frustration being directed at the government through organized protest demonstrations.[24] Following patterns that are familiar in many parts of the world, violence on the part of authorities was publicized by the press and organizations supporting the demonstrators. This served to mobilize broader opposition to the government, and larger demonstrations against it, producing increased strain on its law enforcement institutions. The problems of managing disruptive political opposition in Bihar and Gujarat and militant labor demonstrations throughout much of the country, without further eroding the political base of the Congress party, had become acute by 1975 and appear to have been among the important factors precipitating the declaration of the emergency.

In the months immediately following that declaration, the law and order problem was greatly alleviated. The incarceration of opposition activist leaders, the suspension of their legal rights, the banning of public meetings, and the rigorous censorship of press reports of opposition statements and activities served to both stifle disruptive demonstrations and expand the range of strategies open to police authorities.

It is difficult to anticipate the level of future strains on the law and order bureaucracy. Reports during the early months of 1976 suggest, however, the emergence of a sizable underground opposition movement that may well become a serious challenge to government authorities.[25] The imposition of president's rule for the state of Tamil Nadu will almost certainly lead to the formation of a Tamil nationalist underground opposition movement in that state.

Economic Exploitation

The control of economic exploitation received considerable attention in Mrs. Gandhi's twenty-point program and has figured widely in subsequent press reports about early achievements under the emergency. Mrs. Gandhi promised action against smugglers, urban land speculators, tax evaders, hoarders, and those who misuse import licenses. In discussing measures to be taken against them, she referred specifically to stern and severe punishment, summary trials, the end to the release of smugglers on anticipatory bail and technical points and the confiscation of their property, and speedy trials and confiscation of goods for those who violate import regulations.

Subsequent campaigns did lead to arrests of alleged smugglers, the marketing of commodities that might otherwise have been withheld pending increases in price levels, and the declaration of—and payment of taxes on—vast amounts of income that had been circulating in black market channels. Such activities clearly have beneficial effects not only on public morale but on government revenues and the country's capital markets. The freedom of government authorities to punish suspected violators without having to observe elaborate procedural requirements and satisfy legal demands for evidence, combined with public fears of such arbitrary actions, produced dramatic short-term results.

The substitution of arbitrary for procedurally and legally constrained police action does not guarantee, however, longer-term improvements in enforcement of economic regulations. As new regulatory practices become routinized, patterns of corruption and evasion will be reestablished unless new developments in the incentive structures or ideological environment dictate otherwise. In discussing the possibilities that the black market might be permanently reduced in size and importance, Jayanta Sarkar and Philip Bowring suggest that one means of assuring such a change would be

> a reduction in the plethora of rules by which the Government has vainly attempted to control what is still primarily a market economy. So all-encompassing had these controls, combined with shortages, become that many businessmen considered that it was impossible not to engage in illegal deals and bribe the bureaucracy and the political sector if they were to survive.[26]

Mrs. Gandhi's twenty-point program indicates some sensitivity to the argument that controls must be modified to reduce their counterproductive consequences. She called for simplified licensing procedures, the raising of the investment limit on industries that require neither imports nor government help, and the reduction of constraints on commodity movement by train through introduction of a permit system. Further simplification and relaxation of control regulations would clearly have a major impact on public bureaucracies by reducing their administrative loads, but it is as yet too early to determine whether there is a long-term trend toward more elaborate or more simple control mechanisms. Of potential significance, however, is the growing political prominence of Mrs. Gandhi's younger son, Sanjay, whose experience as an entrepreneur in the auto manufacturing sector has apparently convinced him of the need to remove many of the control regulations that cause delays in industrial development and create opportunities for dishonesty.[27]

Redistributive Programs

Since 1971 Mrs. Gandhi's rhetoric has emphasized the use of redistributive mechanisms to achieve the goal of *garibi hatao*— the abolition of poverty. The continuity implied in her 1975 twenty-point program is suggested by the dominant role that that document gives to redistributive programs. The abolition of bonded labor, the gradual liquidation of rural indebtedness, the raising of minimum agricultural wages, the establishment of sub- sidies for handloom weavers, the imposition of land ceilings and the redistribution of surplus land, the raising of the minimum exemption level for income tax, and subsidies for university students are all designed primarily to redistribute income and control over income-producing resources. For the most part these programs do not represent new goals, but rather a reaf- firmation of old Congress ideology that has not been effectively implemented in the past.

The failure of these earlier efforts has been attributed by some to the opposition of local Congress officials who represent the interests of well-to-do sectors in both urban and rural areas, and by others to the inability of the bureaucracies to assure the honest and effective implementation of their programs at the local level. The question, in short, is whether Indian bureaucra- cies are permeable only by the representatives of electorally based political parties, or whether—and to what extent—they are also susceptible to the corrupting influences of nonpartisan local interests and internal pathologies that distort the imple- mentation of redistributive programs. Though the continued weakening of local party servicing organizations and the re- newed expressions of dedication to redistributive programs are likely to have marginal impacts on local administration, the management problems that have long been associated with the implementation of such high-priority, nonpoliticized programs as family planning and agricultural extension suggest that changes more fundamental than those represented by the emergency will be required to produce significant improvements in bureaucratic performance.[28]

Economic Growth

To observers accustomed to Western modes of economic management analysis, distributive measures are of distinctly secondary importance to those that will promote and sustain economic growth. This seems especially true in the Indian context not only because of the extremely low level of per capita income, but also because of the inability of the Indian system in a competitive political environment to generate significant patterns of sustained growth. There is little in the twenty-point program, however, to suggest that the increased freedom of the national executive from the redistributive concerns of local political forces will lead to a renewed focus on programs that will foster long-term growth. Apart from a passing reference to taking "a series of steps to stimulate production" as part of an anti-inflation strategy and the simplifications of licensing procedures, only two points are devoted to growth measures. These call for an increase in the land area under irrigation and an expansion of the country's effective power-generating capacity. Both have long been important elements in Indian development planning, but neither has been opposed by political forces in the past and there is no apparent reason to believe that progress toward achieving these goals will be more rapid under an emergency regime than it had been previously.

Many other problems, meanwhile, continue to plague efforts to stimulate sustained economic growth. The development of improved food-grain seeds, related production inputs, and the economic conditions to encourage innovative investments have lagged severely since the late 1960s. And the failure of state-run factories to produce at or near anticipated levels reflects an inadequacy in public administration that is not likely to be remedied by changes undertaken in the wake of the emergency declaration.

In the months immediately following the declaration of the emergency there was clearly a significant improvement in both indicators of economic development and appearances of administrative diligence and efficiency. The above analysis, however, suggests that this improvement could well turn out to be of a temporary nature. Discipline and commitment can be induced for short periods of time by fear and appeals to national goals. Indeed, the widely acclaimed effect of the emergency in getting civil servants to arrive at work by the official start of the day rather than one or two hours later could undoubtedly be perpetuated by a policy commitment to the continued enforcement of that rule. Few serious observers of Indian administration would argue, however, that the output of already overstaffed ministries is likely to be significantly increased as a result of such a strategy.

Discipline and commitment are clearly of critical importance in promoting administrative efficiency. An important element of effective leadership is the ability to define and promote a coherent and credible view of the exemplary character of an organization's goals, procedures, employees, and traditions. I have suggested elsewhere that this task is complicated in India because its administration has inherited from the British a tradition of distrust, and its more positive ideologies of the post-independence era were superimposed on an existing tradition in such a way as to create conflicts and organizational pathologies that limit efficiency and engender widespread demoralization.[29]

The enthusiasm and dedication occasioned by the emergency declaration provide an opportunity for the beginning of a long-term reformation and rationalization of Indian administration. That task is one that requires the extensive redefinition of Indian principles of public administration, the detailed restructuring of many of its institutions, and the close attention of political authorities to the process of transformation. The first six months of emergency rule give no indication, however, that such dramatic changes will soon be forthcoming.

In the absence of such changes, there is real danger that the quality of Indian administration will deteriorate rather than improve. As political control has become more highly centralized, the lines of bureaucratic authority are necessarily lengthened. Innovative programs and responses to local needs are less likely to be initiated at the state level. And the problems of designing effective and relevant programs from a central government office in a country of India's size and diversity would strain the most efficient and creative of bureaucracies.

The administrative structures in postemergency India will also be in danger of suffering from a serious decline in the extent and accuracy of information on which their actions must be based. The deterioration of the Congress party grass roots organization, the censorship of the press, and the weakening of competing centers of political power will force the bureaucracy into increasing reliance on internally generated information. Its already dubious reliability will be further threatened by the fear among subordinates of submitting unsatisfactory program results and the absence of independent checks that might act as deterrents to systematic falsifications.

Bureaucratic responsiveness to the public interest as represented by the country's servicing-oriented politicians was a source of much inefficiency and corruption in India's postindependence efforts to promote social justice and economic development. The question, however, is what the bureaucracy will respond to now that the competitive political process has been so severely crippled. One would hope that its efforts would be directed more single-mindedly to the implementation of rational programs designed by the intelligent and capable planners who surround Mrs. Gandhi. Unless their ability to make their will felt through the long and complicated channels of the Indian administrative command is dramatically improved, however, the more likely result is that the lower levels of the hierarchies—the individuals in positions to actually implement programs—will increasingly respond to the personalistic and idiosyncratic interests of their own families and of the more wealthy and influential citizens of the communities they serve.

NOTES

[1] Since implementation of orders restricting civil liberties had in most cases to be passed through the state governments, special problems arose in Gujarat and Tamil Nadu, whose governments were controlled by opponents of Mrs. Gandhi. Indications are that many fewer arrests were made in these states and that implementation of restrictive mandates was much less comprehensive than in other states. The apparent unacceptability of this situation in Tamil Nadu from Mrs. Gandhi's perspective led to the central government's takeover of that state's administration seven months after the emergency was declared.

2 For samples of reports on early retirements, see the *Deccan Chronicle*, Sept. 16, 1975, and *Andhra Jyoti* (a Telugu language daily), Aug. 24, 29, Sept. 14, 18, and Oct. 5, 1975. I am indebted to Narayana Rao at the University of Wisconsin for translating these documents and calling them to my attention.

3 C. P. Bhambhri, *Bureaucracy and Politics in India* (Delhi: Vikas Publications, 1971), p. 63.

4 N. Raghavan Pillai, "The Civil Service as a Profession," in Kewal L. Panjabi, ed., *The Civil Servant in India* (Bombay: Bharatiya Vidya Bhavan, 1965), p. 27.

5 G. D. Khosla, "My Work in the I.C.S.," in Panjabi, *The Civil Servant in India*, pp. 109-10.

6 Ibid., p. 113.

7 Ibid., p. 115.

8 Quoted in Bhambhri, *Bureaucracy and Politics in India*, pp. 78-79.

9 Ibid.

10 Precisely this question has now been answered, for the United States, by Edward Weisband and Thomas M. Frank, *Resignation in Protest* (New York: Grossman, 1975).

11 B. S. Khanna, "Bureaucracy and Development in India," in Edward W. Weidner, ed., *Development Administration in Asia* (Durham: Duke University Press, 1970), p. 244.

12 David C. Potter, "Bureaucratic Change in India," in Ralph Braibanti, ed., *Asian Bureaucratic Systems Emergent from the British Imperial Tradition* (Durham, N. C.: Duke University Press, 1966), p. 160.

13 Robert K. Merton, *Social Theory and Social Structure*, enlarged ed. (New York: Free Press, 1968), pp. 253-55.

14 The following discussion draws heavily on my *Cultures in Conflict: The Four Faces of Indian Bureaucracy* (New York: Columbia University Press, 1975); see especially pp. 20-44, 159-71 and 212-15.

15 Ibid., pp. 20-34.

16 This is a central theme of Myron Weiner, *Party-Building in a New Nation: The Indian National Congress* (Chicago: University of Chicago Press, 1967).

17 See Duncan B. Forrester, "Indian State Ministers and Their Roles," *Asian Survey* 10 (June 1970): 472-82.

18 For a discussion of the *panchayati raj* institutions, see A. H. Hanson, *The Process of Planning: A Study of India's Five-Year Plans, 1950-1964* (London: Oxford University Press, 1966); and Henry C. Hart, "The Village and Development Administration," in James S. Heaphey, ed., *Spatial Dimensions of Development* (Durham, N.C.: Duke University Press, 1970).

19 For a discussion of differing perceptions of democracy within India, see Myron Weiner, "India's Two Political Cultures," in Lucian W. Pye and Sidney Verba, eds., *Political Culture and Political Development* (Princeton, N.J.: Princeton University Press, 1965).

20 The traditional role of "expediting" bureaucratic decisions is seen by Myron Weiner as an important basis for the successful party-building efforts of the Indian National Congress. See his "Traditional Role Performance and the Development of Modern Political Parties: Reflections on the Indian Case," *Journal of Politics* 26 (Nov. 1964): 830-49.

21 See my "The 1971 Revolution in Indian Voting Behavior," *Asian Survey* 11 (Dec. 1971): 1133-52.

22 See my discussion in *Cultures in Conflict*, pp. 32-34 and 208-9.

23 Mrs. Gandhi's twenty-point economic program was presented in a speech delivered July 1, 1975. Quotations are taken from the transcript published in the *Indian Express*, July 2, 1975.

24 For two of the more perceptive discussions of this period, see Ram Joshi, "India 1974: Growing Political Crisis," *Asian Survey* 15 (Feb. 1975): 85-95, and Rajni Kothari, "End of an Era," *Seminar* 197 (Jan. 1976): 22-28.

25 See, especially, "Yes, There Is an Underground," *Economist* (London) Jan. 24, 1976, pp. 32-35.

26 Jayanta Sarkar and Philip Bowring, "India: Exposing Hidden Funds," *Far Eastern Economic Review*, Oct. 31, 1975, p. 66. See also Deepak Lal, "The Twenty Points," *Seminar* 197 (Jan. 1976): 54-56, for an insightful analysis of both the economic controls and redistributive aspects of Mrs. Gandhi's program.

27 *Statesman* (Delhi), January 24, 1976, quoting an unnamed Bombay weekly as its source.

28 For an extended treatment of the bureaucratic pathologies limiting the effectiveness of agricultural extension efforts in Tamil Nadu, see my *Cultures in Conflict*, chaps. 3, 7, and 8.

29 Ibid.

4

Mrs. Gandhi's Pyramid: The New Congress

Stanley A. Kochanek

The elections of 1971 and 1972 in India marked the restoration of Congress dominance at the center and in the states, a return to strong central leadership, and the apparent emergence of a more broadly based, ideologically coherent party. On the surface, the "Indira wave" appeared to have restored the pattern of a one-party dominance that characterized the Nehru era. Yet a closer analysis reveals a distinctly different pattern of dominance that contributed to a severe political crisis in the midst of the gravest economic crisis in postindependence India. These simultaneous crises of political and economic performance threatened the legitimacy of the system and ended in the declaration of an internal emergency in June 1975, the first such domestic emergency since independence. The declaration of the emergency, the decision to postpone elections scheduled for March 1976, and talk of revising the constitution mark the end of the political system that has existed since 1947 and the beginning of a new phase of Indian political development. What were the characteristics of the new pattern of Congress dominance? How did it differ from the period of centralization and convergence of the Nehru era? What were some of the inherent dilemmas or tensions of the new system? What were the consequences of

The preparation of this manuscript was made possible by financial support received from the Central Fund for Research of The Pennsylvania State University.

93

these tensions and how were these consequences related to the declaration of a national emergency in June 1975? What were the implications of these developments for the Congress and the future of the Indian political system? In short, was the declaration of an emergency in June 1975 a reversal of trends or the culmination of a process of systematic change?

SHAPE OF THE INDIRA WAVE

Sources

The end of the Nehru era and the process of succession had resulted in the emergence of a collective leadership in the Congress and a decision-making process based on consensus. Unlike the centralized pattern under Nehru, the period from 1963-69 had been marked by divergence. Party leaders had pressed the prime minister and cabinet for a share of power, as had the chief ministers of the states, and major policies could be decided only with the assent of the state governments.[1] Lal Bahadur Shastri, Nehru's immediate successor, had shown a decision-making style and temperament that was well suited to these new circumstances.

Although the same combination of forces that had managed to smooth the succession of Shastri had managed a similarly successful, if not as smooth, succession of Mrs. Indira Gandhi, the new prime minister had proved unwilling to accept the restraints imposed on Shastri.[2] The result had been six years of conflict, factional intrigue, and the first major split in the Congress at the national level since independence.[3] During her struggle for control over party and government from 1966 to 1972, Indira Gandhi had found herself challenged, or potentially threatened, by almost every major institutional structure in India, including the central cabinet, the president of the republic, the courts, the president of the Congress party, the Working Committee of the Congress, and the chief ministers of the states.

Design

In the course of meeting these challenges, Mrs. Gandhi had promised to create a new political process, based on a restoration of strong central rule which had become eroded over the years since her father's death, and free from the evils of bossism. The new political process which Mrs. Gandhi created, however, proved to be more highly centralized and personalized and less institutional than Nehru's. It had three major characteristics. First, it involved an unprecedented centralization of power in party and government with the prime minister at the top of the decision-making pyramid. Second, Mrs. Gandhi made a major effort to modify the federal character of party and government by strengthening their unitary tendencies and thereby reinforcing the centralization of power. Third, she tried, unsuccessfully, to change the support base of the Congress from above by recruiting underrepresented sectors of society, such as youth, women, intellectuals, minorities, the backward castes and tribes, and the poor, into the party organization and into the Congress legislative parties.

Since the formal structure of power outlined in both the Indian constitution and the constitution of the Congress party were federal with strong unitary and centralizing features, the initiation of this new process did not require major structural change.[4] A new pattern of centralized dominance could be instituted by invoking previously dormant constitutional powers and employing political mechanisms to reverse the pattern of devolution of power to the states and the emergence of a variety of strata within the party, each of which operated with a considerable degree of independence.

Apparatus

The centralization of power in party and government was a critical part of the new pattern of dominance. In order to attain control over the party, Mrs. Gandhi had to ensure control over the appointment of members of the Working Committee, the Parliamentary Board, and the Central Election Committee (C.E.C.). Collectively, these functionally distinct central organs of the party, composed of interlocking and overlapping personnel, comprised the Congress high command. By energizing the power of these central party organs, Mrs. Gandhi would be able to intervene directly in the affairs of the state and district party organizations, the operations of state legislative parties, and the selection of the state and national legislative elites.

Having experienced considerable difficulty in her relations with the last two presidents of the undivided Congress, K. Kamaraj and S. Nijalingappa, Mrs. Gandhi, for a time, thought of taking over the position herself, as her father had done in the early 1950s.[5] Instead, she made sure that only her trusted lieutenants would be named to the post, and that no one would remain in the position long enough to build an independent base of power.[6]

Since the split in the Congress in November 1969, the party has had five presidents: C. Subramaniam (November to December 1969), Jagjivan Ram (December 1969 to March 1971), D. Sanjivayya (March 1971 to May 1972), Dr. Shankar Dayal Sharma (May 1972 to October 1974), and D. K. Barooah (October 1974 to the present). The extremely high turnover at the top of the Congress organization was only partly accidental. C. Subramaniam served as an interim president for only two months, pending the official selection of a president of the Bombay Session of the Congress in December 1969. Although Mrs. Gandhi wanted to select former Congress president D. Sanjivayya, a young Harijan from Andhra, as leader of the party organization, her move was blocked for personal and factional reasons by the Andhra chief minister, K. Brahmananda Reddy. She therefore turned to Jagjivan Ram, one of her senior cabinet ministers and leader of the Harijan community. However, after her massive victory at the midterm Lok Sabha poll in 1971, she forced Jagjivan Ram out as Congress president and replaced him by Sanjivayya.[7] Unlike Jagjivan Ram, Sanjivayya had no strong political base. He was totally dependent on the prime minister, and his appointment could be used as a mechanism for forcing Brahmananda Reddy to give up his position as chief minister of Andhra.[8] Unfortunately for Mrs. Gandhi, Sanjivayya died in May 1972. He was replaced by Dr. S. D. Sharma, former general secretary of the Congress, who also lacked an independent political base in the party. Sharma was supplanted in October 1974, as part of a general reshuffle of the central cabinet, by D. K. Barooah, one of Mrs. Gandhi's ministers, in a move that appeared to be aimed at balancing ideological groups in party and government.[9] Thus, following Mrs. Gandhi's election victory of 1971, Congress presidents have been selected because of their personal loyalty to the prime minister and their lack of an independent political base of support, and high turnover— apparently designed to prevent institutional consolidation of power by any potential political challenger—has been part of Mrs. Gandhi's style.

Control of the Congress presidency is critical for control of the Working Committee, Parliamentary Board, and the Central Election Committee. The Working Committee is composed of the Congress president and twenty members. Ten are elected by the All-India Congress Committee (A.I.C.C.), and ten are appointed by the Congress president. Because elections to the Working Committee are very carefully managed by the party leadership through the use of official lists, dissident groups have had considerable difficulty getting representation.[10] Members of the committee continue to be drawn from the central cabinet, state chief ministers, and members of Parliament. This gives the ministerial wing of the party a preeminent position, and the committee has taken on the same character as the Working Committee of the undivided Congress. Ministerial dominance had ensured party-government coordination and prevented the kind of factional challenge to the government by the party organization that in 1969 precipitated the split in Congress.

The Parliamentary Board is composed of eight members selected by the Congress president upon authorization of the Working Committee. Board members are usually appointed from among the members of the Working Committee and constitute an inner circle of it. The board plays a critical role in supervising the activities of Congress legislative parties in the states. It also forms the core of the fifteen-member Central Election Committee, which is composed of the members of the Parliamentary Board and seven members elected prior to each general election by the A.I.C.C. The C.E.C. has the final authority to select Congress candidates for national and state legislatures. The Parliamentary Board, however, performs this function between general elections. Thus, while the Parliamentary Board selected the candidates for the 1971 midterm Lok Sabha election, the C.E.C. selected candidates for the 1972 state legislative elections.

Since the constitution of the Congress party gives the Working Committee, Parliamentary Board, and C.E.C. extraordinary formal powers in conducting party affairs, control over these central organs of the party gives the Congress leadership a potentially dominant voice in party organizational affairs and the recruitment of central and state legislative party elites. Unlike her predecessors, Mrs. Gandhi has attempted to use these centralizing powers to intervene directly in the affairs of the state parties. She has tried to break the hold of party bosses and to prevent the emergence of independent power centers in the states.

The Working Committee has inherited from the preindependence period extraordinary powers as chief executive of the party organization. The committee has the power to superintend, direct, and control all subordinate Congress committees; to invoke sanctions for breaches of party discipline; and to take all action in the interest of the Congress that it deems fit.[11] In the past, these powers were used with considerable restraint, but following the split in Congress, the Working Committee used its powers in a highly interventionist way to dissolve the existing Pradesh Congress Committees (P.C.C.s) in several states, nominate P.C.C. presidents, and appoint ad hoc committees composed of personnel selected directly by Mrs. Gandhi.[12] These appointed P.C.C.s, in turn, nominated ad hoc District Congress Committees (D.C.C.s). In addition, despite resistance from the states, the central party leadership has bypassed the state party organization and has established direct contact with party cadre at the district level. Congress presidents since 1971 have convened periodic meetings of presidents and secretaries of the D.C.C.s to discuss organizational issues and party program and to chalk out a specific work schedule for the D.C.C.s and lower-level committees.[13] Finally, the central leadership has attempted to penetrate lower-level committees by giving the Congress president the power to nominate two representatives to each Congress committee.[14] Despite these efforts at creating a highly centralized party, however, the leadership has found it extremely difficult to run a complex organization like the Congress from New Delhi.[15]

Centralizing a Federal Party

Since the Congress split, the Parliamentary Board has also become increasingly interventionist as part of Mrs. Gandhi's overall effort to reshape the party and restore central control. From June 1970 to September 1971, for example, the board met thirty-two times.[16] Although most of these meetings involved the selection of candidates for the midterm Lok Sabha poll, the Parliamentary Board has intervened in other areas as well.

Under Mrs. Gandhi's supervision, the board has nominated chief ministers in Congress-dominated states, determined the composition of state cabinets, and forced the resignation of recalcitrant chief ministers, in addition to performing its traditional role of mediating and arbitrating disputes between factions within the state Congress legislative parties.[17] Where the board has found itself unable to maintain stability in a state, Mrs. Gandhi, upon the advice of the governor of the state and acting through the president of the republic, has simply suspended or dissolved the state legislature and declared president's rule under Article 356 of the constitution. President's rule was ended whenever Mrs. Gandhi felt the state Congress was again in a position to form a stable government. The most far-reaching example of the intervention of the Parliamentary Board in state Congress affairs came in January 1974 in the state of Gujarat. Following a series of riots and student agitations against an allegedly corrupt and inept Congress government in Gujarat, the central government imposed president's rule. The legislature was not dissolved as demanded by the demonstrators; it was simply suspended pending a return to normalcy. Chimanbhai Patel, the leader of the Congress legislative party in Gujarat, refused to step down as leader and instead resigned from the Assembly. He intended to facilitate dissolution of the legislature and force new elections as demanded by the demonstrators. Since this was against the directives of the Congress high command, Patel was suspended from the party for six years.[18] Such vigorous interventions by central government and party were rare in post-independence India.

A similar shift in roles has occurred in the activities of the Central Election Committee of the Congress. Over the years since independence, the C.E.C.'s authority in selecting Congress candidates for state and national legislatures had slowly eroded.[19] State leaders, through their control over Pradesh Election Committees (P.E.C.s), came to dominate the selection process for their state, and the C.E.C. played a role only in those states that were badly factionalized or unable to reach a negotiated settlement. Since the Congress split, the decentralization of the selection process has been reversed. The reversal of the process was especially evident in 1972 when Mrs. Gandhi removed strongly entrenched chief ministers in Rajasthan, Andhra, Assam, and Madhya Pradesh prior to the election, forced the resignation of a number of elected P.C.C.s, and replaced several P.E.C.s by ad hoc committees nominated by the central party leadership.[20] Then, using the criteria established by the C.E.C. of retiring one-third of the sitting members, allotting 15 percent of the seats to women, and ensuring representation for minorities, intellectuals, youth, labor, and "weaker sections of society,"[21] the C.E.C., under Mrs. Gandhi's direction, attempted to restructure state legislative elites from above. Although Mrs. Gandhi was able to distribute tickets in such a way as to give her nominees for state leadership a majority, she had to be sure to compromise sufficiently with dominant groups in the states to prevent disgruntled Congressmen from sabotaging the official candidates at the polls. The influence of formerly entrenched groups was thus "curbed and contained," but not eliminated.[22] This method of C.E.C. intervention was deeply resented by local Congressmen in the states.[23]

The formal centralized constitutional powers of the central party organization, which had become increasingly dormant in the years since independence, were thus revived by Mrs. Gandhi. She put them to work to restore central control over the mass organization, the legislative parties in the states, and national and state legislative elites.

Subordinating the President

A similar effort at centralization of power took place at the government level. Mrs. Gandhi took a variety of political steps to consolidate her power and prevent the emergence of independent power blocks or institutional threats to her authority. These actions focused especially on the president of the republic, the cabinet, and the Congress party in Parliament.

Mrs. Gandhi's opponents in the undivided Congress had tried to create an activist president of the republic whom they could control as a device to challenge the prime minister. The lesson was not lost on Mrs. Gandhi. The immediate cause of the split in the Congress was, in the final analysis, a direct result of a factional dispute over the election of the president of the republic. The Congress Parliamentary Board, dominated by the "Syndicate" (an informal coalition of state bosses), voted to nominate Sanjiva Reddy as the Congress candidate over the objections of Mrs. Gandhi. Mrs. Gandhi, convinced that this move was designed to challenge her position as prime minister, supported the non-Congress nominee, V. V. Giri. As a result of Mrs. Gandhi's support, Giri succeeded in defeating Reddy by a narrow margin. The Syndicate, which also controlled eleven of the twenty-one seats in the Working Committee, decided to take disciplinary action against Mrs. Gandhi, and thereby precipitated the split in Congress.[24]

V. V. Giri's term as president expired in 1974. Despite his desire to remain for a second term, Mrs. Gandhi decided to nominate Fakhruddin Ali Ahmed for the post. Ahmed, a seventy-year-old Muslim from the small state of Assam and a loyal colleague, was certainly in no position to challenge Mrs. Gandhi.[25] The strategy of selecting someone like Ahmed as president proved to be especially critical in June 1975, when the prime minister advised the president to declare a national emergency under Article 352 of the constitution. Ahmed could be counted upon to act only on the advice of the prime minister, even under the extraordinary circumstances which had given rise to the emergency. Had the president balked, Mrs. Gandhi's position would have been seriously undermined and a severe crisis would have developed.

A Dependent Cabinet

As prime minister, Indira Gandhi has also attempted to ensure complete and full control over her cabinet. Unlike Nehru, she has tended to recruit a large number of young intellectuals with little or no political base in the party.[26] Moreover, in order to keep ministers off-balance and prevent the consolidation of power of some of her senior colleagues like Y. B. Chavan and Jagjivan Ram, she has resorted to the technique of frequent minor reshuffling of ministers and portfolios with a promise that a major change would take place in the near future. She has also retained a variety of key portfolios under her direct control, centralized key governmental functions such as security and intelligence directly under the prime minister, and following Shastri's example, has greatly expanded the role of the prime minister's secretariat. These techniques have strengthened the position of the prime minister and have kept any potential challenger completely off-balance.[27] Finally, while still making use of the Political Affairs Committee of the cabinet to ratify major decisions,[28] Mrs. Gandhi has also been known for her frequent consultation with her own unofficial kitchen cabinet.[29] Yet, even here, the individuals so designated have tended to change over time and lose favor. Thus, Dinesh Singh, a prominent member of the kitchen cabinet in 1969, has ceased even to be a minister.[30] The current favorites seem to be D. K. Barooah, president of the Congress; Sidharatha Shankar Ray, chief minister of West Bengal; Bansi Lal, former chief minister of Haryana; Sanjay Gandhi, her son; and Rajni Patel, Bombay P.C.C. president.[31] This entire process has tended to emphasize personal power at the cost of institutionalized power.

Countercurrents in the Parliamentary Party

One of Mrs. Gandhi's strongest assets has been her ability to retain the loyalty of the majority of the members of the Congress Party in Parliament (CPP). The vast majority of the CPP members supported her in her battle with the Syndicate and have rallied to her support during every major crisis. Despite her limited influence in selecting candidates for the 1971 Lok Sabha midterm poll, the election victories of 1971 and 1972 and the promise of ministerial positions in the government have made members of the CPP dependent on the patronage of the prime minister, rather than of the chief minister of a member's home state. Congress M.P.s have come to look to Mrs. Gandhi for promotion, patronage, and electoral support.

The newer members of the CPP, as shown by a *Times of India* study of Congressmen entering the Lok Sabha for the first time in 1971, are younger, better educated, and reflect a significant increase in intellectuals as opposed to landowners. (The higher levels of education reflect the increasing spread of education to the rural areas and represent a new bridge between urban and rural India.[32]) They have tended to be somewhat more ideologically oriented than their predecessors.

Although the vast majority of Congress M.P.s have traditionally been more or less nonideological in their orientation and have focused upon their primary role as expeditors in pressing for benefits for their constituents, there emerged within the CPP in the late 1950s several formal and informal ideological pressure groups. The most organized and vocal was called the Socialist Forum. It rejected factional intrigue and insisted its primary role was to educate, propagandize, and press for the implementation of the declared socialist goals of the party. The Socialist Forum was reorganized after the 1962 general election and renamed the Congress Forum for Socialist Action (C.F.S.A.). The position of the C.F.S.A. was especially strengthened after the 1967 general election with the entry into the CPP of several former members of the Communist Party of India (CPI) and the Praja Socialist Party (PSP). The group became increasingly vocal, demanding the implementation of the ten-point program adopted by the Congress after its 1967 election debacle as a mechanism for refurbishing the party's image. The program included abolition of privy purses, social control of banks, and nationalization of general insurance. Mrs. Gandhi encouraged the members of the C.F.S.A. to attack the more conservative leaders of the Syndicate in her battle for control of the Congress. After the split in the Congress in 1969, C.F.S.A. members succeeded in getting elected to the Executive Committee of the CPP and attempted to use the CPP executive as a mechanism to build up the tempo of pressure for the implementation of a radical policy by the central and state leadership. In fact from 1969 until 1972, the C.F.S.A. members, who had little real support in the party organization, were able to use the CPP Executive Committee as a kind of super Working Committee to influence the party leadership.[33]

By 1972, however, the influence of the C.F.S.A. began to decline. There were three main reasons. In the first place, Mrs. Gandhi, having consolidated her power in party and government, became increasingly annoyed with the constant criticism being leveled by the ultraleft of the C.F.S.A. against the leadership. The group, therefore, found it increasingly difficult to press for action in her name. Second, the C.F.S.A. split into two groups. One group, composed of former PSP members like Chandra Shekhar, Mohan Dharia, Krishan Kant, and Ram Dhan, was called the "young Turks." They tended to be more moderate, strongly anti-Communist, but committed to implementation of the socialist policies outlined in various Congress resolutions. The second group, on the other hand, was small, but highly vocal, and consisted of former members of the pro-Soviet CPI. They demanded a more radical economic policy and rebuilding of the Congress around an organizing cadre. They had strong supporters among ministers (K. R. Ganesh, K. D. Malaviya, and the late Mohan Kumaramangalam), the members of the Working Committee (Chandrajit Yadav, Vayalar Ravi, and possibly Congress President D. K. Barooah), and the chief ministers of a few states (Nandini Satpathy of Orissa and Zail Singh of Punjab).[34] The pro-CPI lobby in the CPP came largely from the Hindi-speaking states of northern India—Bihar, Uttar Pradesh, Madhya Pradesh, Rajasthan, and Harayana.[35] As early as the summer of 1973, one of their members, Shashi Bhushan, had called for the creation of a limited dictatorship in India.[36]

Although Mrs. Gandhi's majority was dependent upon CPI support from 1969 to 1971, this dependence ceased with the restoration of Congress dominance. In the states, however, the Congress continued to be dependent upon CPI support in West Bengal, Orissa, and Kerala, and individual Congress leaders used CPI support in intrafactional battles in Bihar and Uttar Pradesh. Many pro-CPI Congressmen even went so far as to argue that India's special relationship with the Soviet Union required close cooperation and even a sharing of power between the Congress and the CPI.

A third reason for the decline of the C.F.S.A. was the creation of the Nehru Forum. In an effort to offset the growing influence of the C.F.S.A., a group of Congressmen led by Uma Shankar Dikshit, a close colleague and friend of Mrs. Gandhi, created the Nehru Forum in August 1972. The forum worked to counter the pro-CPI lobby in its alleged attempts to undermine Mrs. Gandhi's confidence in such key ministers as Dikshit, Jagjivan Ram, Y. B. Chavan, Kamlapati Tripathi, C. Subramaniam, and T. A. Pai, all of whom were dubbed rightist. This anti-CPI group felt that the strength of the Congress in the rural areas was more than enough to offset the urban base of support of the pro-CPI group. Although both the C.F.S.A. and the Nehru Forum were officially requested to disband by Mrs. Gandhi in 1973, the two groups, plus the "young Turks," continued to function as informal, ideological pressure groups with the CPP.[37]

Thus, after six years of conflict over control of party and government, Mrs. Gandhi was not content to dominate the Congress solely through her charisma. The conflict of 1966 to 1972 had taught her a bitter lesson that led her to consolidate her power so that no potential challenger could emerge. Mrs. Gandhi's consolidation of power resulted in the creation of a pyramidal decision-making structure in party and government in which all key institutional positions were staffed by loyal and trusted followers. Although the decision-making structure prevented threats to her personal power, it tended to centralize decision making, weaken institutionalization, and create an overly personalized regime. Moreover, the new political process proved unable to manage the tensions and cleavages of a heterogeneous party operating in a heterogeneous society, federally governed. A major crisis in the system followed.

VULNERABILITIES OF THE
NEW CONGRESS DOMINANCE

Since Mrs. Gandhi's new politics were superimposed upon the old, the Congress remained vulnerable to the twin threats of factionalism from within and opposition alliance politics from without. These inherent vulnerabilities threatened the stability of continued Congress dominance.[38] Internal tensions in particular were aggravated by the prime minister's apparent manipulative style, her use of populist ideology for political mobilization, and her emphasis on economic performance. These factors combined to make the management of one-party dominance extremely difficult and complex.

Several factors tended to make Mrs. Gandhi's new Congress look very much like the old. In the first place, an incongruity persisted between the desire for cohesion and the need to restore Congress dominance in a highly segmented society. Second, the dilemmas generated by the unwieldy character of a historically open, mass party remained unsolved. Finally, tension persisted as a result of the structural incompatability of trying to operate a centralized party in a federal system, resulting in severe problems of conflict management.

Centrifugal Pulls

The need to restore Congress dominance was clearly a precondition of the creation of a new political process. Yet, the restoration of dominance could not be achieved solely by Mrs. Gandhi's charisma. It involved considerable compromise with the segmented character of Indian society. The limitations of restructuring the Congress from above were clearly visible during the process of candidate selection in 1971 and 1972.

Despite greater control and direction of the process of candidate selection, the overwhelming need to select candidates who were not just acceptable to Mrs. Gandhi, but who could also win at the polls meant that even Mrs. Gandhi could not bypass local caste, regional, communal, and factional alignments. Although Mrs. Gandhi clearly attempted to manipulate state and local situations to her advantage, the Congress continued to remain a broadly aggregative electoral coalition, rather than a cohesive ideologically coherent party.

Mrs. Gandhi's opportunities to restructure the party varied over time and from state to state. In the 1971 midterm Lok Sabha poll, her freedom of action was still limited. Despite an attempt to give a new look to the party, Mrs. Gandhi was able to have a decisive voice in the selection of candidates in only four states—Uttar Pradesh, Punjab, Haryana, and Jammu and Kashmir—where the Congress was badly divided and thus susceptible to central management. In states like Andhra, Rajasthan, Maharashtra, Assam, and Bihar, on the other hand, state leaders continued to dominate the selection process and there was little change in the composition of the party. In a variety of instances, moreover, the Congress was compelled to grant tickets to defectors in an effort to bolster its local electoral support and ensure victory.[39]

Similarly, despite her stronger position within the Congress as a result of the 1971 midterm poll victory and the popularity of her role in the Bangladesh civil war, Mrs. Gandhi's ability to restructure the party at the time of the 1972 state elections was also limited. Again, Mrs. Gandhi had to succumb to a variety of local pressures of caste, community, region, and party factional alignments, and her success in restructuring the party varied from state to state.[40]

The most dramatic changes were evident in Andhra and Mysore as the power of older landed castes was diminished in favor of newly mobilized groups belonging to the less privileged sectors of society. However, even in successful cases such as Andhra, the attempt to rebuild the party on a nondominant caste basis did not go unchallenged. The formerly factionalized, but dominant, Reddy caste immediately unified in an effort to reverse the onslaught, and there was a sizable revolt as 200 Congressmen rebelled and contested as independents. Although the central leadership responded with massive expulsions, those suspended were later quietly reinstated. As one observer noted,

"Half-way through, the expulsions reached such proportions that they became untenable and the campaign was stopped. Possibly the central leadership realized that it is still impossible to lead the party through direct contact with the base, that the relays of factional leaders who act as middlemen between the leaderships at the state and central level and the grass roots cannot yet be ignored."[41]

In most other states, no such massive transformation was attempted and in no state were previously dominant factions totally eliminated. In Rajasthan, Haryana, and Jammu and Kashmir new leaders were imposed on the party, but the socioeconomic base of support remained unchanged. In Assam, Maharashtra, and Madhya Pradesh there was a drastic turnover of candidates and an infusion of new and younger faces, but those recruited continued to be drawn from the same socioeconomic base as in the past. In states such as Gujarat, Punjab, Bihar, and West Bengal, on the other hand, the strong desire to restore Congress dominance required winning back old supporters who had defected from the Congress in the past.[42] Thus, Congress dominance at the center and in the states was restored by selecting candidates who could win. This, in turn, tended to make the new Congress look very much like the old. Since Congress dominance remains tenuous in the face of factional revolt or opposition alliance, attempts to restructure the Congress from above had to be tempered by the need to maintain a strong electoral base below.

Nonhierarchical Party

The compromises made to restore Congress dominance were reinforced by the open, mass character of the Congress organization. The pyramidal structure of Mrs. Gandhi's Congress rests, by tradition, on a wide-open base. The base consists of two types of members: primary and active. Primary members are recruited biennially and pay one rupee (presently, eleven cents) dues. Any person who has been a primary member for two years may become an active member upon paying a subscription fee of twenty-five rupees, or on enrolling twenty-five primary members biennially. An active member must also subscribe to the traditional Congress values of *khadi* ("home-spun cloth"), prohibition, communal unity, and Harijan uplift.[43] In practice, membership tends to be enrolled on a competitive basis by Congress factions attempting to control the party organization to maintain power, or as a springboard for gaining control of the state government. This practice has not changed.

Following the Congress split in 1969, the central leadership repeatedly extended enrollment deadlines for membership and postponed organizational elections due to the "large number of Congressmen returning to the fold."[44] By the time the Working Committee set a final deadline of August 15, 1972, Congress dominance had been restored and there was a mad rush to join the party. Congress membership rolls reached a near record of 10 million primary members and 300,000 active members.[45] During the last membership drive of the undivided Congress in 1966-67, the Congress had enrolled 11 million primary and 208,000 active members.[46] Although a good portion of this membership was bogus and based on the payments of membership fees of fictitious members, the membership rolls are used as the basis for party organizational elections. Primary members act as an electoral college at the lowest level of a basic unit, but only active members are eligible for election as a member of any Congress committee. Control of the party organization, however, is essential because of the party's role in candidate selection.

Several factors contributed to the massive influx of members, both real and fictitious. In the first place, a wave of popular enthusiasm in support of Mrs. Gandhi and the Congress following the "Indira wave" of 1971-72 brought a large number of new recruits to the party. They were attracted by the central leadership's call to youth, intellectuals, minorities, and the underprivileged who had worked for Mrs. Gandhi during the elections to join the party on a permanent basis.[47] Second, there was an influx of ex-Congressmen and even opposition party members into the newly restored dominant party, which again controlled the major sources of patronage and benefits. Third, the entry of both new and old recruits was facilitated by the competitive enrollment of Congress factions attempting to gain control of the party organization. Chief ministers selected by Mrs. Gandhi and without a local base of support tried to strengthen their power base in the party organization. Dissident factions, especially those groups that had seen their positions in the party undercut at the time of candidate selection and ministry making in 1971 and 1972, sought to strengthen their positions within the party organization as a base from which to attack those in control of the state government and to place themselves in a strategic position for the next general elections.[48]

The frenzied pace of mobilization affected the Congress organization in a variety of ways. In the first place, it restored the pre-1969 character of the Congress. Veteran Congressmen, using the time-tested technique of bogus enrollment and checkbook party building, involving the payment of all required fees for nonexistent members, were able to reestablish their control of the Congress organization. As a result, newly mobilized sectors such as youth, intellectuals, scheduled castes, and backward classes lost out to formerly dominant groups.[49] Congress youth wings, for example, were unable to survive as an effective force, except in states like Kerala and West Bengal, where they were effectively organized. Second, the ability of formerly dominant groups to reassert their positions within the Congress organization resulted in the outbreak of rampant factionalism in almost every state. Party dissidents, their positions strengthened within the party organization, joined with their supporters in the state legislative assemblies to launch a major attack against state leaders nominated by Mrs. Gandhi. Chief ministers, finding their positions in the organization undercut, were forced to turn to the central leadership for support, only to find that this was not sufficient to keep them in power. Third, Mrs. Gandhi's nominees, challenged by dissident groups in state after state, were unable to survive the factional onslaught. Chief ministers in Andhra, Bihar, and Gujarat were forced to resign.[50] Mrs. Gandhi's call for a restoration of Congress hegemony to ensure strong, stable, and effective government in India appeared hollow when even Mrs. Gandhi proved unable to sustain her nominees in office.

Collapsing State Power Bases

The segmented nature of Indian society and the open character of the Congress exacerbated the structural incompatibility of a centralized party in a federal system, creating severe problems of conflict management. One of the most important functions traditionally performed by the Congress high command was the management of conflict within the party. During the Nehru era, the high command acted as an appellate structure to arbitrate and mediate state level conflicts, ensure fair procedures, and confirm newly emerged state leaders in office. It could not impose leaders on a reluctant party, nor could it sustain leaders in power who had lost the confidence of the majority of the state legislative party. During the period from 1963 to 1969, the passing of the old nationalist leadership eroded the effective power of the high command, and power in the Congress became more decentralized. District and state levels of the party operated with a considerable degree of independence, and there was a general dilution of power throughout the party structure. Although each level in the structure looked to the next level for patronage and dispute settlement, the system began to break down because factionalism had begun to penetrate every level, including the high command itself. Thus, the high command became increasingly unable to act as a point of appeal for dissident groups, with the result that many felt compelled to leave the party and function as opposition parties. The emergence of Congress splinter parties in almost every state at the time of the 1967 general elections was a telling example of this organizational breakdown.[51]

Mrs. Gandhi reestablished centralized control of the Congress, but in a totally new way, which ultimately proved unworkable. In an effort to restructure the party and reduce the power of state leaders, she eased out of office the very state leaders who had supported her during her struggle for control of the Congress against the Syndicate. The first to go was Mohanlal Sukhadia, chief minister of Rajasthan for over a decade. He was followed by K. Brahmananda Reddy of Andhra, Mohinder Mohan Chaudhury of Assam, S. C. Shukla of Madhya Pradesh, and even V. P. Naik of Maharashtra. The departure of such dominant state leaders, coupled with the split in the Congress and the defeat of the Syndicate, gave Mrs. Gandhi an almost free hand to restructure the state party leadership of the Congress. She used the technique of nominating candidates for chief minister for each state, who were then ratified in office by the dominant state Congress legislative party. Most of Mrs. Gandhi's nominees were former members of her council of ministers, were personally loyal to her, and had no established local bases of power in their home states.[52] Although state Congress legislative parties dutifully endorsed their new leaders unanimously, they deeply resented the imposition of outsiders from above.

Following the organization elections in the fall of 1972, dissident factions began to mobilize from below to challenge the leadership of Mrs. Gandhi's nominees. The credibility and authority of most nominated chief ministers was so weak that they constantly had to turn to New Delhi for political support to stay in office. Moreover, although Mrs. Gandhi remained free of factional alignment and played the role of final arbitrator and mediator in state factional disputes, central cabinet ministers, members of the Working Committee, and even members of the CPP became closely allied with one faction or another in their home states. To many it appeared that the new Congress pyramid of command, instead of facilitating the emergence of a new, stable, and effective state leadership with a strong local base of support, was deliberately manipulating Congresss factionalism to prevent a healthy consolidation of power in the states.[53] The result was weak, ineffective, and inept leadership incapable of dealing with the mounting economic hardship of the population.

By the middle of 1973, Mrs. Gandhi was unable to sustain this pattern any longer, as one nominated chief minister after another was voted out of office by the state party or was being severely challenged by dissident Congressmen. Surveying the increasing instability and disorder in her party, Mrs. Gandhi tried to disassociate herself from her nominees by arguing that she had selected these leaders upon the recommendations of others. More significantly, Mrs. Gandhi changed her style of management. Rajasthan and Gujarat were given a free hand to select their own leader, the chief minister of Uttar Pradesh was forced out following a revolt of the state police, and Andhra and Bihar were encouraged to nominate their own compromise candidates, who only then received the endorsement of Mrs. Gandhi. Thus, the centralized unity of command adopted by Mrs. Gandhi began slowly to give way to a devolution of power to lower-level party structures. Mrs. Gandhi's interventionist role in managing state legislative party affairs began to decline and it appeared that she might permit some consolidation of power in the states and play a more traditional role of coordinating and trouble shooting, rather than controlling and managing.[54]

In many ways, however, the damage was already done. People began to question the utility of the Congress style of "governmental stability." More significantly, inept chief ministers had to spend all their time trying to stay in power and were unable to cope with the problems generated by thirty months of economic crisis, food shortages, and uncontrolled inflation. Agitations that originated as localized expressions of grievance against incompetent state leaders blossomed into large movements, which ultimately came to challenge the political power of the Congress at the center.

In a heterogeneous, segmented society like India, there exists a political and functional interdependence that cannot be sustained by the kind of centralized control Mrs. Gandhi has attempted to employ. Nehru learned the lessons of overcentralization and the limits of central manipulation in the early 1950s in dealing with the problems of the state of Andhra. A central leadership may facilitate the emergence of a new leadership; it cannot invent that leadership where it does not exist.[55] Because of the complexities of social, religious, subregional, and ethnic differences, the Indian political system faces severe problems of political cohesion and stability reflected in its style of factional and alliance politics. Some degree of layering within the party is essential to its stability and survival. Even though state leaders may become powerful through a healthy consolidation of power, they will still remain factionally vulnerable and, thus, will still depend upon the vital brokerage function which only a strong, unified, central leadership can provide. Even strong state leaders will still be dependent upon the center. The refusal to permit the development of the state leadership based on support from below threatens the party with stagnation.

The center itself, in turn, is more dependent upon the states than it is prepared to admit. The states play a critical role in the development and maintenance of political support and in implementing those policies that have the widest impact on the population at large in the fields of agriculture, education, and welfare. Mrs. Gandhi's new political process, while definitely preventing any challenge to her personal power, contributed to a major political crisis and undermined her claim that Congress dominance was essential to continued political stability and development. The resultant shift in focus from nation building to regime building has inherent within it the seeds of disintegration.

THE CRISIS OF CONGRESS DOMINANCE

The mounting factional instability of the Congress governments in the states developed in the midst of the severest economic crisis in India since independence. The cumulative impact of the financial consequences of the 1971 Bangladesh war, the sharp drop in food production brought on by two successive droughts, and the sudden international energy and fertilizer crisis that grew out of the Arab-Israeli war of October 1973 touched off a wave of unprecedented inflation, widespread food shortages, isolated outbreaks of famine, recession, and further economic stagnation and unemployment.[56] The hopes generated by Mrs. Gandhi's populist rhetoric suddenly collapsed, for both urban and rural sectors of Indian society were experiencing severe deprivation. Spontaneous outbreaks of violence and protest against ineffective Congress governments occurred first in Gujarat and then in Bihar. Slowly, the inchoate nature of these regional explosions was galvanized into a significant new political movement led by Jayaprakash Narayan, who threatened to translate these regional protests into a national, anti-Congress alliance. India was suddenly confronted by a simultaneous economic and political crisis which seemed to threaten the survival of the Indian political system.[57]

The Narayan movement had an impact on national politics in three ways: (1) a symbolic appeal to urban intellectuals and students with its emphasis on Gandhian morality and tactics; (2) resusitation of the fragmented political opposition; and (3) threat of a possible split in the Congress.[58] The opposition uniting behind Janata candidates could, as in 1967, translate the fragmented votes of diverse parties into pluralities in single-member districts. Congress dominance might not survive.

Mrs. Gandhi's centralized pyramid of power, once subjected to this stress, ironically contributed to its further development. In the first place, Mrs. Gandhi's technique of frequent shifts of cabinet personnel created political and administrative chaos. The central ministers found it very difficult to deal with the economic crisis that confronted the nation. Repeated shifts in policy due to unresolved ideological tensions had disastrous economic consequences. The failure of the government's attempt to take over wholesale trade in wheat aggravated the food shortage, debates over monopoly and the joint sector created confusion among the industrialists, the unemployment problem intensified, and massive deficit financing fanned the flames of inflation.

Second, the tendency to treat the states as potential threats to the center resulted in weak and ineffective state governments whose leaders were too busy maneuvering to stay in power to be capable of coping with the growing hardship experienced by the population. Moreover, since these weak and ineffective state governments tended to be closely identified with the central Congress leadership, local discontent was easily translated into a threat to the national government itself. The crises in Gujarat and Bihar were notable examples.

Third, Mrs. Gandhi's Congress became increasingly intolerant of dissent and came to rely more and more on coercion in an attempt to control it. Dissent within the Congress, party opposition, and press criticism ceased to function as thermostats measuring discontent. They were now interpreted as antiparty, antinational, and traitorous, or even foreign inspired. Congressmen who called for a dialogue with Jayaprakash Narayan were expelled from the party. Opposition party attempts to mobilize and express local grievances, valid or not, were perceived as law and order problems. Increasing press criticism was dismissed as the voice of monopoly capital destroying the people's confidence.

Fourth, the system became highly personalized. Yet, curiously, by the fall of 1974, Mrs. Gandhi's charisma began to suffer. Until 1972, people in India were likely to separate Indira Gandhi from her party. By 1974, they tended to identify her with her party, while at the same time the image of both declined severely.[59] By the fall of 1974, the prime minister's popularity had fallen to an all-time low.[60] Charges of corruption leveled against state leaders and central cabinet ministers now touched the prime minister herself.

Finally, there emerged a serious factional split within the Congress party in Parliament, based on ideological and tactical differences. The former PSP "young Turks" were strongly anti-Communist and sympathetic to their older leader, Jayaprakash Narayan. The pro-CPI group in the Congress dubbed the Narayan movement a manifestation of rightist reaction and supported Mrs. Gandhi's treatment of the movement as an antigovernment plot. A large number of Congress centrists were extremely sympathetic to the Gandhian appeals of Narayan and were especially fearful of the impact his appeal might have at the polls. These fears were, in fact, born out by the result of the 1975 Gujarat elections. Thus, the Congress response to the Narayan movement had the added potential danger of creating a split in the Congress itself.[61]

It was this growing political crisis that translated the June 12, 1975, Allahabad High Court judgment that Mrs. Gandhi had been guilty of corrupt election practices from a legal issue into a threat to Mrs. Gandhi's personal power and to the political system itself.[62] Mrs. Gandhi responded on June 26, 1975, by declaring a state of national emergency under Article 352 of the Indian constitution, arresting major opposition leaders, and imposing rigid press censorship throughout India.

THE EMERGENCY AND AFTER

The declaration of a state of emergency was, therefore, not simply a sudden turn of events, but the end product of a process which saw the weakening of political support for Mrs. Gandhi and the Congress party, the emergence of a revitalized opposition, the development of increased tensions and factionalism within the Congress, and a seeming lack of governmental capacity to govern despite massive Congress majorities. Mrs. Gandhi's legal problems simply compounded the difficulties of an existing crisis of economic performance and political legitimacy.

Survival

During her rise to power, Mrs. Gandhi had effectively destroyed the major regulating mechanisms within the old Congress system of one-party dominance. However, the pyramid of power she had created from 1966 to 1975 foreclosed revolt within the party against her leadership, and this ensured her survival. Following the Allahabad High Court's decision, the party had little choice but to rally to her support. Senior cabinet ministers, Congress M.P.s, and chief ministers feared her departure from office, even for a short period, would result in a debilitating schism within the party that would destroy the party's dominance, not only at the center, but in the states as well. The absence of any layering of effectively organized state units based on strong local support from below left the party too weak institutionally to absorb such a shock.

Mrs. Gandhi's decision not to step down pending her appeal to the Supreme Court was made with the full support of the top party leaders. The party held together because the elite held together, an elite that had been hand picked by the prime minister and owed their political survival to her. As one of her chief supporters noted, "A difficult situation could arise only if there were any groups within the party, or any other party men who would stake his claim for leadership. This has not happened and she should, therefore, continue. There would be no political stability without her."[63]

Both Jagjivan Ram and Y. B. Chavan, her only potential challengers, realized that if Mrs. Gandhi were to step down neither could become prime minister without a contest. They therefore decided to support her continuation in office rather than inherit a divided party. Although Jagjivan Ram hedged somewhat more than Chavan by emphasizing the need to await a final court decision, he too realized he could not become prime minister without a bitterly divisive fight that could split the party for a second time.

The CPP, fearful of the consequences of a succession struggle on the eve of the 1976 general elections, reiterated its faith in Mrs. Gandhi and declared that her continued leadership was indispensable to the nation.[64] Similarly, the chief ministers of Congress-dominated states, recognizing their factional vulnerability, declared that Mrs. Gandhi's resignation would result in conditions of "instability, not only at the national level, but also in various states."[65] Yet it must have been personally significant that, for the first time since she had reached the pinnacle of her power in March 1972, Indira Gandhi had been compelled to turn to a variety of individuals and institutions within the party for support.

The new system built by Mrs. Gandhi, having ensured her personal survival, now reinforced itself so thoroughly as to mark a significant redirection of political development in India.

Further Centralization

Since the emergency, there have been two major cabinet reshuffles, by which such senior leaders as Swaran Singh and Uma Shankar Dikshit have been replaced by younger supporters of Mrs. Gandhi.[66] Power in the government has become concentrated in the hands of a small political elite around the prime minister, aided by the bureaucracy and the military.[67] The thrust toward centralizing power is apparent in the discussions initiated in December upon proposed major constitutional changes along Gaullist lines.

Since the emergency, the party has neither been mobilized nor energized to assist the government in the implementation of its newly proclaimed twenty-point program. Although all party organizational elections were suspended indefinitely, even before the emergency, the Congress held its seventy-fifth session on schedule at the end of 1975. This session passed a series of resolutions without opposition which endorsed the continuation of the emergency, ordered a reexamination of the Indian constitution with a view to amending it, and recommended extending the life of Parliament by one year. Thus, the party has been used as a major mechanism for legitimizing the political actions taken by the government.[68]

At the same time, Mrs. Gandhi has taken several steps to restore Congress dominance to all twenty-two states. In Gujarat she has succeeded in getting Hitendra Desai, former chief minister and leader of the old Congress, to rejoin the Congress party along with his followers.[69] This action has helped to strengthen the Congress in the state. In Tamil Nadu, not content with persuading a large number of former supporters of the late Syndicate leader, K. Kamaraj, to rejoin the party, thereby strengthening one of the weakest Congress units in India, she has dissolved the state government which has been controlled by the DMK since 1967.[70] In this move she used the power of the central government to eliminate opposition government in the states.

Finally, Mrs. Gandhi has attempted to consolidate her hold over the Congress party in the Hindi heartland states by declaring president's rule and replacing the Congress leadership in Uttar Pradesh,[71] restoring S. C. Shulka to power in Madhya Pradesh,[72] and bringing Bansi Lal, chief minister of Haryana, into the central cabinet.[73] Thus, Mrs. Gandhi continues to manipulate state and local situations to her advantage in an attempt to consolidate her hold over the party.

Vulnerabilities Remain

Although Mrs. Gandhi has succeeded in restoring her supremacy in both party and government, there remain fundamental problems which pose a dilemma to continued Congress dominance and the survival of Indian unity and the Indian political system.

Brittle center. In the first place, India is entirely too large, diverse, and fragmented to be governed by a clear and rigid hierarchy centered in New Delhi. Decision making must include bargaining and negotiating among a variety of actors, each holding some power on his own. Such a system requires a restoration of some degree of state autonomy and state leaders supported from below, not from New Delhi.

Mrs. Gandhi's centralized style of command is already encountering resistance from the periphery. The proposed constitutional reforms are, it appears, running into difficulty because of concern on the part of Congressmen from the south that a changed constitutional structure might upset the center-state balance of the past. The decision to dissolve the DMK government in Tamil Nadu may strengthen feelings of Tamil nationalism and is, therefore, fraught with danger. In fact, repressive policies, even if carried out in the name of socioeconomic reform, may spark separatist or breakaway movements, not only in the south, but also in such critical areas as Bengal, Kashmir, Punjab, and Gujarat.

Reforming the bottom from the top. A second problem involves the possibility of implementing reforms from above, without a corresponding pressure from below. Neither the Indian bureaucracy nor the Congress party as presently constituted is capable of implementing basic reforms unless prodded by organized groups capable of pressing claims on the political system. But, of course, such groups must have the freedom to mobilize, organize, and agitate, either within the Congress or from outside.[74] For example, even the Communist-controlled government in Kerala had difficulty implementing land reforms, despite the best of intentions. A recent study concluded, "Even if a political elite, responsive to the demands and expectations of the poor, initiates radical legislation, their implementation will be subverted, unless there is pressure built from below through militant protest movements."[75] A closed Congress and an opposition operating under the restrictions of the emergency could hardly mobilize such pressures.

Today, both local Congress organizations and local *panchayats* continue to be controlled by the very agrarian interests that would be disadvantaged by Mrs. Gandhi's program of land reforms, ceilings on land ownership, and an agriculture income tax. For example, a study of the Andhra Congress demonstrated that, despite Mrs. Gandhi's attempt to restructure the party from above, the base of the party continues to be controlled by the forward castes, who are also the dominant landowners.[76] Reform will require more, not less, political dynamism, more, not less, mobilization at the base—and neither is permitted under the emergency.

Reform vs. reconciliation. A third problem is reflected in the inability of the Congress to reconcile the tensions between the need for organizational mobilization and the need for reconciliation. The twin problems of poverty and diversity pull in different directions. As Mark Franda has observed, "To attack poverty and bring about economic development, Indian political parties are tempted to seek the widespread mobilization of India's vast population behind concrete programmes. Yet, because of the great diversity of India, widespread mobilization is frequently possible only through a series of negotiations and compromises that tend to dilute such programmes."[77] This is precisely Mrs. Gandhi's dilemma with the twenty-point program. It cannot be solved by mere centralization, bureaucratization, or even by the use of coercion.

Deinstitutionalization. Finally, the new Congress system is too personalized. It has failed to establish mechanisms for building support other than through the use of populist slogans. Mrs. Gandhi is not institutionalizing her charisma so much as creating a severe long-term problem of succession. The Indian political system, prior to the emergency, had successfully managed three successions. Mrs. Gandhi's Congress was unable to manage even one. Mrs. Gandhi could not step down, even temporarily, without fear of the system collapsing.

The opposition parties, the groups behind Jayaprakash Narayan, and perhaps even the courts may have behaved irresponsibly, but to a large extent their actions were in response to severe economic hardships and a growing intolerance and arrogance on the part of Mrs. Gandhi's Congress. Surely, Congress will not be less arrogant under a one-party dictatorship, and yet it will not be able indefinitely to suppress local or national explosions of discontent. A short emergency may have positive results, but the restoration of the normal functioning of the political system is essential for long-term unity, stability, and development. This normal functioning will have to apply to the Congress as well. It must include a healthy consolidation of power by state Congress leaders, the restoration of a less interventionist umpire role for the Congress high command, and the development of a new consensus about the aims and objectives of the Congress. The highly personalized style of Mrs. Gandhi must give way to a more systematic effort of institutionalization of roles and functions within the Congress and the government.

NOTES

[1] For a detailed discussion of the development of the Congress party from 1947 to 1968 see Stanley A. Kochanek, *The Congress Party in India* (Princeton: Princeton University Press, 1968).

[2] For a detailed discussion of the succession process in India see Michael Brecher, *Nehru's Mantle: The Politics of Succession in India* (New York: Frederick A. Praeger, 1966); and Brecher, "Succession in India: The Routinization of Political Change," *Asian Survey* 7 (July 1967): 423-43.

[3] For details of the split see A. M. Zaidi, *The Great Upheaval '69-'72* (New Delhi: Orientalia, 1972); and Mahrendra Pratap Singh, "The 1969 Split in the Indian National Congress," *Journal of the Society for Study of State Governments* 7 (Jan.-March 1974): 52-68.

[4] For a discussion of the distribution of power in the Congress see Kochanek, *The Congress Party in India*, pp. 111-316. For an excellent study of the Indian constitution see Granville Austin, *The Indian Constitution* (New York: Oxford University Press, 1966).

[5] Haridwar Rai and Jawhar Lal Pandy, "Intra-Party Democracy: The Experience of the Indian National Congress," *Journal of Constitutional and Parliamentary Studies* 5 (Oct.-Dec. 1971): 431.

[6] H. M. Jain, "Changing Role of the Prime Minister—Is India Moving Towards a Priministerial System?," *Journal of the Society for Study of State Governments* 6 (April-June and July-Sept. 1973): 143.

[7] See *Times of India* (Bombay), Sept. 18, 1971.

[8] *Link* (Delhi), May 1, 1971, pp. 901-2; *Times of India* (Bombay), March 19, 1971.

[9] *Overseas Hindustan Times*, Oct. 24, 1974.

[10] See *Economic Times*, Nov. 24 and 29, and Dec. 28, 30, and 31, 1969, for election of Working Committee members.

[11] Kochanek, *The Congress Party in India*, p. 211.

[12] Iqbal Narain and Mohan Lal Sharma, "The Fifth State Assembly Elections of India," *Asian Survey* 13 (March 1973): 324; *Times of India* (Bombay), Sept. 10, 1971.

13 *Link*, May 9, 1971, pp. 8-9; *Times of India*, Sept. 18, 1971.

14 *Link*, Aug. 15, 1971, p. 51.

15 See *Times of India* editorial, Oct. 29, 1971.

16 All India Congress Committee, *Report of the General Secretaries June 1970-September 1971* (New Delhi: A.I.C.C. 1971), p. 1.

17 Ramashray Roy, "India 1972: Fissure in the Fortress," *Asian Survey* 13 (Feb. 1973): 235-36.

18 A. M. Zaidi, ed., *Annual Register of Indian Political Parties 1973-74* (New Delhi: Orientalia, 1975); All India Congress Committee, *Report of the General Secretaries September 1973-June 1974* (New Delhi: A.I.C.C., 1974), p. 16.

19 Kochanek, *The Congress Party in India*, pp. 288-98, 438-39.

20 Marcus F. Franda, "India's 1972 State Elections," *American Universities Fieldstaff Reports*, South Asia Series 16, no. 1 (April 1972); Norman D. Palmer, *Elections and Political Development: The South Asian Experience* (Durham, N.C.: Duke University Press, 1975), pp. 115-25.

21 All India Congress Committee, *Report of the General Secretaries October 1971-May 1972* (New Delhi: A.I.C.C. 1972), p. 9.

22 Narain and Sharma, "The Fifth State Assembly Elections," pp. 323-26.

23 *Times of India* editorial, Dec. 2, 1972; V. S. K. Haranath, "Undemocratic Trends in the Congress Party of India: A View Point," *Indian Journal of Social Science* 2 (May-Aug. 1973): 142-56.

24 See R. P. Rao, *The Congress Splits* (Bombay: Lalvani Publishing House, 1971), pp. 91-162.

25 *Overseas Hindustan Times*, Aug. 29, 1974, p. 1.

26 Satish K. Arora, "Social Background of the Indian Cabinet," *Economic and Political Weekly* 7 (Special Number, 1972): 1523-32.

27 Krishan Bhatia, *Indira* (New York: Praeger Publishers, 1974), pp. 204-5; S. C. Gangal, *Prime Minister and the Cabinet in India* (New Delhi: Navachetna, 1972).

28 H. M. Jain, "Decision-making at the Centre: Role of the Prime Minister of India," *Journal of the Society for Study of State Governments* 7 (Jan.-March 1974): 1-12.

29 Jain, "Changing Role of the Prime Minister," p. 123.

30 *Times of India*, April 14, 1971.

31 *Hindu* (Madras), June 26, 1975.

32 Palmer, *Elections and Political Development*, pp. 43-44; *Times of India*, March 31, 1971; *The Hindu*, May 28, 1972.

[33]See *Link,* May 20, 1973, pp. 27-28; ibid., April 22, 1973, pp. 10-11; and the *Times of India,* April 17 and 21, 1973.

[34]*Overseas Hindustan Times,* Feb. 13, 1975, pp. 1, 7.

[35]Ibid.

[36]*Hindustan Times* (New Delhi), July 13, 1975.

[37]See the *Times of India,* Feb. 9, 1974; and *Statesman Weekly,* April 5, 1975, p. 5.

[38]Palmer, *Elections and Political Development,* pp. 143-147.

[39]See *Times of India,* Feb. 6, 1971; Iqbal Narain and Mohan Lal Sharma, "Election Politics, Secularization and Political Development: The 5th Lok Sabha Elections in Rajasthan," *Asian Survey* 12 (April 1972): 294-309; Padma Srivastava, "Selection of Congress Party (R) Candidates for Parliamentary Seats in Delhi (1971)," *The Indian Political Science Review* 4 (Oct. 1971-March 1972): 29-38.

[40]See Franda, "India's 1972 State Elections," pp. 10-11; Narain and Sharma, "The Fifth State Assembly Elections"; Partap Singh, "Haryana State Assembly Polls of 1968 and 1972," *Indian Journal of Political Science* 7 (April-Sept. 1973): 143-64; and G. Ram Reddy, "The 1972 Assembly Elections in Andhra Pradesh," *Indian Journal of Social Science* 1 (June -Aug. 1972): 87-93.

[41]Dagmar Bernstorff, "Eclipse of 'Reddy Raj'? The Attempted Restructuring of Congress Party Leadership in Andhra Pradesh," *Asian Survey* 8 (Oct. 1973): 973-74.

[42]Franda, "India's 1972 State Elections," p. 11.

[43]Text of Congress constitution of 1969, in Zaidi, *The Great Upheaval,* pp. 581-82.

[44]All India Congress Committee, *Report of the General Secretaries,* 1970-1971, p. 30.

[45]A. M. Zaidi, *Annual Register of Indian Political Parties, 1972-73* (New Delhi: Orientalia, 1973), p. 38; *Times of India,* Dec. 23 and 30, 1972.

[46]Kochanek, *The Congress Party in India,* p. 345.

[47]Link, April 25, 1971. pp. 15-16.

[48]Ibid., Sept. 2, 1972, pp. 15, 17.

[49]*Times of India,* Dec. 23 and 30, 1972.

[50]*Statesman* (Calcutta), June 24, 1973.

[51]Kochanek, *The Congress Party in India,* pp. 437-41.

[52]J. C. Johari, *Reflections on Indian Politics* (New Delhi: S. Chand 1974), pp. 243-311.

[53]See Romesh Thapar, *Economic and Political Weekly* 10 (April 19, 1975): 648-49; and ibid, (May 10, 1975): 744-45.

[54]Ramashray Roy, "India: 1973: A Year of Discontent," *Asian Survey* 14 (Feb. 1975): 85-94.

[55]See Kochanek, *The Congress Party in India*, pp. 223-24, 304-5.

[56]Ram Joshi, "India 1974: Growing Political Crisis," *Asian Survey* 15 (Feb. 1975): 85-94.

[57]Rajni Kothari, "Year of Turmoil, *Seminar* 185 (Jan. 1975): 1035-54.

[58]See the *Times of India*, Jan. 29, 1975; the *Statesman Weekly*, March 22, 1975, p. 10, and April 5, 1975, p. 10; and John Wood, "Extra-Parliamentary Opposition in India," *Pacific Affairs* 49 (Fall 1975): 313-34.

[59]Indian Institute of Public Opinion, "The Images Behind the Uttar Pradesh Elections: 1974," *Monthly Public Opinion Surveys* 19 (Feb. 1974): 211.

[60]Indian Institute of Public Opinion, "The Prime Minister's Popularity: September 1974, The Unprecedented Fall," *Monthly Public Opinion Surveys* 19 (Aug. 1974): 5-6; idem, "Indian Popular Expectations for 1974: Increasing Pessimism," *Monthly Public Opinion Surveys* 19 (Dec. 1973): I-III.

[61]*Overseas Hindustan Times*, Feb. 13, 1975, pp. 1, 7.

[62]For a detailed summary of the events of June 1975, see Norman D. Palmer, "The Crisis of Democracy in India," *Orbis* 19(Summer 1975): 379-401; and Richard Park, "Political Crisis in India, 1975" *Asian Survey* 15 (Nov. 1975): 996-1013.

[63]*Economic Times*, June 13, 1975.

[64]Ibid., June 19, 1975.

[65]In a memorandum to President Ahmed, ibid., June 21, 1975.

[66]See the *Overseas Hindustan Times*, Dec. 11, 1975, and Jan. 1. 1976.

[67]The new inner circle is composed of Sanjay Gandhi, Bansi Lal, D. K. Barooah, S. S. Ray, and Rajni Patel. Among this group, Sanjay Gandhi is emerging as a key figure and has been given an official position in the party as a member of the executive committee of the Youth Congress.

[68]See the *Overseas Hindustan Times*, Jan. 8, 1976.

[69]Ibid., Sept. 25, 1975.

[70]*Washington Post*, Feb. 1, 1976

[71]*Overseas Hindustan Times*, Jan. 21, 1976.

[72]Ibid., Jan. 1, 1976.

[73]Ibid., Dec. 11, 1975.

124

[74]Angela S. Burger, *Opposition in a Dominant-Party System* (Berkeley: University of California Press, 1969): 282-84.

[75]T. K. Oommen, "Agrarian Legislations and Movements as Sources of Change: The Case of Kerala," *Economic and Political Weekly* 10 (Oct. 4, 1975): 1571.

[76]Bernstorff, "Eclipse of 'Reddy Raj,'" p. 959.

[77]Asoka Mehta et al., "Forum: Relationship between the Organizational and Parliamentary Wings of the Congress Party," *The Indian Political Science Review* 4 (April 1970-Sept. 1970): 269.

5

The Industrialists
Howard L. Erdman

We receive counterindications of the position of India's corporate owners and executives on the emergency and the accompanying economic program. Mrs. Gandhi *seems* to place them in the camp of the enemy:

> A vociferous minority, which has the support of big money, big press—and, some say, influential interests abroad—[sought] to force its views on the majority.[1]

> The antagonists of socialism have started joining forces. . . . the persons who oppose us within the country derive their inspiration from without.[2]

> Powerful classes and powerful forces are against the implementation [of our econmic program.] These forces must be combatted with all the strength at our command.[3]

The industrialists define their position on Mrs. Gandhi's side. This they do, not only in their public resolutions supporting her, but in their statements to their own stockholders. These are two of the more powerful voices:

> Thanks to the positive and bold approach and the pragmatic decisions taken by the Government for resolving the problems facing the country, the condition was perceptibly eased . . .: K. K. Birla, Chairman India Steamship Company Ltd.[4]

125

Government have in the recent past shown encouraging signs of being willing to reconsider some of their economic policies in the interest of stimulating production . . .: J. R. D. Tata, Chairman, Tata Oil Mills.[5]

Some probing seems warranted to get behind these conflicting images.

THE NEHRU YEARS: ASPIRATIONS AND ACTUALITIES

Hostilities between the Congress leadership and large-scale industrialists[6] were not new to modern India. Under the British raj, to be sure, Indian industry generally languished. Facing indifference if not hostility, captains of industry were for the most part strong supporters of the nationalist movement. The advent of independence, it was hoped, would usher in an era of rapid growth. In the broadest terms, industrialists favored a policy of maximum state assistance with minimum state control. Concern for "social justice" was in some cases sincere; but this could not obscure the fact that most wanted government intervention not to protect the weak but to help the private sector to flourish.[7]

The *sine qua non* was of course a stable regime congenial to private enterprise. This entailed: (1) central government initiatives to maximize coherent national development, avoiding the fragmentation and parochialism that might result from devolution to states within the union;[8] (2) incentives, including tariff protection, tax concessions, and loans on favorable terms; (3) government action to assure adequate raw materials, power, and transportation; (4) public sector industries complementary to the private sector where the latter would not enter because of limited capital, unacceptable risk, or dim prospects of desired profitability; (5) labor policy based on discipline of the work force, to maximize output and to tie wages to productivity and to the ability of industry to pay; and (6) miscellanea such as government assistance in acquiring land—especially where it was good agricultural land—needed for industrial growth.[9] All of this went beyond making the world safe for private enterprise; it tended toward a guarantee that the private sector would prosper.

These were the hopes, but industrialists had cause to doubt that postindependence policy would fulfill them. The Gandhian commitment to technological primitivism was never seen as a serious problem.[10] In somewhat the same category were those who favored an agriculture-first policy: they might retard industrial expansion, but they were not hostile to it in a fundamental way. They might be misguided, but not menacing. Most troublesome were those who inveighed against the private sector from the perspective of socialism and who favored industrial development under the aegis of the state. Nehru was seen to be among them. There were others, of course—including the other post-1947 "duumvir," Sardar Patel—who were considered sympathetic to the private sector. But few if any expected even the powerful Patel to prevail over a determined Nehru.[11] A leading industrialist, G. D. Birla, was not alone in urging the British to come to terms with Gandhi before Nehru could impose more radical solutions to the country's problems.[12] There was considerable anxiety, but no fear of extinction.

The Climate of Opinion

A climate of opinion overwhelmingly favorable to the private sector was a luxury which industrialists never enjoyed. Rather, there was an abundance of both socialist and nonsocialist rhetoric which portrayed industrialists as rapacious exploiters who might be grudgingly tolerated but whose motives and actions would always be suspect. Efforts were made to counter this image, ranging from local programs to broad, occasionally nationwide activities. Most notable among the latter for its explicit and forthright defense of the private sector was the Forum of Free Enterprise (1956), largely sponsored by Bombay industrialists, especially the Tata family. But even this group did not convert many to the cause of free enterprise.[13] In fact, given the abuse that Nehru heaped upon it, it is possible that it was counterproductive. However, the policies acutally pursued by the government of India and the states during the Nehru years stopped far short of driving industrialists to the wall. This being so, most industrialists accepted a poor public image as a fact of life. Nehru's bark was far worse than his bite.

Policies

Self-reliance. The Nehru government was committed to increasing economic self-reliance, including industrialization, through a mixed economy. To achieve this a substantial measure of central planning was favored, to channel limited resources (including foreign exchange) into those sectors deemed important to the national effort. At this general level industrialists had few complaints. The balance between agriculture and industry or among different sectors of industry was not uniformly acceptable; but industrialists had enough opportunities to sustain themselves comfortably.

Public vs. private sectors. A number of industrial policy resolutions and enactments reserved certain sectors of the economy for principal or exclusive development by the public sector on the one hand and by medium- and small-scale ventures on the other. While not opposed to the public sector in principle, industrialists certainly criticized it amply in practice. For example, some public sector ventures in pharmaceuticals were opposed on the grounds that the private sector could easily have done the job. As a minimum, industrialists desired the opportunity to compete with such public sector units, which they regarded as inefficient, rather than have the latter given special standing by government action.[14]

Exclusion in favor of medium and small ventures certainly rankled, especially where the big industrialists could have moved easily into high-profit areas. But as in the previous case, this did not deprive industrialists of anything that they already had; it simply limited their access to potentially attractive areas.

Constraints on entering open areas and on management. Even in areas where they were permitted to enter, industrialists faced a variety of vexatious and often frustrating constraints. A major irritant was the system of government industrial licensing. While a few argued that the entire system could be abolished to good effect, most criticized the forms, supplementary materials, personal representations, and the like which meant, as an inevitable concomitant, considerable delay.

Government action to eliminate the so-called managing agency system, whereby a large number of diverse industries were firmly under the control of a single management group (usually associated with the major industrial houses), also caused concern, as limits were placed on the number of units that could be so managed and as interlocking directorates, inter-company investments, and the like came under attack. The Company Law (1956) defined acceptable managerial structures, compensation for executives, etc., further limiting freedom of action. Also troublesome was the pattern of taxation of corporate and individual wealth, and a few government sorties into the realm of price ceilings, pharmaceuticals again being a case in point.

Labor. An area of major concern to industrialists and one which was almost uniformly linked to ideological bias on the one hand and the compulsions of democratic politics on the other was that of labor. While conceding that the central government and the states could legitimately protect labor against indiscriminate exploitation, industrialists contended that standards of compensation, factory conditions, etc., had to be within the capacity of the private sector to pay, with due regard for funds for ploughing back and for profits. This, they held, was not the case. An ideological commitment to socialism and the desire, inspired by competitive electoral politics, to cultivate the labor vote had combined to produce a labor force that demanded more and more benefits and engaged in work slowdowns and strikes upon the slightest provocation. With troubled industrial relations, it was held, profits (and in some cases physical safety) were too uncertain to encourage private sector activity.[15] In this area, variations over time and space were of great importance, as, e.g., industrialists sought out states where the investment climate was better—Gujarat as opposed to Bengal.[16]

Nationalization. As already implied, there was a generally remote threat of nationalization during the Nehru years. Whatever the socialist rhetoric, the emphasis was on "nationalization of the vacuum" in key areas, not a takeover of existing enterprises. The few cases of nationalization in the 1950s and early 1960s were special in one way or another, and few industrialists were troubled by them.

Overall, industrialists had much for which to be thankful, along with undesired constraints. And in addressing themselves to the constraints, they recognized certain facts of life. The ruling Congress party, especially at the center, was seen responsible for troublesome policies, but it was also the source, the only sure source, of political stability. Here, too, circumstances at the state level varied considerably, leading to different stategies over space.

Another perception was that, if India were not a paradise for profit-hungry industrialists, it was still a very far cry from rigorous imprisonment, let alone the firing squad. With all the socialist rhetoric, in short, the private sector had sufficient scope to pursue its interests; if there was no plausible alternative regime, there was little reason for industrialists to take to the barricades in what would be largely a sham battle.17

Responses: Devious Practices

While lobbying and negotiating for additional opportunities and benefits, industrialists went about their business in ways which often hurt their image and led to constraints. Many industrialists demonstrated a marked propensity for quick and large profits. There were strikes of capital, even threats to close down existing plants altogether.

This range of behavior was, of course, entirely legal, but it contributed to something of a vicious circle involving government and industry. Seeing huge profits in some fields and a reluctance to invest in others, the government often castigated industry, or imposed curbs on profits (in drugs, e.g.). This, in turn, prompted some industrialists to resort to devious practices and/or further to withhold investment. This pattern was quite common in the Nehru era.

A major element in industry's response to a relatively hostile environment was willful disregard of undesirable legislation. Excluded from certain sectors reserved for medium- and small-scale ventures, major industrialists set up fully controlled subsidiaries through roundabout routes, violating the spirit, if not the letter, of the law. Unable to secure sanction for additional capacity, industrialists installed it illegally. Unable legally to secure necessary raw materials at home or abroad, they entered the black market and dealt in smuggled goods. Bribery, tax evasion, and the like became, for some, integral components of economic life. Altogether these activities led to massive economic activity outside the law—the realm of "black money" and the parallel economy.

The Case of the Fertilizer Industry

The cycle of interaction between the Congress government and major industrialists during the 1960s with regard to expansion of fertilizer production[18] provides a foretaste of what might be a corresponding cycle under the present emergency. Then, as now, stepped-up production was sorely needed. In the case of fertilizer, Green Revolution technology depended on it. Until the early 1960s, synthesis of nitrogen was virtually a monopoly of the public sector. The urgent need for more production, however, overcame ideological scruples, and the government encouraged both foreign and domestic investors to enter the field, side-by-side with expanding state-run enterprises. The private sector responded cautiously; this was a high-cost, capital-intensive undustry which at best would yield profits only after some years.

The government's adaptation to this caution is revealing. In a major concession, private producers were given autonomy in pricing and marketing for a period of seven years. At the same time, however, public sector capacity was increased; government spokesmen refused to give any assurances about policy after the seven years, and official pronouncements made clear that private entry into this industry was a temporary expedient. Moreover, in the late 1960s, after Nehru's death, the government reneged on its promise of a free hand in pricing and marketing, reminding industrialists of their dependent position.

Many of India's major fertilizer ventures date from this period, and have been highly profitable. Nevertheless, the whole experience suggests the inhibitions under which large-scale private enterprise operates, even when the needs of the economy and the variations of public policy may offer points of entry.

Overt Political Activities of Business[19]

In his major study of India's industrialists, Kochanek has described in detail the political activities of principal business organizations. He notes that in the view of some observers the Federation of Indian Chambers of Commerce and Industry

(FICCI) had a veto over selection of the government's finance minister.[20] Unfortunately, this kind of assertion is almost impossible to prove with compelling evidence; but whether it be true or not, it is important. If it is true, it is no small achievement, and business obviously had friends in high places. If it is false, those who make this assertion obviously expect it to find a receptive audience.

In any event, industrialists have been able to find ample opportunities for private sector enterprise. Whether this is due to their intrinsic strength as the "national bourgeoisie" of Marxist analysis or to the very pragmatic concessions of the central and state governments cannot be resolved here, although it is a central issue. My own inclination is toward the latter view, but either way, industrialists have not been able to keep off the books very troublesome legislation. It is also clear, however, that during the Nehru years industrialists were not engaged in a life-and-death struggle with the government.[21]

MRS. GANDHI'S PRIME MINISTERSHIP

Well before Nehru died, a number of observers posed the question, "After Nehru, what"? The implication was that India might have in store fundamental changes of policy and of constitutional form. Industrialists pinned a good deal of hope upon Lal Bahadur Shastri, Nehru's immediate successor.[22] He died before this optimism could be tested.

Mrs. Gandhi, when she came to the prime minstership in 1966, was viewed as more impulsive and more leftist than both Shastri and Morarji Desai, her only serious competitor, and hence potentially more troublesome. Balancing this was the feeling that she lacked substantial roots in the Congress party and thus could be managed by the power brokers in the party, who were seen to be generally less leftist than she. Combined with the feeling that she would have some mass appeal, this produced a curious and qualified optimism. Her appeal to the electorate would secure support for the Congress and thus contribute to political stability; but she would not be able to impose herself on the Congress, thus limiting her capacity for harm.

Business had some success in the 1967 elections; several articulate spokesmen for the private sector won seats in Parlia-

ment on the Swatantra ticket. That gain was offset by the instability of many state governments occasioned by the anti-
Congress electoral swing. West Bengal was the extreme case.

Policies

Causing further apprehension among industrialists was evidence of a significant move to the left on the part of Congress.
In the aftermath of electoral reverses in 1967 many Congressmen concluded that the party had failed to deliver the goods
to India's suffering masses and that a more radical posture and
policy were required.[23] Thus, at a time when some developments suggested support for the Congress, others suggested
opposition, or a variant: energetic boring from within the ruling
party. Among the policies that troubled industry during the
early Gandhi years were the following.

Nationalization of private banks.[24] In the mid-1960s the
Congress party had committed itself to a vague goal of "social
control" of leading private sector banks. Even with this loose
formulation, many industrialists felt that this meant de facto
nationalization of companies by control over a major source of
investment funds. With Mrs. Gandhi's outright nationalization
of the banks (1969), most industrialists joined in the chorus
to criticize industry inasmuch as the other major source of
investment funds, special industrial development institutions,
was government sponsored. In many cities industrialists established cooperative banks to provide an alternative source of
short-term capital, but for major borrowing and underwriting
they remained dependent on government-dominated institutions.[25] Even though most personnel in the nationalized banks
were retained and even though big business was well represented on the boards of the lending institutions, industrialists
felt that their freedom of movement was diminished. To the
more nervous, bank nationalization was but another step on the
road to eventual demise.

Restrictions on major houses.[26] Following a number of
studies on the concentration of economic power in the hands of
leading industrial families—including new industrial licenses
issued and access to support from major public lending institutions—Parliament passed the Monopoly and Restrictive Trade
Practices (MRTP) Act (1969), which imposed another hurdle

in the path of major industrialists. The intent of the MRTP Act was to exclude larger houses from additional investment in fields where they had "monopoly" or "dominant" position in existing markets. Major houses could still enter areas where they were not dominant, and in this respect the MRTP Act was not a blanket curb on big business. But the general aim was seen to be further limitation of the scope of activity by the captains of industry. As in other areas, industrialists were not able to prevent passage of this undesirable legislation, but they sought to clarify provisions to their own advantage, as in the criteria for defining areas of production. It would make a difference, e.g., if there were a category of "pharmaceuticals" as opposed to smaller categories such as "antibiotics" or "penicillin." The anti-MRTP Act campaign was waged on a variety of fronts, more often than not behind the scenes.

Conflict

These and other measures, including the government's use of its powers to convert loans to private industries into equity,[27] convinced the industrial community that Mrs. Gandhi's government intended slowly to strangle the private sector, ultimately to convert management into paid government functionaries—albeit well paid ones. This fear was probably unwarranted, but some industrialists were worried enough to counter Mrs. Gandhi's "*garibi hatao*" (abolish poverty") slogan with an "Indira *hatao*" ("get rid of Indira") slogan in the 1971 elections, and supported the 1971 "grand alliance" of opposition groups that has as its main—if not only—theme the defeat of Mrs. Gandhi and her cohorts.

Illustrative of the friction between Gandhi and the industrial community was her off-the-cuff, sharp retort to a group of Gujarat's leading industrialists in late 1970, when most of the latter continued to support the Old (anti-Gandhi) Congress. After listening the the familiar litany about the problems of the private sector, Mrs. Gandhi took her audience very much by surprise when she stated: "You can bully the Gujarat Government but there is a lot of difference between the Gujarat and the Central Government. You cannot bully me."[28] Mrs. Gandhi was opposed by most local industrialists in the 1971 parliamentary elections in Gujarat, and, to a lesser extent, in the

1972 state assembly elections. In both cases another facet of the industrialists' activites was revealed: prominent Ahmedabad businessmen strongly supported Mahatma Gandhi-influenced, nonstrike unions against organizers of a more militant labor movement in the city.[29]

With the rout of the opposition parties by Mrs. Gandhi in both the 1971 and 1972 elections, most of the anti-Gandhi industrialists went into at least temporary hiding. The effective demise of the Swatantra party was a factor here. It was time to abandon the overt campaigns which were evident in the mid-1960s and early 1970s, in favor of less conspicuous and more familiar approaches of boring from within the Congress and working at many levels behind the scenes. Even as this was done—and, it must be stressed, this was done before the June 1975 declaration of emergency—industrialists received other warnings from leading government figures. Prominent themes included the following:

1. Many Indian industrialists had in the past compared their country's sluggish rate of growth with Pakistan's; but, it was asked, where did that get Pakistan or her industrialists? Growth without social justice would lead to unrest and to danger to industrialists. Behave.
2. The ministers were dressed in white *khadi* (Gandhian hand-woven) clothing when they spoke to business groups, but without social justice the next minister might be wearing a red shirt. Which did they prefer? Behave.
3. India's sluggish rate of growth was not due to government policy but was the fault of industrialists who refused to take even modest risks as good entrepreneurs had done in the past. The medium- and small-scale sectors had made great progress, the larger houses had not. Shape up.[30]

And so it went throughout the early 1970s: most audiences were not converted, but most were certainly chastened, as their reluctance to challenge central government spokesmen suggested.

Harassment

Off and on during the Nehru years, some industrialists held that their freedom to criticize the Congress was impaired because they were dependent upon the government for industrial licenses, import allocations, loans, and the like. A few cited specific cases where, after opposing the ruling party, they were allegedly denied access to government largesse. Such comments continued during the Gandhi period, and in 1972, in Ahmedabad (Gujarat), an event occurred which was widely taken as a warning to industrialists who challenged the ruling Congress: there was a raid on a suburban house owned by prominent industrialists, who were caught drinking in violation of the state's dry law. Such penalities as were eventually imposed were of a trivial character, but for many industrialists this was not the point: it was merely one sign of things to come if they persisted in opposing the ruling party.[31]

These were some of the developments that led to abundant caution on the part of the industrial elite. There were, however, other developments that have to be kept in mind for a proper perspective of the post-June 1975 period. One was Mrs. Gandhi's resistance to the most leftist members of her own party and to pressure from the CPI. More to the present point were two preemergency measures. The first was a 1972 memorandum on speeding industrial development, requested by the government from J. R. D. Tata, head of India's leading business house. The second was Mrs. Gandhi's response to a strike by railway unions in the spring of 1974.

Convergence

The Tata Memorandum. Entitled "Suggestions for Accelerating Industrial Growth," the Tata Memorandum was one of a long line of such submittals by the private sector to the government. What is significant about this one is that it was solicited at precisely the time when anti-Congress activity by industrialists had met with a severe setback and when industrialists were being warned repeatedly to behave themselves. And even though Tata opened his remarks by saying that he proposed no radical transformation of government thinking about industrial policy, he was widely and explicitly critical of many specifics of that policy, as they adversely affected private sector industrial development. Whether for full utilization of installed capacity or for addition to capacity, reliable and adequate power, transport, raw materials, and labor were absolutely essential. At least with respect to the first three items there was no fear of government hostility: the government was as anxious as the private sector to provide essential inputs and infrastructure. In the same category was the insistence on a streamlined and expeditious licensing process, both for substantial expansion of existing plant and for installation of new plant. (The issue of labor was more problematical, for a variety of obvious reasons.)

Tata went beyond this, however, in insisting that for a great leap forward in industrial production certain policies had to be changed. The bias against larger houses, as reflected in the MRTP Act, would have to be overcome, as only they had the capital and the expertise to succeed *quickly* in many areas. The conversion of loans into equity would have to be modified drastically (if not scrapped completely) if fresh private sector investments were to be forthcoming. And, of course, decent return on capital and provisions for accruing development reserves were an integral part of private sector activity.

Somewhat more obscure in its import was a suggestion that in massive ventures the central government would of necessity have to be the partner of private sector entrepreneurs, but that in other ventures the states were the most appropriate partners for the private sector. Many industrialists had learned to work effectively with state governments. And most states, including some influenced by Communists, were anxious to increase industrial investment from all conceivable sources and had few scruples about inviting captains of industry into their midst.[32] Without arguing that Tata became the de facto minister of industrial development, it is evident that most of his main points found a place in Mrs. Gandhi's twenty-point program.

The 1974 railway strike. Another prevision of things to come was the severity with which the central government handled a strike by railway workers. The strike was not only denounced by the government, but in an uncommon act of firmness Mrs. Gandhi jailed many union leaders, including George Fernandes, union leader and chairman of the Socialist party. Other strikers had their services terminated or lost seniority (and associated benefits) when they returned to work. Significantly these measures were justified on the grounds that (1) the organized workers were not the neediest sector of the population and (2) economic recovery could not tolerate disruption of such an essential service.[33] Both of these themes have been echoed repeatedly during the emergency.

THE EMERGENCY AND THE INDUSTRIALISTS

The full impact of the government's activities under the emergency cannot be gauged accurately at this juncture. Mrs. Gandhi and others have repeatedly stated that the twenty-point program is not definitive, and, in fact, there have been some modifications since its first presentation. Even after the promised economic blueprint (due in 1976) is available it will still be premature to pass anything like definitive judgment. Nonetheless, a number of industry-related propositions have been set forth already and have been reiterated. These at least suggest the drift of government thinking.

As concerns the industrial sector, it is clear that to this juncture (February 1976) there has been no menacing, radically left-wing posture on the part of the government. Mrs. Gandhi sometimes seemed, in justifying the emergency, to include industrialists among those status quo and reactionary forces that were bringing the country to the verge of chaos, but there has been no concerted attack on them since June 1975. Traders, especially those dealing in basic commodities, have been warned to avoid hoarding and price gouging and have been the target of much criticism, but the captains of industry have been left relatively unscathed.

Economic policy under the emergency has stressed rapid economic recovery through full utilization of installed capacity and additions of new capacity; and throughout the process, discipline and efficiency have been the watchwords. More or less routinely the government has also stated that every effort would be made to provide adequate power, transport, and raw materials—persistent problems all—and has promised speed in industrial licensing. In the latter case, special licensing committees of top officials (as suggested in the Tata Memorandum) have worked energetically to clear the backlog and to gear up for expeditious handling of new proposals. As part of this process certain industries have been delicensed completely, provided that they did not require foreign exchange or significant government financial assistance—quite substantial limitations if one contemplates major projects. Even with such complications the aim is clear: to speed private sector activity as part of economic recovery. Thus far, however, we have not encountered any significant departures from past policy. But what of major issue areas, such as those raised in the Tata Memorandum? There have been significant departures.

The Climate of Opinion

Mrs. Gandhi's public statements did not rehabilitate the image of private sector industrialists. There were many sharp attacks on rapacious businessmen, especially traders and merchants, who would be dealt with "firmly and ruthlessly" if they did not behave properly.[34] At the same time, Mrs. Gandhi told a meeting of chief secretaries of state governments that, while the guilty should be ferreted out and punished, "our attitude towards those who are engaged in productive processes—whether as farmers, industrialists, traders, transport operators—should be friendly and helpful."[35] This is quite far from an announcement that what is good for the Tatas and Birlas is good for India; but even so, industrialists could be thankful. As before, most industrialists seem happy enough if opportunities exist, even with a poor public image.

One of Mrs. Gandhi's principal themes, an attack on the black money economy, reflects her often ambivalent approach to the business community. The prime minister has understandably attacked those who have become rich and preserved their wealth through devious practices. She announced that malefactors' wealth would be subject to summary confiscation when unearthed by teams of special investigators who were organized in most major cities. At the same time she announced that, if the corrupt would confess their crimes and make a full accounting of accumulated wealth to the income tax department, the latter would keep this secret from other government bodies, sparing further penalities. In addition to paying full taxes on illegal wealth, the government's policy required the culprits to invest 5 percent of their black money in nonnegotiable but interest-bearing "social welfare" bonds.[36] There is little likelihood that without some prior understanding, if then, anyone would take the risk to confess; and there is also little likelihood that any captains of industry will be publicly humiliated and subjected to severe penalties. There have been reports, however, that some industrialists have been visited by the special teams and that in isolated cases local industrialists have been paraded in public as social parasites.[37] Likely to be more troublesome are the proposals for a ceiling on urban wealth; but even these will not frighten industrialists unduly.[38]

Industry's General Response

Following the declaration of emergency and the presentation of the twenty-point program, industrialists have been quite cautious in their public statements. But they have, of course, expressed their support of Mrs. Gandhi's aims. A FICCI spokesman called Gandhi's program a "sensitive and realistic programme of action which must be supported by all responsible sections of the public."[39] The FICCI president, Harish Mahendra, stated that the central government had taken "appropriate policy actions" and he urged his colleagues to accept the government guidelines and make them work. He stated that "it is entirely up to us to ensure that while augmenting production and distribution, we always remember that first and foremost we are part and parcel of the mainstream of national life and act accordingly."[40] At the same time, industrialists have not entirely refrained from criticism, although the criticism has admittedly been guarded. Patriotism would, of course, carry industrialists a certain distance, but patriotism had to be supplemented with a healthly investment climate. If, for example, prices were to be frozen or lowered (as they were in a few cases, including fertilizer), input costs would also have to be controlled, because "prices are rooted in costs" and modest profits would not attract fresh investment. A review of tax policy, among other proposals, was part of the probing. The give-and-take continued in various forms and at various levels.[41]

Government Policy

Within this broad framework the drift of the twenty-point program with its ad hoc modifications is very favorable to the large-scale private sector industrialists, as a review of some key issues will indicate.

Public vs. private sectors and nationalization. The earliest policy statements were almost uniformly taken to mean that there would be a moratorium on nationalization of existing industries, although in view of the government's past policy shifts, industrialists might be pardoned if they displayed some residual skepticism. More significant were statements attributed to the prime minister's son Sanjay to the effect that the public sector was hopelessly inefficient and that significant progress would depend on the private sector. Yet further, T. A. Pai, who even before the emergency had favored greater latitude for the private sector, was promoted to the post of union minister for industry and supply, in the face of vehement opposition from leftists within the Congress and the CPI; and, as will be seen, he had persisted in this posture during the emergency. Taken together, these developments were construed by left-wing critics as a virtually complete sellout to the private sector. Subsequent clarifications of Sanjay Gandhi's remarks, assertions that the public sector industries were making spectacular progress, and statements by Finance Minister Subramaiam that official policy was "not a declaration of no nationalization at all" have thus far done little to modify the no-nationalization interpretation.[42]

A major policy change allows larger houses to enter certain areas that earlier had been off limits to them. First, some areas previously reserved to the public sector are to be opened to the private sector, generally on a case-by-case basis. Second, the application of the MRTP Act is to be substantially modified, perhaps fully, if only temporarily, suspended, allowing monopoly and dominant houses to become active in areas which were earlier de facto limited to medium- and small-scale enterprises. In a related matter, Pai has stated that economic parochialism, as manifested in the "sons of the soil" policies of some state governments, is a problem with which the government will deal, further to the advantage of larger houses.[43]

Of considerable potential gain for the private sector—especially the larger houses—are two government proposals concerning the public sector. A suggestive general statement holds that "we [the government] want to encourage both [public and private sectors] for the sake of production."[44] But other statements have gone beyond this essentially harmless remark. The government announced that public sector units would have to fend for themselves in the market place, without government intervention to prop them up against competition.[45] Of much greater interest is the suggestion—it is yet nothing more that that—that existing public sector units might be opened up to private investors, as part of a "national sector" where all could participate cooperatively. This idea was also set forth prior to the emergency by Pai, in the face of left-wing hostility.

It is most unlikely that the government would divest itself of a significant percentage of shares to place affected companies under substantial private influence, but private industry does not need this to benefit. As in the case of government-dominated "joint sector" projects, private sector participation provides opportunities for industry as suppliers, marketers, ancillary manufacturers, and applicants for important licenses for "downstream" industries.[46] There is no guarantee of such a payoff for the private sector, but participation with such benefits in mind is a very low-risk activity which industrialists will surely seek. The upshot of this and preceding discussions is that the private sector in general and the major industrialists in particular will have greater scope for development.

Labor policy. A major part of the economic program is the maintenance of peaceful industrial relations, which, for the moment, has been construed as meaning first and foremost a ban on strikes and, second, a linking of various forms of compensation to productivity. Long convinced that in a democratic framework with leaders of socialist orientation labor policy could not be "sound," industrialists must have been almost ecstatic when guidelines for organized labor were set forth by the government. It is certain that the last word has not yet been heard on this subject, given the strength of organized labor, but official pronouncements over a span of several weeks have all tended in the direction of a fairly severe labor policy. A complete reversal is unlikely, and proponents of such a policy can cite approvingly the handling of the 1974 railway workers strike.

Nearly all major figures in the cabinet and in the Congress party have expressed themselves on the general subject of labor discipline and limitations on compensation. Congress president Barooah urged trade unions to work for greater productivity and he criticized reactionary and status quo forces for trying to mislead the working class and through it to sabotage production.[47] Pai stressed the importance of a production orientation on the part of labor, and in this connection he cautioned against pressures to hire only "sons of the soil," as such action would be detrimental to the national effort.[48] Prime Minister Gandhi appealed to workers to refrain from agitations, go-slow tactics, and strikes in order to "strengthen the economic structure and increase production."[49] Most forceful to date has been the statement of Union Minister of Finance Subramanium, who said, apropos the policy on compensation, that it "was not a pleasant decision" but that economic recovery required it, even if it hurt the workers.[50] In addressing itself to this issue the government has approached business and labor groups separately and in tripartite discussions, the latter being a widely-used mechanism in preemergency years, as, e.g., in wage boards for specified industries.[51] Thus far the government has held a number of such meetings, mainly of an exploratory nature, with business and labor representatives. It is significant, however, that the latter have been drawn from Congress, CPI, and, to a lesser extent, Socialist unions, apparently excluding leaders from unions controlled by the CPM and the Jan Sangh.

In its pronouncements in this area the government has insisted that the trade union sector is not the neediest in India and that the reduction of prices as part of the campaign against inflation rendered less urgent the demands of organized labor. In light of a decline in workers' real income in recent years, unions may not easily reconcile themselves to a ban on strikes and to productivity-related compensation. And given the supporters of trade unions in the government, some prolabor clarifications are almost inescapable, and much tough bargaining is on the horizon. If, following the example of the railway strike, the administration can make its policy stick, it will be something of a minor miracle for which the major industrialists will be very grateful indeed.[52]

Problems and portents. On the other side of the twenty-point ledger are some entries that have the potential for being troublesome to big business. As already noted, there has been ample praise of late for the performance of public sector units; but along with this has come some criticism of sluggishness in the private sector.[53] This may be taken as a modest warning to the latter to get down to business energetically. In addition, in some areas, notably the highly charged field of pharmaceuticals (where well before the emergency the government has enforced lower prices due to alleged profiteering), the government has reaffirmed its intention of having public sector units dominate new ventures.[54] Also of modest import was the announcement that production of certain consumer goods, up to now dominated by private sector companies exploiting brand name power, would be shifted to small-scale and cooperative units to enhance competition.[55]

Delicensing of certain categories of industries was announced in part as a measure to encourage the less-than-giant entrepreneures to come forth without having to go through the often sluggish review bodies; but no larger houses seemed at all concerned. That delicensing applies only to those proposals that do not require foreign exchange or loans from public lending institutions suggests that entry by lesser lights will be limited. Moreover, big industry remains convinced that it alone has the capital and the expertise to assure rapid progress, and there is some expectation that many of these new areas will be open to it by default.[56]

Another area of modest concern for industrialists was the statement—significantly, in response to criticism from smaller industry—that the government would not regularly bail out "sick" private sector companies and then return them to private sector hands.[57] It remains doubtful that the central and/or state governments would allow major undertakings to collapse at a time when maximum output and more jobs were the main goals of policy; and it seems more likely that after a rescue operation the government(s) would keep the affected companies in the joint sector.

In the broad area of labor affairs the government has in the first instance stressed reciprocity: no strikes or slow-downs must be matched by no-lockouts, union busting, and the like.[58] Somewhat more problematical are proposals to associate workers with management at various levels within individual companies. It is significant that while some favored this as a mandatory proposition, the government has left it on a voluntary basis, with companies employing more than 500 workers strongly urged to adopt the practice. It is surely significant that in justifying this Mrs. Gandhi and others have stressed the higher productivity expected if workers' alienation is reduced: it is not intended to enable labor to extract maximum concessions, but to "strengthen the economic structure and increase production."[59] Industry must certainly have some residual fears about the eventual impact of this provision, which may come back to haunt them. For this, among other reasons, industrialists are sure to keep a close watch on trade unions and to seek to deradicalize them when the opportunity arises, as they have done in the past.60 Greater caution in this effort is also likely, however.

Another area in which the administration is seeking to diminish the impact of larger houses is through the proposal to abolish the marketing arrangement known as the "sole selling agency" system, in which a manufacturer can assign exclusive marketing rights to one company, often a company affiliated with the producer. Coupled with the sole supplying agent at the other end, this permits considerable maneuvering with respect to prices and profits. At the time of writing, the sole selling agencies in two basic commodities, suger and vegetable oil, have been banned for a period of five years. Even with an extension into other sectors this is not likely to trouble many industrialists, who are likely to find ways to circumvent the intent of the legislation. The government will then have to decide whether it means seriously to attack those who do.61

Finally, despite industry's plea that prices are rooted in costs, the government has committed itself to hold the price line and in some cases rolling prices back. In one major area, fertilizers, prices have been reduced and a higher commission given to marketers, to enhance fertilizer use. In the short run this is not likely to become a major issue with producers (many of whom are in the public sector Fertilizer Corporation of India) because of large accumulated stocks. Industry may become more vocal after inventories are reduced. In a related case, a new four-year wage settlement for the steel industry was arranged, but producers (also with accumulated stocks) were not permitted to meet the higher wages with increased prices, only with greater efficiency at various points in the manufacturing process.62

Overall, one can readily see why industry should be pleased with the measures taken under the emergency and why their statements of support for Mrs. Gandhi's program are more than a ritual exercise. There will certainly be clarifications and modifications. If the past be any guide, there will also be some studied ambiguities that will allow ample scope for private enterprise, but that will simultaneously reassure those hostile to the private sector that the government is maintaining constant vigilance and firm control.63 It would appear necessary, however, that the private sector set aside some of its doubts and shake off some of its lethargy. Mrs. Gandhi has made too many commitments and accommodated too much to big business for her to tolerate "business as usual." In view of the concessions, however, big business should be able to do quite nicely. Industrialists are not likely to apply much, if any, pressure to restore the status quo ante in India.[64]

NOTES

[1] Interview in *Saturday Review,* Aug. 9, 1975, p. 10.

[2] Interview for distribution at Congress annual meeting, *Times of India* (Bombay), Dec. 28, 1975.

[3] Lok Sabha speech, *Economic Times* (Bombay), Jan. 10, 1976.

[4] *Commerce* (Calcutta), Oct. 4, 1975.

[5] Ibid, Aug. 23, 1975.

[6] As used here, "industrialists" will refer to India's major families/houses, including those of nationwide prominence (Notably the Tatas and the Birlas) and those of great regional (and increasing national) activity (e.g., the Kirloskars in Majarashtra and the Amins in Gujarat). For capsule summaries of the top twenty houses see Stanley A. Kochanek, *Business and Politics in India* (Berkeley: University of California Press, 1974), Appendix.

[7] Some Muslim industrialists were obviously apprehensive; but some Parsis were also concerned about their position in a Hindu-dominated independent India. Kochanek, *Business and Politics,* explores such matters in considerable detail.

[8] India's leading industrialists were very wary about a bias in favor of local industrialists, as against nationwide firms, if the constitutional structure were too decentralized. See Kochanek, *Business and Politics;* also Kochanek, "The Entrepreneurial Elite and Federalism in India" (mimeo, prepared for a conference on federalism at the Christian-Albrechts Universität, Kiel, Germany, June 29-July 1, 1975).

[9] These points are explored in detail for a regional industrial group in Howard L Erdman, *Political Attitudes of Indian Industry* (London: Athlone Press, 1971).

[10] Marxists viewed Gandhi as a petit bourgeois or utopian socialist whose preferences in the economic sphere were naive and fundamentally inconsequential. India's major industrialists concurred.

[11] The use of "duumvir" and a useful examination of Nehru-Patel relations will be found in Michael Brecher, *Nehru: A Political Biography* (London: Oxford University Press, 1959).

[12] G. D. Birla, *In the Shadow of the Mahatma* (Bombay: Orient Longman's, 1955), pp. xv, 48.

[13] For a discussion of the forum, see Howard L. Erdman, *The Swatantra Party and Indian Conservatism* (Cambridge: Cambridge University Press, 1967), pp. 65-71, 78-80. Kochaneck, *Business and Politics,* also provides good coverage.

[14] For specific applications see Erdman, *Political Attitudes;* and Howard L. Erdman, *Politics and Economic Development in India* (Delhi: D. K. Publishing House, 1973).

[15] See Erdman, *Political Attitudes,* pp. 27-30, for labor.

[16] Kochanek, *Business and Politics,* and Erdman, *Political Attitudes,* cover many of these regional variations.

[17] *Kochanek, Business and Politics,* Erdman, *Swatantra Party,* and Brecher, *Nehru,* provide general background on this point.

[18] A fuller account may be found in Erdman, *Politics and Economic Development.*

[19] Erdman, *Swatantra Party,* describes the most prominent of these activities, omitted here for want of space.

[20] Kochanek, *Business and Politics,* explores this and other matters pertaining to the personnel of and access to the central government.

[21] Supporters of the Swatantra party were inclined to argue that the government was slowly strangling the private-sector industrialists, a judgment that had greater force from the time of Nehru's death.

[22] See Erdman, *Political Attitudes,* pp. 38ff.

[23] Stanley A. Kochanek, *The Congress Party of India* (Princeton, N. J.: Princeton University Press, 1968), Postscript, discusses the postelection analysis by the Congress. His *Business and Politics* explores the same issue at a later juncture.

[24] Erdman, *Political Attitudes,* and Kochanek, *Business and Politics,* present discussions of this from a regional and a national perspective, respectively.

[25] During 1971-1972 when the author was carrying on research in Ahmedabad, many industrialists had already formed highly specialized cooperative banks for short-term capital.

[26] The MRTP Act did not exist *in vacuo.* Larger houses were at the same time urged to consider investment in economically backward areas and in certain "core sector" industries, where the full force of the MRTP Act would not be felt. Such policies were intended to force the major private-sector industrialists into areas where only they (or the national government)

could go. The response to such "invitations" was not overwhelming. See J. R. D. Tata, "Suggestions for Accelerating Industrial Growth" (memorandum submitted to the government of India, May 17, 1972.) Tata's memorandum will be discussed in more detail later in the chapter.

[27] Ibid. For a specific case see Erdman, *Politics and Economic Development,* pp. 112 ff.

[28] From an address quoted in Erdman, *Politics and Economic Development,* pp. 38-39.

[29] Based on the author's interviews in Ahmedabad, 1971-1972,

[30] Remarks were made in an address to Ahmedabad industrialists in 1972 by the then minister of industrial development, Moinul Huq Chaudhry, known widely in Gujarat as the minister of industrial decay. The author was present at the address, and some of the minister's remarks were not in the prepared text distributed prior to the meeting.

[31] The industrialists were not uniformly opposed to Mrs. Gandhi, but some of those present were known supporters of the Old Congress. According to local industrialists and journalists (based on interviews by the author) the target of the raid was Jaykrishna Harivallabhdas, who was not present when the raid occurred—according to some because he had been warned by authorities beforehand. Harivallabhdas had been a leading industrialist-politician in the city, had served as mayor, but had lost some luster as the 1960s proceeded. Remaining with the Old Congress, he was also serving as the chairman of the board of the Gujarat State Fertilizers Company (GSFC), an enormously successful "joint sector" company, to which position he had been appointed bythe government of Gujarat in the early 1960s. He resigned from this position to campaign for an Ahmedabad parliamentary seat in the 1971 elections, and during the campaign he and his followers made very strong attacks on Mrs. Gandhi. After his defeat at the hands of a Congress candidate, Harivallabhdas was reappointed to the chairmanship of the GSFC, which office had been kept open by the Old Congress in the state. This was widely cited as an example of collusion between the state government and the industrialists in the state and it contributed to the growing demand that the GSFC be taken over fully by the state government, which held 49 percent of the shares.

[32] It would appear that Bengal was the most troublesome, but industrialists seem to have found Kerala, also with a communist-influenced ministry, a reasonably attractive state in which to invest. Gujarat actively courted Bengal industrialists when the latter were under severe local pressure.

[33] At this juncture Mrs. Gandhi evidently felt quite secure in her position vis-a-vis organized labor, as she did vis-a-vis the industrialists. She could then be "pragmatic" in dealing with such groups, as suited her analysis of

desirable lines of development in the economic sphere. More recent (early 1976) evidence suggests that Mrs. Gandhi is fully prepared to consult with important groups, provided they do not represent a significant challenge to her position. Further attention will be given later in the chapter to the range of issues and patterns of activity since the emergency.

34 *Statesman Weekly* (henceforth *SW*), Aug. 9, 1975, p. 9.

35 *SW*, Sept, 6, 1975, p. 5.

36 *SW* contains many references to aspects of the attack from the beginning of July 1975 to the present. Representative statements will be found in: *SW*, July 5, 1975, pp. 1, 4, 9; July 12, 1975, pp. 1, 4; July 19, 1975, p. 4; Aug. 2, 1975, p. 13; Aug. 9, 1975, p. 13; Aug. 13, 1975, p. 1 (sugar traders warned that they will face stringent action "if the trade does not discipline itself"); Sept. 6, 1975, pp. 5,9; Sept. 13, 1975, pp. 1, 5, 7; Sept. 20, 1975, p. 1; Oct. 18, 1975, p. 6 (concerning black money, voluntary disclosures, and confiscation, with over 2,000 raids netting assets of 180 million rupees); Oct. 25, 1975, p. 10 (compulsory investment of 5 percent of illegally held wealth in special nonnegotiable but interest-bearing "social welfare" bonds). Along with urban land ceilings, this general issue has received extensive and sustained coverage.

37 Based on statements by recent visitors to India. Mrs. Gandhi has pledged recently to deal firmly and directly with cases of harassment where adequate information is provided (*SW*, Jan. 3, 1976, p. 3).

38 See, e.g., *SW*, July 12, 1975, p. 4; Aug. 9, 1975, p. 13; Sept. 6, 1975, p. 9; Sept. 20, 1975, p. 1.

39 *SW*, July 5, 1975, p. 1.

40 *SW*, Aug. 16, 1975, p. 3.

41 *SW*, July 12, 1975, p. 1; Aug. 16, 1975, p. 3; Oct. 25, 1975, p. 6.

42 *SW*, Aug. 9, 1975, pp. 1, 10, for the quotation. Cf. *SW*, July 5, 1975, p. 5, where the emphasis is clearly seen to be on a moratorium on nationization and other controls short of that.

43 *SW*, Sept. 20, 1975, p. 3. "Sons of the soil" means hiring state natives.

44 *SW*, Oct. 4, 1975, p. 14, from a statement by A. P. Sharma, minister of state for supply and industries.

45 *SW*, Sept. 6, 1975, p. 7, from an address by Mrs. Gandhi.

46 Gujarat industrialists in many cases invested in the Gujarat State Fertilizers Company not so much for short-run profits but for an "inside track" on downstream industrial licenses. In some important cases the hoped-for advantage did not materialize. Details are found in Erdman, *Politics and Economic Development.*

47 *SW*, July 5, 1975, p. 1.

48 *SW,* Sept. 20, 1975, p. 3.

49 *SW,* July 12, 1975, p. 9.

50 *SW,* Oct. 4, 1975, p. 10.

51 There are many formal and ad hoc tripartite boards (Government, labor, industry) and advisory bodies to discuss wages, working conditions, and other industrial matters. Industrialists generally argue that they are invited only to give the appearance of openness on the part of the administration, which is presumed to be partial to labor. Be that as it may, many decisions that are received unhappily by industry are well watered down at the implementation stage, often with enthusiastic support from state governments.

52 In view of the judgments by Baroda industrialists in the mid-1960s (Erdman, *Political Attitudes*), labor discipline is certainly the last thing that the government could enforce. It would require remarkable persistence and perhaps heavy-handedness to secure it, for which reason the 1974 railway strike and certain postemergency developments are examined so closely. With much *garibi hatao* rhetoric, certain wage increases already granted (and *not* matched by price increases), and a "routinization" of the emergency, I would expect far more prolabor legislation than has thus far—January 1976—been the case.

53 E.g., *SW,* Aug. 9, 1975, p. 1; Aug. 16, 1975, p. 10. Some statements suggest that it will take a while for fresh private-sector activity to emerge, but the implication of many remarks is that the industrialists are not coming up to the mark. See also note 30. A recent statement concerning the steel industry indicated that the private-sector firms might rise shortly to the level of the public-sector firms in terms of output. It should be noted here that major steel producers are under the umbrella of the Steel Authority of India Ltd. (SAIL), a government-sponsored holding company of sorts, whose managing director is now Wadud Khan, on deputation from Tata Iron and Steel. This kind of interpenetration is becoming increasingly common and provides much food for thought for those who worry about who is controlling/influencing whom.

54 *SW,* Oct, 18, 1975, p. 1.

55 *SW,* Sept, 13, 1975, p. 1.

56 "Accent on Production," *Economic and Political Weekly* (Bombay) 10 (July 5, 1975): 983-84; *SW,* Sept. 6, 1975, p. 1; Sept. 20, 1975, p. 1; Nov. 13, 1975, p. 13. See *SW,* Sept. 13, 1975, p. 1, for a statement that smaller industrialists had failed to do the job in areas reserved for them and that the larger houses could well move in by default.

57 *SW,* Sept, 13, 1975, p. 5.

58 *SW*, July 12, 1975, p. 1, reporting a statement by Mrs. Gandhi to leaders of India's major industrial organizations.

59 See note 50.

60 In the recent past, e.g., Gujarat industrialists supported no-strike labor leaders against those who would intensify the labor-managment struggle; in Bombay city industrialists supported some Shiv Sena labor organizers against Congress, Socialist, and Communist union leaders/organizers; and in Tamil Nadu (Madras) industrialists have tried to curry favor with the incumbent ministry and to deradicalize labor by supporting the DMK union effort.

61 *SW*, Sept, 6, 1975, p. 10; Sept. 13, 1975, p. 10; Sept. 20, 1975, p. 1.

62 *SW*, Aug. 9, 1975, p. 1, for price reductions in fertilizers; p. 5 for the wage settlement in the steel industry.

63 For exploitation of ambiguities, see Erdman, *Politics and Economic Development*, pp. 55 ff.

64 Kochanek, *Business and Politics*, and Erdman, *Political Attitudes*, both discuss business support for "presidential" and expert-oriented regimes. No doubt many state-based entrepreneurs would oppose a significant move toward centralization of power, insofar as it would deprive them of easy access to sympathetic governments.

6

Communism Further Divided
Bhabani Sen Gupta

In declaring the national internal emergency on June 26, 1975, Prime Minister Indira Gandhi pitted the ruling Congress party against all of the other political groups in India, with the sole exception of the Communist Party of India (CPI). In the split spectrum of the Indian Communist movement, the two other Communist groups—the Communist Party of India (Marxist), or CPM, and the Communist Party of India (Marxist-Leninist) (CPML)—are, on the other hand, among the authoritarian regime's mortal enemies.[1] The gravest political crisis in the world's largest democracy was in no way the creation of the Indian Communists. It resulted from a grim polarization in the national bourgeoisie, a confrontation between Mrs. Gandhi's government and party on the one hand and the major opposition parties of northern India on the other. Among these opposition parties are rightist groups like the Jan Sangh and the Old Congress as well as the non-Communist leftist groups and the populist elements represented by Jayaprakash Narayan. Opposing each other, the two main Communist parties (the CPI and the CPM) have taken on opposing bourgeois bedfellows, Congress and the anti-Congress conglomerate.

153

It is characteristic of inter-Communist conflict situations that Communists find it easier to cooperate with the bourgeoisie than with rivals professing the same basic doctrine. The present polarization has widened the divide between the CPI and the CPM. It has also pitted the CPM and the CPML against the Congress-CPI combination.

The various factions of the CPML, banned in September 1975, are already functioning underground. It is entirely possible that the CPM may have to follow, assuming it demonstrates against the increasingly authoritarian regime.

Looming on the horizon, then, is this question: Will the two major Communist groups be able to function as parliamentary parties under a prolonged state of emergency? For twenty-five years the mainstream of Indian communism has flowed along parliamentary channels. Parliamentary politics, however, have always been supplemented by mass mobilization and agitation; the combination of the two has enabled the Communists to gain whatever support base they have in a number of states. Tension between these two political roles has been perennial. Indeed, the inner-party differences in the united CPI even in the 1950s centered basically on the style and content of revolutionary parliamentarianism: whether and to what extent and on which specific issues the Communists should support and collaborate with the bourgeois government, and the relative priorities that should be given to parliamentary and extraparliamentary activity. As the CPM weekly expressed it:

> It was precisely on these questions that differences arose in the united Communist Party—the character of the present Indian State, the classes in power, the leadership of these classes, the class front that has to be forged to complete the democratic revolution, the leadership of this front, the tactics that have to be evolved to forge the front and so on.[2]

There were other factors behind the division of the CPI in 1964, including conflict among its leading personalities, factional infighting, and the split between Moscow and Peking with its impact on India's relations with the Soviet Union and China. However, the present widening of the breach between the Communist parties arises from that old question—who are the enemies, thus who are viable allies?—now accented by the perception that bourgeois political forces have suddenly become more dynamic, and hence, vastly more dangerous.

THE FRUITS OF REVOLUTIONARY
PARLIAMENTARIANISM

Indian independence was won by the national bourgeoisie rather than by the Communists. During the 1940s, the CPI was at war with the Congress and with the regime set up in Delhi under Jawaharlal Nehru's leadership; it lost all positions of strategic importance within the political system. To break out from its isolation, the CPI adopted the parliamentary line in 1952, and in five years was able to capture the government in Kerala in a free and fair election. Thirty years of parliamentary politics have determined the currently prevailing framework of the Indian Communist movement.

There have been two splits. The CPI divided in 1964, producing the CPM. Out of an extremist fringe of the CPM emerged the CPML in 1969. This Naxalite group—named for Naxalbari, the area in West Bengal in which it sought to seize control in 1967—shunned parliamentary politics and espoused the cause of protracted peasant guerrilla warfare, on the Chinese model. This, then, is the splintered framework of the movement that, as noted, is both discordant and competitive. Another aspect of that framework is the predominantly regional character of Indian communism. Communism thrives in two extreme corners of India—in the southwestern coastal state of Kerala, and the eastern state of West Bengal. Its once strong base in Andhra Pradesh has disintegrated largely because of intraparty and, then, interparty conflicts, and also because the urban-oriented parent CPI rapidly lost ground as soon as the Congress party was able to identify itself with the linguistic subnationalism of the Telugu-speaking elite.

State Support Bases

In the elections between 1967 and 1972—a period which displayed contemporary political forces at a fluid stage—the combined Communist electoral vote remained at 25 percent or more in Kerala and West Bengal. In no other state did it hold above 10 percent, though it was still at 15 percent in Andhra Pradesh in 1967, and peaked in Bihar at 11 percent in 1969. The combined Communist vote remained over 5 percent in those four states, plus Punjab, Assam, and Orissa, across the 1967 to 1972 state elections. In the rest of the country, the total Communist vote has been negligible. It is true that the actual political effectiveness of the Communist movement, even of the two parties, cannot be determined by electoral showing. Nevertheless, the movement remains strong only in two states; it shows a modest promise in three or four others; while in the rest of India it is almost nonexistent. Clearly, Indian communism is regionally distributed, strong in the east and the extreme south, feeble in the sprawling central Indian plains of Rajasthan and Madhya Pradesh.[3]

The loss of the Communist support base in Andhra Pradesh appears to have been somewhat compensated by the CPI's recent success in Bihar, in which state the party now claims to have one-third of its total membership of 550,000. The CPI, which after the 1964 split was able to retain its Bihar apparatus more or less intact, has made itself one of the influential opposition parties in the Bihar legislature, with around 10 percent of the seats: 24 in 1967, 25 in 1969, and 35 in 1972. The Marxists have not formed a base in Bihar.

Even in Bihar the CPI support base is unstable. It has failed to build its independent constituencies, and therefore must rely for major electoral success on a compact with the Congress party.[4]

Problems of a Multicultural Society

The regional character of the Communist support base creates organizational as well as social-psychological problems for both major Communist groups (as for other national parties in India). The CPM spelled these out in a document issued in 1968. It was "curious to note" that while the central committee of the CPM was "compelled to be content with running an English weekly as its organ, in a language not known to 99 percent of the people in any state, seven state committees run their language weeklies and three among them run their daily organs." The language barrier "prevents the central leadership from coming into direct and close contact with the cadres and their day-to-day work in different states." "Localism" was found to be rampant. "A sort of state exclusiveness and the absence of an all-India consciousness is gaining currency in the party leadership, let alone the bulk of our party members."[5]

Regionalism, however, has helped both parties only temporarily to harness the forces of linguistic nationalism in the language-oriented states. For when the demands for linguistic boundaries, or for cultural autonomy, have been mobilized, either the central government has granted the demands or non-Communist parties have preempted the issue. In either case the Communist support base built upon this appeal has collapsed. The Communist vote for the state legislature in Andhra was 22 percent of the total in 1952 and 29 percent in 1957 at the peak of linguistic mobilization; it fell away to 19 and 15 percent in the succeeding state elections. The CPI received 18 percent of the Punjab vote by championing Sikh demands for a separate state in 1957; the Akali and Congress parties stole the issue, and the Communist vote dropped to 10 and then 8 percent. In Tamil Nadu the Communist vote, which had run between 7 and 8 percent, dropped to 6 and then 4 percent upon the victory of the DMK in 1967.[6]

A Communist support base can be stable and strong only if it is built upon exploited elements of the working class and peasantry rather than upon culturally oriented middle classes.

Economic Mobilization

The two main Communist parties cultivate such economic bases through their trade unions and the *kisan sabhas* (peasant organizations). The CPI's trade union arm is the All-India Trade Union Congress (AITUC); the CPM's, the Center of Indian Trade Unions (CITU). The AITUC, with over 1 million members, contests with the Congress's INTUC (Indian National Trade Union Congress) the claim to be the largest trade union organization in India. It is strong in Maharashtra, especially in the Bombay-Ahmedabad-Poona industrial belt, in Kanpur (Uttar Pradesh), and to a lesser degree, in West Bengal, Punjab, and Tamil Nadu. CITU's strong base is in the Calcutta industrial zone, Tamil Nadu, and Delhi-Haryana-Punjab. Each Communist party's leadership is drawn partly from the trade unions. The CPI's chairman is S. A. Dange, a veteran trade union leader; in the Marxist party, the majority of the politbureau members are trade unionists. The AITUC at times is inclined to act independently of the CPI leadership, while the CPM seems to have a tighter control of CITU.

Both major Communist parties have their *kisan sabhas*, which have been increasingly active since 1968. The Marxists, as Robert L. Hardgrave accurately points out, have "retained their base of support among the poor and the landless in Kerala."7 Their agrarian base in West Bengal we will examine below. The CPI's peasant organizations have been active in Bihar and Punjab. A certain amount of peasant mobilization has occurred also in Orissa, Andhra Pradesh, Tamil Nadu, and Maharashtra. However, the peasant organizations of both Communist groups are still weak; this is true even of the CPM in Kerala. Cadres effective at agrarian organization are hard to come by. The death of Harekrishna Konar in 1970 deprived the Marxists of the one leader who could give a new radical direction to the party's peasant mobilization.8

In their thirty years of parliamentary politics, the two Communist groups in India have crossed the threshold of power at the state level, and have made their mark as oppositionists at the national center. However, it is only since the late 1960s that they have addressed their attention systematically to the rural poor, the largest Indian constituency still to be politically mobilized.

Maoist Challenge

The Marxist shift in strategy away from a parliamentary emphasis to the mobilization of the agrarian have-nots was spurred by the Naxalite movement, which sprouted in a small area of West Bengal in 1967. A rebellion of poor peasants in three villages in this remote northern area was spearheaded by CPM radicals who objected to their party's contesting the 1967 state elections. They demanded recognition of the tiny area of rebel control from the new united front government the CPM had succeeded in establishing. But the police broke the rebel hold, with bloodshed on both sides, and the CPM expelled its radical champions. One of these was Charu Mazumdar. With encouragement from Peking, he became the leader of Indian Maoism. When uprisings of the landless broke out in other isolated pockets of West Bengal, Andhra Pradesh, Orissa, Uttar Pradesh, and Bihar, he drew some of the instigators into an uneasy coalition which in 1969 designated itself as the Communist Party of India (Marxist-Leninist), or CPML. All the Communists entering the new party were formerly of the CPM.9

Police action, some of it massive and ruthless, put down all these uprisings. The mountains and jungles of Srikakulam provided the most determined local guerrillas (exploited tribesmen), but even that base collapsed. Mazumdar moved his guerrilla action into the urban sprawl of Calcutta. A bloody, protracted struggle ensued between the CPML, CPM, and police. After Mazumdar's death in 1972, the CPML broke into several splinters. Most of these have been hibernating, but they represent some potential for rural violent protest, even after being outlawed in 1975 under the emergency.

Failing in its own cause, the Naxalite movement nevertheless had powerful indirect effects upon the government of India and Indian communism. In 1969 the Indian Home Ministry issued a survey of agrarian unrest which concluded that without rapid land reforms the Green Revolution would turn red.[10] Several state governments, hitherto indifferent to the Congress pronouncements about redistribution of large holdings, lowered their ceilings on agricultural land holdings. The preconception that the landless of India were too docile or divided to fight for the rights to which virtually all politicians gave lip-service was shattered.

On the CPM itself the impact of the Naxalite movement was even more decisive. The Marxist party had, after all, split away from the CPI in 1964, committed to a more radical line. After it lost governing power, in both Kerala and West Bengal in 1969, the party decided upon a more revolutionary line, accepting some of the premises of the CPML. For the first time, the rural poor received priority over the urban industrial workers.[11]

Power and the Rural Poor

The revolutionary pull of the Maoist threat encountered an almost directly contrary pull, that of the opportunity to govern, in the two states where communism is strong, Kerala and West Bengal.

In Kerala, the undivided CPI ruled for two years following the 1957 election until it was dispossessed by president's rule from Delhi (largely at Indira Gandhi's initiative). Both Communist parties entered a ruling coalition in Kerala again after the 1967 election. This was supplanted in 1970 by a CPI coalition without the Marxists. With various additions of support—first from the Congress, more recently from the largely Christian

Kerala Congress—this CPI-led government has become the most stable in Kerala's history. The CPM, meanwhile, provides the principal opposition to that government.[12]

The West Bengal CPM, whose coalition had lost control of government due to the defections of allies in 1969, responded seriously to the Naxalite challenge. When it gained a second chance by the formation of a new united front government in 1969, it used its power over land revenue and police to conduct officially inspired and protected seizures of rural power in large contiguous areas of the state. *Jotedars*—landlords wielding moneylending and grain dealing powers—were dispossessed of government land they were alleged to have taken illegally, forced to limit their crop shares to the legal maximum, and stripped of their de facto police power in the villages. The Marxists were thus able to build, in two years, a base of controlled rural militancy. The electoral results of this strategy—of which Harekrishna Konar was the principal designer—were remarkable.[13] Amidst the Indira Gandhi sweep of 1971, the CMP won 111 seats in the West Bengal legislature, 123 counting its allies, of the total of 277. But the CPI had fielded an opposing left front. It won only 25 seats, but it got the support of the Congress, with 105 seats. An anti-CPM coalition was hastily put together, so unstable that it lasted but a month, and was succeeded by rule from Delhi. The CPM was thus kept from governing upon its new power base of the agrarian underclass.

The experiences in Kerala and West Bengal hold profound lessons as to the impact of the Communist mobilization of the rural poor upon the larger role of Communist parties in the political system. Where landlord power has been oppressive, where it has been backed by local government authority, great political strength—perhaps enough to win elections in an agrarian society—can be released by upsetting it. Such an upset is possible if there is determined effort from below (e.g., through the work of CPM cadres) and above (through control of the police and land revenue apparatus). But such a thrust galvanizes the resistance of the Congress, not only locally but nationally. It frightens the middle classes by the violence it manifests. Its success would seem, therefore, to demand Communist unity.

There's the rub. The CPI in West Bengal found the pursuit of such a policy would make it much the junior partner of the CPM. On the other hand, the Congress of Indira Gandhi, hard pressed after its own party split in 1969, and locked in an all-out struggle with the CPM in West Bengal, would bid high for cooperation. Thus, the very success of the agrarian class conflict strategy polarized the opposition of the two Communist parties: the CPI as supporter-critic of the prime minister's party, the CPM as spearhead of its class opposition.

IDEOLOGICAL BEARINGS

Whether these opposing tactical lines of the two Communist groups give rise to their diverging ideological perceptions of class dynamics in Indian society, or (as Marxists are convinced) vice versa, differences in "scientific" analysis of "objective" class forces powerfully reinforce and entrench tactical differences. And for the Communists, the relevant perceptions of class dynamics are international as well as Indian. Each party analyzes the current emergency and plans its response from its own ideological perspective.

All of the three groups see India overtaken by the crisis of capitalist development. This crisis is reflected in the increasing gap between the few rich and the vast multitude of the poor, in economic stagnation, rising prises, and the immutable power of the hoarders and profiteers, of big business and the big landlords. The current political crisis is seen in itself as a crisis of capitalist development.

Moving from the CPI to the CPM to the CPML, each party defines the class base of the present regime in India in successively narrower terms. The CPI image of the Indian state is, then, the most accepting, the Maoist view the most condemning.

CPI

The CPI perceives the Indian state as the "organ of class rule of the national bourgeoisie as a whole."[14] The party believes that capitalist growth in India has strengthened the economic base of nationalism; India has undergone *independent* capitalist development, and is not a mere creature of the world capitalist system. The national bourgeoisie who control state power comprise capitalist monopolists and big landlords, but also smaller, middle-class elements. Consequently, supporters may be found within these strata for both reactionary and progressive policies.

Independent capitalist development and the diminished political power of big business and big landlords have been possible because of India's close ties with the Soviet Union and the Socialist bloc. India belongs to the peace-loving, anti-imperialist national liberation zone.

The CPI strategic objective is a "State of National Democracy." This political concept was worked out between the Communist Party of the Soviet Union (CPSU) and the CPI during the world Communist conference in Moscow in 1960. In a "national-democratic" state, political power is wielded by a coalition of progressive democratic forces including the Communists, who, however, are not in the driver's seat. Such a state has very close political, economic, and strategic relations with the Socialist bloc.

The fit with the CPI's tactical line is obvious. Communists must cooperate with all democratic and progressive forces including the center and the left of the Congress party, which represents the national bourgeoisie. A national-democratic front of all progressive forces, built from above, is the best instrument with which to strive for a national-democratic state. Among the potential partners in such a front are the broad majority of the capitalists (except the monopolies) and the entire land-owning peasantry as well as the rural poor. The CPI hopes to enlarge its parliamentary strength through electoral pacts with the ruling party. It is willing to be junior partner to the Congress party on the basis of a common program of social change. But it will not submerge its identity in the ruling party, nor its support base.

CPM

In the CPM view, political power in India is controlled by big business and, particularly at the state level, by the big landlords.[15] The capitalist economy tends to strengthen the position of the monopolies; even the state sector sustains the capitalist industry and feudalist hold on the peasantry. The Indian monopolists have strong linkages with the international monopolies, and the government is neither willing nor in a position to curb the interests of either. At the state level, the ministers and the bureaucracy openly defend the landlords' interests. This is why the publicized reforms remain only on paper insofar as they are intended to curb the powers and privileges of the big and middle-level landlords. In the Marxist party's perception, the Indian revolution is now essentially in an agrarian stage; it must be directed against the ramparts of feudal power and privilege. The feudal chieftains are, however, in league with big business and the national bureaucracy and can summon the state's coercive power to the defense of their interests.

The CPM strategic objective is a "State of People's Democracy." It is a coalition of leftist and democratic forces in which the proletariat, in alliance with the peasantry, must hold the dominant position. This coalition or united front must be built from below—in the crucible of struggle against the class enemy—not from above. The agrarian revolution in India can begin and gather momentum only at the state level, and then advance toward the center of national power. In those states where the Marxist party is strong, the task is to forge the united front through militant, though not necessarily violent, struggles for the rights of the urban and rural poor, the middle classes, and the intelligentsia. Power captured by the CPM at the state level has to be used as an instrument of mass mobilization on the one hand and class struggle with the center on the other. There can be no cooperation with the party of the bourgeoisie, whose progressive rhetoric is a mere camouflage to deceive the masses and scatter the forces of radical change. At the same time, every sign of disarray or split in the ranks of the bourgeoisie is welcome and needs to be exploited to the advantage of the agrarian revolution.

To wage this revolution in India, it is necessary to isolate the big landlords from the middle-range and small landholders, and to establish dynamic linkages between the struggles of the urban and rural poor. The Indian agrarian revolution cannot copy the Chinese because the two countries and the two situations are entirely different. There is no objective possibility in India for protracted guerrilla warfare, at least at the present time, although the peasants must learn how to defend their interests and gains, if necessary, with violence.

CPML

According to the CPML, the Indian ruling elite represent the interests of the big landlords and of the comprador-bureaucratic capitalism that has grown in the country since independence. The government is a hostage to international imperialism, which includes "social imperialism"—i.e., the Chinese Communist conceptualization of the class character of the Soviet Union. The basic task of the Indian revolution is to overthrow the rule of feudalism and comprador-bureaucratic capitalism. According to the Maoist party, the two basic contradictions in India are, first, the one between imperialism and the people, and, second, the contradiction between feudalism and the broad masses. The Indian revolution, then, is essentially antifeudal, just as the Chinese revolution was in the 1940s. To crush the feudal fortresses of power, the peasants have to take to arms and to protracted people's war, build rural bases in the Maoist style, and advance from these bases toward the urban centers of power. The CPML is ambivalent on the question of united front and mass struggles. It rejects parliamentary politics. Legislative pursuits can only denature the revolutionaries, co-opting them into the bourgeois political system.[16]

Relation of Ideology to Tactics

Taking a closer look at the ideological positions of the two major Communist parties, we see a good deal of coincidence with the actual mass bases they have been able to establish in the different parts of India. The Marxists are within reach of power in two states, weak elsewhere. Their line is to advance from state power to national. Since their chance to gain power in these states is through encouraging class conflict in the countryside and mobilizing the rural poor, they are bound to collide with the Congress, whose support depends on delivery of the votes of the rural poor through the landed Congress stalwarts in village, taluk, and district. Struggle with the Congress creates opportunities for alliances with non-Congress parties, both left and right. Thus, limited cooperation was possible with the populist cause of Jayaprakash Narayan, even where it drew also upon the Jan Sangh.

The CPI, lacking enough following to win a statewide election anywhere, but having tiny followings in many places and a few prominent legislators, is drawn to cooperating with progressive elements of the Congress as its avenue to power. Its trade union strength is a political resource in this game. Its strategy is not revolution, but incremental change. The five-year-old Kerala government is its model, and that government, headed by a CPI chief minister but deriving many more votes from the Congress, has in fact implemented many of the programs first enunciated by the CPM-led united front and now included in Indira Gandhi's economic program.

Both parties have bent their strategic lines to suit the exigencies of India's diverse political mosaic. The CPI during 1967-72 supported non-Congress coalitions in Bihar, Uttar Pradesh, and Punjab, and has even shared power with one or more of them. Both Communist groups have been inconsistent in their relations with the DMK regime in Tamil Nadu, offering cooperation and opposition at different points of time. In 1974 the CPI supported the DMK regime in Tamil Nadu, but opposed the DMK party in the election in Pondicherry. In 1976 the CPI became highly critical of the DMK government in Madras and welcomed its dismissal by the central government. The Marxists opposed the DMK bitterly in 1972-75 by organizing industrial protests in several cities, but took a benign view of the DMK regime under the present emergency.

EXTERNAL ORIENTATIONS

CPI

In relating the Indian situation to the world situations, as Communist analysis requires, the CPI finds itself in the more comfortable and stable position of the two parties. The CPI is the leading pro-Soviet Communist party in contemporary Asia. Its perceptions of the international political realities are identical to Soviet perceptions. For its part, the official Soviet view of the Indian situation approximates that of the CPI. The question of whether the Indian bourgeois government or the CPI is more important to the U.S.S.R., though often asked, is (with an exception we will note below) hypothetical. Those Indian Communists who saw a contradiction between the Indian revolution and the relations between New Delhi and Moscow left the CPI in 1964 to form the Marxist party.

The CPI's analysis of the Indian political situation is determined principally by the fact of India's close relations with the Soviet bloc. Not only has India's foreign policy become sharply anti-imperialist as a result of the Soviet connection, according to this view, but Indo-Soviet collaboration has left its mark on the domestic political front also. Such antimonopoly and democratic measures as the nationalization of the Indian banking system, the takeover of the foreign-owned oil refineries, and the changing pattern of exports and imports might not have been possible without Soviet friendship. The Soviet connection has, in the CPI perception, severed India's defense linkages with the capitalist world. By enabling India to proceed firmly along the path of independent economic development, the Soviet connection has, in summary, created a favorable condition for CPI-Congress collaboration.[17]

These CPI arguments, which mirror Soviet articulations on India and the third world, have not been formulated in isolation. There are regular annual consultations between the CPI and the CPSU. Since 1971, the CPSU has been maintaining certain organizational contacts with the Congress party also, a policy that presumably facilitates CPI-Congress collaboration. When Leonid Brezhnev visited New Delhi in November 1973, he had separate meetings with the Congress party president and leaders of the CPI. When the Soviet defense minister, Marshal Grechko, visited New Delhi in March 1975, CPI and Congress leaders were invited to an official dinner hosted by him. The Indian delegation to the World Peace Congress in 1973 included a large number of Congress party officers.

If there is one question regarding the CPI's current role which the Soviet's and the CPI's perceptions may diverge, that question concerns the party's bid for a share of political power. At the Tenth Congress of the CPI at Vijaywada in February 1975, the leader of the fraternal delegation from the CPSU, Rashidov, described the Indian party as "an active, influential force in Indian politics." The CPSU's fraternal message stressed the CPI's role in the "patriotic anti-imperialist struggle for consolidating the country's political and economic independence, for its social and economic progress."[18] The role sketched in Rashidov's speech was more modest than that in the fraternal message. It seems reasonable to speculate that Moscow does not want the CPI to divert the Indian government from its friendly collaboration with the U.S.S.R.

If this interpretation is correct, the Soviet expectation seemed to be somewhat at variance with the CPI's self-perception during its Tenth Congress. The leaders seemed to entertain rather high expectations of the party's sharing political power with the Congress party in several states (and, less probably, nationally) after the 1976 elections.[19] (Postponement of the elections now makes the issue academic.)

For different reasons, neither the CPSU nor the CPI wants a return to the political situation of the late 1960s, when the CPI and CPM worked together in two state coalitions. This kind of a situation polarizes Indian politics too fast, tends to create agrarian unrest, and leads to a confrontation between the Congress and the Communists. It creates a situation not particularly favorable for Moscow's Indian diplomacy.

The Soviets have not excommunicated the CPM as an ideological rebel. The Soviet media refer to the CPM (though this is rarely done at all) as the "parallel Communist party"; they are critical when the party shows signs of success or when it is severely repressed by the authorities.[20] At times the Soviets seem to have intervened to lower the scale of interparty conflict between the two major Indian Communist groups.

CPM

The CPM has organizational links neither with Moscow nor with Peking. It is South Asia's only independent Communist party. It criticizes policies and conduct of both the Soviet Union and China, and it wants India to have friendly relations with both. The CPM's ambivalence stems from the fact that, while it supports close Indo-Soviet relations, it is irked by the profuse praises showered by the Soviet leaders on its mortal enemy, the government of Indira Gandhi. After Brezhnev's visit to India in 1973, a CPM party organ published this comment by its editor:

> It would . . . be an illusion to think that the economic problems facing the nation can be solved only by strengthening relations with the Soviet Union. . . . While we welcome every step that is taken to strengthen the relations of friendship and cooperation between the two countries, we deplore that the Soviet leaders go on praising the bourgeois-landlord Government in our country as progressive *in every respect*, totally ignoring the basic class character of the regime. How could Brezhnev himself and all the other leaders of the Soviet Union have made such pronouncements . . . ?[21]

THE EMERGENCY: PERCEPTIONS, POLICIES, PROBLEMS, AND PROSPECTS

Guided by its strategic objectives and tactical line, each Indian Communist party is now attempting to formulate its posture with reference to the emergency declared by Indira Gandhi in June 1975. The crucial question is whether there will be scope for parliamentary communism if the Indian democracy is repressed as a result of the current train of political developments. For purposes of this discussion, we assume that constraints on free speech, political dissent, opposition government, and collective bargaining will continue for a matter of years.[22]

Orientations

CPI. The CPI, which stood firmly and closely with the Congress party and its government during the political confrontation of 1974-75, formulated its perception of the emergency in a long statement issued by its Central Executive Committee on July 2, 1975. The CPI saw a gigantic ramified conspiracy being organized against the legally established, progressive government of Indira Gandhi by the "different leaders" of the "right, reactionary" parties helped by "foreign imperialist agencies." The conspirators "were using all the rights and liberties of the parliamentary democratic setup in order to destroy the freedom of our country." In June 1975 these forces were poised for a decisive attack, for a final push for power.[23] Imperialism is part of the conspiracy. Balked elsewhere, "U.S. imperialism has stepped up its neocolonialist attacks in the South Asian region. India is the main target of this attack today in this region."[24]

The CPI therefore saw as "necessary and justified" the "swift and stern measures taken by the Prime Minister and the Government of India against the right reactionary and counterrevolutionary forces."

The CPI approved the economic policies and measures set out by Indira Gandhi against "the neocolonialists, monopolists, landlords, hoarders and speculators." Nevertheless, the party showed a keen concern that the extra powers obtained by the bureaucracy and police might be misused:

Emergency powers are taken advantage of by the monopolists and other anti-social exploiters as well as the bureaucrats to strengthen their grip on the economic life and administration of the country. This must not be allowed to happen.

. . . Under no circumstances must the emergency be used against the legitimate democratic agitations and movements of the working people. This warning is particularly necessary in view of the fact that in the past such powers have been grossly misused.[25]

In its more theoretical analysis the CPI saw the "differentiation and conflict inside the Indian bourgeoisie" as having reached "a new stage" in which "those representing the anti-imperialist democratic sections . . . have been forced into using the repressive organs of state power against those representing the pro-imperialist, most reactionary, pro-monopoly, pro-landlord, anti-communist sections." This intrabourgeoisie polarization offered "the most favorable possibilities for strengthening the united front of the working people, peasantry and other toiling sections with the anti-imperialist democratic national bourgeoisie."

From this perspective, the central executive charted the CPI's course of political action:

1. Continuing pressure on the government to direct its efforts to further weaken the reactionary forces and their social base of power. This called for a "nationwide mass mobilization campaign" jointly, "wherever possible," with the Congress party.
2. Effective implementation of the prime minister's twenty-point economic program, through active participation of the democratic forces and the people.
3. Implementation of the CPI's political and economic policies during the emergency. These included nationalization of "some" industries, "stern action" against the CIA and its agents, granting the vote to eighteen-year-olds, and "democratizing" the education system.[26]

CPM. The CPM took an entirely different view of the emergency. Taking advantage of the challenge of the rightist parties and the populist forces, the prime minister, according to this view, had struck at the root of Indian democracy and was moving toward the establishment of a one-party state. Her economic program was a deceptive screen behind which her government had set out to deny the Indian people the political rights they had won after many decades of struggle with British imperialism. The CPM saw three "broad segments" working in the country:

> One, the ruling party and the right communists; two, the parties of the right opposition; three, the parties of the left and democratic opposition. . . . The recognition of this fact should imply the recognition of another fact also: that the masses are divided between all these three segments.

> The task of the Left and democratic forces, especially of the Communist Party, is to draw all the masses, whomsoever they follow now, into a common front and establish the leadership of the working class in such a front.[27]

For the CPI, the struggle is still basically "anti-imperialist," since the counterrevolutionary forces are acting with the help of imperialism and imperialist interests. The ruling Congress party and the CPI constitute the antiimperialist forces; these are receiving valuable and welcome support from the Soviet Union. The Marxists' struggle, on the other hand, is not against imperialism, but against an Indian regime that is about to destroy democracy and deprive the people of their civil liberties and democratic rights. This done, the democratic struggle in India would fall back by decades. In fighting for civil liberties and democratic rights the Marxists are prepared to work with all political forces that value these rights, including the "reactionary" parties and groups.[28]

The CPM has not so far issued a comprehensive analysis of the emergency, nor a plan of action. (It is possible that censorship has not permitted the printing of all that the party's leaders might have wished to say.) Isolated in Kerala and hibernating in West Bengal, the Marxist leadership is probably anticipating governmental suppression. Reports say that its cadres have gone underground, although an "overground" apparatus is being maintained. The party's Tenth Congress is scheduled for 1976, but it is not certain that the congress will be held. The leadership has not convened any meeting of the politburo nor even of the central committee. Innerparty consultations have been confined to informal channels. Evidently the leaders have no wish to gather together to risk wholesale arrests.

Many cadremen are reported to feel that in view of the qualitative change in the political situation in India, the CPM should have a new tactical line. The leadership's predicament stems from the risks of continued hibernation as well as those of going into active opposition. The former may deactivate many of the cadres. The latter course may expose the cadremen to arrest. Underground activity has the risk of radicalizing the cadre and thus widening the gap between the rank and file and the leadership. One report says that the party has thus far not lost much of its cadre strength nor its trade union and peasant following. Passivity may lead to big losses.[29]

Events

CPI. Indira Gandhi has shown no indication that she wishes to move in the direction called for by the CPI. She has announced that there will be no further nationalization. The emergency powers are being used as much against Jan Sangh, Old Congress, and other politicians to her right as against Socialist, CPM, and other left-wing oppositionists. Censorship has been institutionalized; it has been extended to books and pamphlets. In a reshuffle of her Council of Ministers, Mrs. Gandhi has got rid of several "progressives"as well as at least one leading member of the right wing in her party.[30] In short, she seems to have decided to use her authoritarian powers to steer a middle course, not to take a leftward lurch.

This seems to have created a certain amount of friction between her government and the CPI. The CPI leadership was stunned by a presidential ordinance issued in September 1975 slashing the "minimum guaranteed bonus" of industrial workers from 8.33 percent to 4 percent for the year 1974-75 and stopping the bonus entirely thereafter.[31] It was considered a concession to the "monopolies" at the expense of labor.[32] A three-man CPI delegation saw the prime minister and pleaded for the suspension of the measure.[33] When the government refused, the AITUC called a one-day strike of workers all over India. To what extent the call was heeded was not reported in the Indian press, but a *Manchester Guardian* dispatch said that 30,000 to 40,000 workers were arrested on January 6.[34] The CPI chairman, S. A. Dange, declared that the party could not support "certain reactionary trends that had also occured after the declaration of the emergency."

The *Guardian* reported that the "major development" in the Indian Parliament in January was "the growing uneasiness in the current alliance between the Congress party and its loyal supporter, the CPI."[35] The CPI also reportedly opposed the idea of a presidential form of government in India, which was said to be gaining support in the Congress party leadership.[36] At the same time, the CPI supported the dismissal of the DMK government in Tamil Nadu on January 31. But it did not support the proposal to postpone the nationwide elections by one year, and opposed the move to institutionalize press and publications censorship.[37]

Thus, a relationship mixing support with opposition seems to be emerging between the Congress and the CPI. This may not bother the ruling party, because it does not need CPI support to get measures adopted by Parliament, nor to rally people to hold counterdemonstrations, as in Bihar in 1974. With the elections postponed and most opponents cowed, the Congress party needs the CPI less under the emergency than before, a consideration that seems to have been grasped by the chief ministers and the party bosses of the states where the CPI has any sizable support base.

Meanwhile, the CPI plans to further the implementation of the prime minister's redistributive economic reforms by "mobilization of the Masses" for "suitable forms of struggle."[38] Party Secretary Rajeshwara Rao has been asking cadremen to change their lifestyles and to concentrate on grassroot-level mobilization in collaboration with the Congress party, wherever possible.[39] The CPI has been demanding significant participation in the committees that are being set up in the states and districts to watch over implementation.

From the Congress side, how much to cooperate with the CPI has been a divisive issue since long before the emergency was declared. The Nehru Forum vs. Socialist Form rift in the Congress parliamentary party echoed that controversy until both forums were suspended in 1973. At the Narora Congress camp consultation late in 1974, opinion on cooperation with the CPI was divided among the leaders. Jagjivan Ram led the opposition, with support, one report said, from Y. B. Chaven and Uma Shankar Dikshit. Support of collaboration with the CPI came from the Orissa chief minister, Mrs. Nandini Satpati, as well as the Congress party's president, S. D. Sharma.[40] At the Congress cadres' camp at Bordi in January 1975, Ram again opposed cooperation, which was supported by the party president, D. K. Barooah.[41]

Congress-CPI relations vary from state to state; except in Kerala they also fluctuate over time. In those states where the Congress party is faction-ridden and the chief ministers are politically weak, the CPI tends to be needed. Among these vulnerable states are Bihar, Uttar Pradesh, Orissa, and West Bengal. Taking advantage of the bitter factional squabbles in the West Bengal Youth Congress, the CPI was said to have "consolidated its hold on the Congress youth front" in 1974. The CPI has not been equally friendly toward all Congress governments in the states. It fought a mild war of attrition with the West Bengal government in 1973-74, withdrawing from the People's Democratic Alliance, the joint organization set up in 1971 to oversee the performance of the state government. The CPI opposed Congress "misrule" in Gujarat in 1974, and "declared war" on the Congress government in Andhra Pradesh. In 1975 it launched an anti-Congress movement in Uttar Pradesh because the chief minister, Bahuguna, whose installation the Communists had supported in 1973, refused to have a working agreement with the party.[42]

The emergency has put a clamp on factional in-fighting, at least for the time being. Chief ministers are less dependent than before on the shifting support of factions represented in the state legislatures. They need the CPI less and are not anxious to share with the CPI the political gains to be derived from implementation of the prime minister's economic program. They have now adopted Mrs. Gandhi's own public posture on relations with the CPI: the Congress party does not need the CPI's help, but will not spurn offers of cooperation from such like-minded parties. The state governments have sought to give the CPI only a minor role in the implementation committees. In West Bengal, for instance, the CPI has been given only four seats in the fifty-one-member implementation committee set up at the state level.[43] The Andhra Pradesh government has set up a committee to implement land reforms entirely with its own officials.[44] After the factional differences in the West Bengal Youth Congress were resolved in December 1975, the new president of the organization terminated its linkages with the CPI. "The Congress and the CPI are two different organizations," he declared. "Our ideologies and programs are different. We do not recognize any other party's supremacy over us. The question of a joint movement [with the CPI for implementation of the economic program] does not arise."[45] "The CPI is not guided by Congress ideology," retorted a CPI leader; "its political existence does not depend upon the mercy of the Congress party." He proceeded to add, "Hitler once wanted to give leadership to his country. But he was rejected by the people and got ruined."[46]

The CPI, however, claims in *New Age* that the party has been campaigning to enlist popular pressure to carry through economic reforms.[47] For instance, a September 1975 report on such a campaign in Punjab claims that 700 village meetings were held, 29 big public meetings, and 35 conventions. Such mobilization efforts have proved effective only in the areas where meetings and assemblies have not been banned.[48]

The CPI lacks the political strength to push the prime minister toward CPI goals. Nor can it afford to lose its revolutionary image. This is the CPI's chief dilemma. Isolated from the other leftist forces in India, it runs the risk of ending up as a tail of the Congress party. If the CPI actively opposes the government's "anti-people" measures, or plunges into agitational activity to force the government to keep to the left, it may easily incur Indira Gandhi's wrath and lose whatever leverage it currently enjoys with her. What is more important, a policy of abject compromise will be resented by the cadres and make dissent within the party stronger. The National Council has warned the party to be prepared for all possible "twists and turns" in the Indian political situation, which indicates that the CPI leadership is far from certain in what direction politics will move.[49]

CPM. For the CPM, there is no escape from the predicament imposed by the emergency. The strengthening of the CPI-Congress coalition governing Kerala isolates the Marxists; postponement of the 1975 state election in that state denies them the opportunity to expand their base. In Bengal, with much of their new peasant support preempted by police action and Congress organization, they are in hibernation.

According to the CPM strategists, this is a period for waiting while the contradictions within the ruling bourgeoisie, which have aready caused the 1975 crisis, deepen further and make the situation fluid once again. But waiting will not satisfy many cadres. To engage the party's activists there are only two alternatives:

    1. Agitate, expecially among the poor peasants where the CPM has ties, demanding delivery of the land, debt relief,

and minimum wages promised by Congress policy. If such agitation is effective, it will probably provoke government repression, arrests, and perhaps the banning of the party.

2. Go completely underground. Activities then available would presumably be sabotage of various kinds, combined with propaganda and maintenance of the party's inner core. Or, where peasant resentment comes to the surface, the party might spearhead more and more violent peasant protests. This would, of course, mean a tactical line resembling that of the now-splintered Naxalites. But the ideological opposition of the CPM leadership to Maoism for India is sufficiently well formed to make any identification with the Naxalite past or personnel unlikely.

India is a land of acute potential class conflicts. The Communists are the only politicians in the country to pursue class-oriented policies and programs. The electoral system leads inevitably to class cooperation even on the part of the Communists, who in any case paid no systematic attention, until recently, to the class mobilization of the rural poor. If the parliamentary democratic system is supplanted by an authoritarian system, Indian communism will also have to change tactics. Each of the two major Communist parties will then probably be radicalized. Leaders—now mostly elderly people of urban middle-class origin, used to the comforts and rewards of parliamentary communism—will change.[50]

In the current worldwide political temper, radicalization may well mean recourse to violence. Struggles against a common enemy may bring the different Communist groups closer to one another, but this is far from certain. What does seem to be certain is that if the emergency is institutionalized, the Indian Communist movement will become more distinctly class oriented, more radical, and more responsive to violent means. In the context of the Indian countryside—where tensions grow, however suppressed—the impact of a radical militant Communist movement can be highly disruptive.

If Indian democracy changes, so will Indian communism. Both terms of this hypothesis are at this point uncertain. But the indications of change are strong.

NOTES

[1] The best history of the united CPI is Gene D. Overstreet and Marshall Windmiller, *Communism in India* (Berkeley: University of California Press, 1959). On the split in the CPI, see Mohan Ram, *Indian Communism: Split within a Split* (Delhi: Vikas, 1970); and Tulsi Ram Sharma, "1964 Split in the Communist Party of India: A Study in the Interaction of Ideology, Strategy and Power" (Ph.D. dissertation, Himachal Pradesh University, 1976). For a comprehensive study of the Indian Maoist movement see Manoranjan Mohanty, "Strategy and Creativity: The Maoist Movement in India" (Ph.D. dissertation, University of California, Berkeley, 1974); also Mohan Ram, *Maoism in India* (Delhi: Vikas, 1971); and Shankar Ghosh, *The Naxalite Movement* (Calcutta: Orient Longmans, 1974). My *Communism in Indian Politics* (New York: Columbia University Press, 1972) offers a study of the three Communist parties in the context of the Indian political process. Perceptive studies in the same genre include Paul R. Brass and Marcus F. Franda, eds., *Radical Politics in South Asia* (Cambridge, Mass.: MIT Press, 1973); Marcus Franda, *Radical Politics in West Bengal* (Cambridge, Mass.: MIT Press, 1968); and John Osgood and Marcus Franda, *The Communist Parties of West Bengal: Studies in Election Politics in the Indian States,* vol. 1 (Delhi: Manohar Book House, 1974). Two volumes of an official account of CPI history are now available: Ganghadar M. Adhikari, ed., *Documents of the History of the Communist Party of India,* vols. 1 and 2 (New Delhi: People's Publishing House, 1971, 1974). Also of historical value is Muzaffar Ahmed, *Myself and the Communist Party of India* (Calcutta, National Book Agency, 1970); and Gautam Chattopadhayya, *Communism and Bengal's Freedom Movement,* vol. 1, 1917-1929 (New Delhi: People's Publishing House, 1970).

[2] "History will Demand an Answer from Them," *People's Democracy* (Calcutta, CPM weekly), August 17, 1975.

[3] A fuller discussion of the demographic base can be found in Paul Brass's first chapter in Brass and Franda, *Radical Politics in South Asia,* together with a convenient table of Communist election results, pp. 76-77.

[4] Paul R. Brass, "Radical Politics of the Left in Bihar: A Comparison of the SSP and the CPI," in ibid., pp. 394-95.

[5] Communist Party of India (Marxist), *Our Tasks on Party Organization* (Calcutta: CPM, 1968), pp. 17-20.

[6] Vote percentages taken from Brass (see note 3 above).

[7] Hardgrave, "Contradictions of Power," in Brass and Franda, *Radical Politics in South Asia,* p. 179.

[8] For Konar's contribution to the CPM peasant mobilization in West

Bengal, see my "Peasantry and Indian Communism," *Problems of Communism* 21 (Jan-Feb. 1972): 1-17.

9 See my "A Maoist Line for India," *China Quarterly,* no. 33 (Jan.-March 1968): 3-16.

10 "The Causes and Nature of Current Agrarian Tensions" (unpublished monograph, Research and Policy Division, Ministry of Home Affairs, 1969).

11 "It is necessary for the toiling people and the democratic forces to understand that their struggle has reached a new phase. The struggle for defense of democracy will have to be intensified and spread to wider areas and should be linked with the day-to-day struggles of workers and peasants. Just now the peasants are faced with a direct attack. Hence the democratic forces will have to stand by the peasants and the struggle for democracy will have to be taken deep into the villages" (*People's Democracy,* Dec. 24, 1967).

12 Hardgrave, "The Kerala Communists," in Brass and Franda, *Radical Politics in South Asia.*

13 Sen Gupta, *Communism in Indian Politics,* chap. 6.

14 Communist Party in India, *Proceedings of the Seventh Congress of the Communist Party of India: Documents* (Delhi: CPI, 1965); and idem, *Political Report to the Tenth Congress* (Delhi, CPI, 1975).

15 Communist Party of India (Marxist), *Program of the Communist Party of India* (Calcutta: CPM, 1965); idem, *Resolution of the CPI* (Calcutta: CPM, 1965); idem, *Fight Against Revisionism* (Calcutta: CPM, 1965); *People's Democracy,* Nov. 8, 15, 22, 1964; Communist Party of India (Marxist), *Communist Party of India Report of the Ninth Congress* (Calcutta, CPM, 1973).

16 Mohanty, "Strategy and Creativity," chaps. 3 and 5.

17 Communist Party in India, *Political Report to the Tenth Congress,* pp. 16-20.

18 Moscow Radio *Tass* in English 1750 GMT, Jan. 28, 1975; *Tass* in English 0848 GMT, Jan. 29, 1975; *Pravda,* Jan. 27, 1975.

19 *Indian Express* (editorial), Dec. 17, 1975.

20 The Soviet media were highly critical of the "reactionary forces" during the conflict between the West Bengal left united front government and the government in New Delhi; the broadcasts, however, never mentioned the government of India (Sen Gupta, *Communism in Indian Politics,* chap. 6).

21 *People's Democracy,* Dec. 2, 1973. The article was written by M. Vasavapunniah, editor of the paper.

22 This assumption is based on reports in the *New York Times* between Sept. 1975 and Jan. 1976. See William Borders's summing up of the situation in the *New York Times,* Feb. 18, 1976.

23 "National Emergency and Our Party's Task," *New Age* (Delhi CPI weekly), July 6, 1975.

24 Ibid.

25 Ibid.

26 Ibid.

27 *People's Democracy,* Aug. 17, 1975.

28 Bhupesh Gupta, "Whither CPM?," *New Age,* Sept. 28, 1975; *People's Democracy,* Sept. 21, 1975. The CPI saw the coup in Bangladesh on August 14, 1975, in which Sheikh Mujibur Rahman and members of his family were killed, as an offensive on the young republic by the reactionary forces instigated by imperialist agencies like the CIA. For the CPM, the coup stemmed from Mujibur Rahman's own actions—his abrogation of the parliamentary democratic system and promulgation of a one-party system with authoritative powers for himself to rule the country.

29 *Times of India New Service,* quoted in *Frontier* (Calcutta), Sept. 13, 1975; *Statesman* (Calcutta), Dec. 11, 1975.

30 The two leftists eased out were K. R. Ganesh and Hanumanthaya; the portfolios of another leftist, K. D. Malviya, were trimmed. The rightist to leave the cabinet was Umashankar Dixit, once a close confidant of Mrs. Gandhi.

31 A 1965 law provided for payment of a minimum 4 percent bonus to workers even if a company incurred loss. Each year during 1971-74 an ordinance was passed to raise the bonus to 8.33 percent on the basis of interim recommendations of the Bonus Committee.

32 *New Age,* Oct. 5, 1975.

33 Ibid.

34 *Guardian* (Manchester), Jan. 10, 1976.

35 Ibid.

36 *Guardian,* Jan. 6, 1976.

37 *New York Times,* Jan. 30 and Feb. 5, 1976.

38 "New Political Situation, New Form of Struggle," *New Age,* Sept. 7, 1975.

39 *Link* (Delhi), Aug. 10, 1975.

40 M. K. Dhar, "The Bear Hug of the CPI," *Overseas Hindustan Times* (New Delhi), Jan. 18, 1975.

41 Ibid.

42 Ibid.

43 *Statesman,* Dec. 18, 1975.

44 Ibid.

45 Ibid.

46 *Amrita Bazar Patrika* (Calcutta), Dec. 27, 1975.

47 *New Age,* July 20, 1975.

48 *New Age,* Sept. 28, 1975.

49 The National Council resolution said, "Our party must be streamlined so that it is prepared to face all twists and turns, so that its independent activity is increased and its pioneering role and initiative is enhanced" *New Age,* Sept. 7, 1975).

50 For insight on the social background of the two Communist party leaderships, see Hardgrave, "The Kerala Communists," and Sen Gupta, *Communism in Indian Politics,* chap. 11. In his autobiography, the veteran Marxist party leader A. K. Gopalan gives this description of how the Communists' participation in parliamentary politics affected their lifestyle and thinking: "A new life, a new environment, a new alliance. I found myself in an environment calculated to ruin a man. First-class travel, comfortable chambers in Parliament, a surfeit of money, magnificent quarters, and a new life free of heavy responsibility. All circumstances favorable for a life of pleasure. Is anything more necessary to turn a man's head? Daily garden parties and tea parties given either by the Prime Minister, the President or the Vice-President. In addition, there were hosts of invitations from the foreign embassies. This was the setting in which ties of friendship could be established with fashionable men and women who constitute the upper crust of society. . . . On the other hand, people from all strata of society were arriving daily to meet Parliament members to present petitions and memoranda. We were thus faced with a combination of circumstances that brought us face to face with temptations of authoritarianism and luxurious living, as well as self-conceit. Communists like me who had suffered from want of a change of clothes to wear, for want of shelter for a night's sleep, for want of money to pay for our tea and bus fare, and who were scoffed at by the elite of society, were particularly liable to be spoilt by this sudden onset of luxury" (*In the Cause of People* [Delhi: Orient Longmans, 1973], p. 181).

7

India's Rural Poor: What Will Mobilize Them Politically?

F. Tomasson Jannuzi

A continuing state of emergency governs the lives of India's rural poor. Those millions of landless laborers, sharecroppers, and small farmers, who constitute the majority of the people of India, struggle for subsistence against the capricious forces of nature and more powerful men. The rural poor of India, however defined and classified, live within conditions of emergency that are timeless. For them, the suspension of certain civil liberties beginning on June 26, 1975, tends to be a remote happening having no immediate discernible bearing on their lives. What matters is the constant search for employment, the struggle to acquire rights in land or to maintain them, and the needs to satisfy hunger and secure protection from natural elements. There is no fundamental right enshrined in the constitution for the landless laborer to hold land. There is no fundamental right for the sharecropper to receive a fair share of what he produces. There is no fundamental right for the small farmer to hold land without threat of eviction. There is no guarantee that such as these shall receive the benefits of economic growth in rural India, where the rewards of increases in output generally flow in the direction of large landholders with secure rights to land.[1]

Underlying the continuing emergency that grips India's rural poor is the failure of the government of India to effect structural changes, including land reforms, that would permit more

181

equal opportunity to earn a living and to share in economic progress. Further, underlying this continuing economic emergency is the question of whether the rural poor matter, and whether they will claim their rights, either through their own representatives or through outsiders speaking authentically for them.

The perspective of this chapter is framed by the following assumptions. It is assumed that regionally differentiated segments of the Indian peasantry, small farmers having tenuous rights in land as well as sharecroppers and landless laborers, are increasingly capable of placing demands on the political and economic systems of the republic. It is assumed that the rural poor of India, however defined, are heterogeneous in attitudes and interests and will find it difficult in the foreseeable future to establish consensus positions on most economic or political issues that cross extensive areas or cultural divisions. Nonetheless, it is also assumed that the rural poor have political salience in contemporary India[2] and that all political parties increasingly would welcome a nexus with yet-to-be-organized have-not elements in rural India.[3]

The political rhetoric of India's ruling elite in the 1970s[4]— including the promises to implement existing laws on land reform and to check the rich, uplift the poor, and make the country more self-sufficient—documents their efforts to identify with the interests of the rural poor and to respond, at least symbolically, to the demands of weaker sections of the peasantry. Yet no political party, except possibly the CPM in regionally differentiated conditions, has established reliable means over time of enlisting the participation and responding to the legitimate needs of the rural have-nots. All recognize the growth of agrarian tensions.[5] All perceive that promises of future improvements in income and quality of life have not been fulfilled for the majority of India's rural population and that latent anger is being translated into isolated anomic behavior which in time may be transformed into systematically organized forms of political action.

It is time for some definitions. By "rural poor" we mean those living outside urban areas who do not have enough to eat. Economists in India have refined this stark but clear-cut definition, reduced it to rupee equivalents, and made comparative measurements with it. In doing so, they use monthly or annual income data; e.g., fifteen rupees per month per capita (about two dollars) in 1960 buying power defines the poverty line.[6] Our definition, which we use politically, must have another real, but unfortunately less measurable, component. We believe people outside the protection of public welfare and security systems act, must act, on the basis of *expectations* of under-nourishment, which may not be monthly or annual, but occasioned by monsoon failure or other periodic hazards which they perceive as conditions of their lives.[7]

By "have-nots" we mean those who are dependent on agriculture for income but who do not have occupancy rights to land capable of yielding a bare subsistence. This concept must be applied in terms of the productivity of the land and the tenurial institutions of each part of India.[8] There are some tenants farming more than the minimum holding who are (by our definition) have-nots, yet not poor. There are some small-scale landholders of above-minimum farms who are poor, though (by our definition) haves. By and large, however, the categories overlap.

Using ten-year-old annual income data, Dandekar and Rath estimated the rural poor at 40 percent of the rural population. Both because of evidence that the proportion measured in their terms has since grown,[9] and because we are using a broader definition here, we must assume the rural poor to make up at least half the rural population. This estimate leaves out of account an unknown increase in the numbers of those capable of feeling themselves *relatively* poor either because they come to demand more than a caloric minimum of subsistence, or because they compare their progress over periods of time with those of other strata in the population.

This prompts one final assumption. The rural poor, or those who develop the capacity to manipulate them, will be the determinants of the future course of the republic. They are becoming aware of their own intersts. We do not assume that they can act alone politically, or be led easily by outsiders from any of India's political groups. We do assume that no ruling group can long hold power unless it gains the means to respond to the needs of the rural poor. This is a change. The ruling elite have maintained power so far through control of two linked sets of institutions: the large-scale instruments developed for colonial rule, and the local networks of traditional society. We assume the era in which a minority could control and co-opt a majority is ending.

THE RELEVANCE OF THE CASE OF BIHAR

No attempt is made in succeeding pages to suggest that factors governing the mobilization of the rural poor of Bihar will be duplicated in rural areas throughout India. Nonetheless, events in Bihar illustrate broad processes in which rural have-nots may be induced to coalesce around a number of issues linked to the failure of agrarian reforms, persisting exploitation by the traditional landholding elite, and differential benefits from economic development programs.

Bihar (with one-tenth of the people of India within her borders) assumes special significance as the first state to initiate agrarian reforms and possibly the least successful of all in implementing such reforms. The predominantly agrarian economy of Bihar is controlled by landholders whose rights and prerogatives over those below them in the agrarian hierarchy remain extensive, even in 1976.

The subsistence nature of Bihar's agricultural economy is complicated by rapid population growth in a state in which 92 percent of the people live in villages, in which employment opportunities outside of agriculture are limited due to the slow pace of industrialization, in which the net cultivated area per capita is only .42 acres, in which average landholdings are less than three acres, and in which more than 80 percent of all holdings are below five acres in size and splintered into an often bewildering number of noncontiguous plots. The population has grown from roughly 46 million in 1961 to more than 62 million in 1976.

Bihar is recognized as one of the least developed of the Indian states. Yet, the state has land resources that are among the best in India, rivaling those of the Punjab in quality, as well as the most important concentration of mineral resources in the country.[10]

The misery and poverty of the rural poor in Bihar are extreme, even in a country where per capita income is less than $100 per annum.[11]

In Bihar's agrarian setting, land is the primary source of life, status, and power. Land is securely held if rights to it can be defended successfully in a court of law.[12] The have-nots depend on those who control land. Rural economic development programs in Bihar and in India as a whole have tended to benefit landholders with substantial landholdings,[13] rather than the majority of small cultivators. Persisting inequities within the traditional agrarian structure of the society help to determine who will benefit from development programs and who will be denied the benefits of such programs.[14] This is true even of government programs designed to have redistributive effect.

AGRARIAN POLICY

The government of India and the government of the state of Bihar have persistently emphasized rural development programs that would benefit the poor.[15] Verbal commitment to improve conditions for weaker sections of the peasantry began before independence. The election manifesto of the Congress party in 1936 stressed the importance of changing the traditional agrarian structure in India to give relief to the poorest among the peasantry.[16] The central government has issued periodic directives to the states to both legislate and implement agrarian reforms consistent with the "Directive Principles of State Policy" within the constitution of India,[17] but it has lacked the capacity, if not the will, to make certain that this was done.[18] The constitution itself has been used repeatedly by powerful landholding interests in the states who claim constitutional protection of property rights in the courts in order to block land redistribution.

Legislation, 1950

The Bihar Land Reforms Act, 1950, as subsequently amended, remains the most important piece of agrarian reforms legislation in that state.[19] This legislation had the appearance of abolishing the rights in land, as well as the rent-collecting prerogatives, of specified categories of large landholders.[20] In reality, the legislation was designed only to deny certain large landholders their right to continue to act as intermediaries between the state (in legal theory the ultimate landlord in Bihar) and its peasant cultivators. This meant that the state would thereafter have an exclusive right to collect rent from landholders. Those who had previously acted as the state's rent collectors (legally classified as *zamindars* and tenure holders in accordance with the provisions of the Bihar Tenancy Act of 1885)[21] would no longer have this right—and would no longer take an intermediary's share of the rent before passing on the amount due to the state.[22]

What is noteworthy about the Bihar Land Reforms Act, 1950, is that it contained no provisions to directly benefit small farmers (who were rent-paying holders of land on short-term leases), sharecroppers,[23] and landless laborers (having no rights in land). The legislation contained no provisions that would re- distribute the landholdings of large landholders among weaker sections of the peasantry.[24]

The landholders who had acted as the state's intermediaries in the collection of rent were not "abolished." They retained certain portions of their holdings subject to the payment of "rent' to the state, other portions rent-free. Many of them per- sisted as absentee landlords engaged in "personal cultivation" with hired laborers. As such they possessed holdings ranging in size from 500 acres to more than 5,000 acres as recently as November 15, 1975.[25]

By permitting the former intermediaries to retain lands cul- tivated either personally by them or by their servants and hired laborers, the legislation actually sanctioned a process by which peasant cultivators could be denied their rights in the lands they customarily tilled on the often spurious grounds that the cultivators were, in fact, only hired laborers or servants lacking any permanent right of occupancy to the land.

Rural Expectations

No systematic attempt was made by the government of Bihar to inform any section of the peasantry about the provisions of the Bihar Land Reforms Act. What was learned in rural areas about the legislation was through nonofficial channels of com- munication. Many in rural areas developed high expectations of the changes that would be effected. Some anticipated that forms of bonded labor or peonage on the lands of former land- holding intermediaries would be ended. Some anticipated that they would receive more secure rights to the lands they had cus- tomarily tilled for those above them in the agrarian hierarchy. Others, among them the landless who derived the major portion of their incomes from labor in the fields of noncultivating inter- mediaries, expected to receive permanent occupancy rights to lands they have cultivated as wage laborers.

However, the reforms had been enacted by a state legislature controlled by the landholding elite of Bihar. Those hopes were frustrated. The weaker sections of the peasantry did not benefit from the legislation. The former intermediaries were largely successful in preserving their rights in land, within and outside the law. Thousands of cultivators were evicted from holdings they had customarily tilled and were reduced to the status of landless laborers. The civil courts were burdened with cases of litigation over rights in land between rural haves and have-nots. Illegal transfers of land took place to avoid anticipated legislation that would place a ceiling on the size of landholdings. A climate of tension and fear enveloped the countryside.

Ceilings

The principle that there should be in India an absolute limit on the amount of land that an individual or family might hold was commended in the First Five Year Plan (1951-56) and became national policy. Reluctantly responding, Bihar drafted ceilings legislation in 1955. But the bill was referred to a select committee for modification and was shelved until 1961 when a new version of the original bill was enacted.

The legislation clearly favors the former intermediaries who are now classified as cultivators with permanent occupancy rights to the lands tilled personally by them or their servants or hired laborers.[26] The legislation permitted the ceiling to be applied to individual holdings, rather than to family holdings (with family defined to encompass the joint Hindu family). Moreover, the act permitted each landholder to transfer portions of his holding to relatives and nonrelatives within a specified period prior to the commencement of the act. In this fashion, the Bihar ceilings act encouraged pro forma (*benami*) transfers of land within joint families. *Benami* transfers of land became the accepted legal method of preserving rights in land far in excess of the variable ceilings established by law.

There were additional loopholes favoring the interests of the landholding elite. Holdings could exceed the ceiling if they were associated with a landholder's homestead, consolidated blocks used for the production of fodder, pledged to the Bhoodan (land gift) movement, or licensed as a sugarcane farm.

The ceilings act of 1961 has never been fully implemented. Even before it passed, however, it had a profound effect on conditions in rural areas of Bihar. The landlords' strategy has been to delay the act's effective date and to use the time to protect their interests by engaging in fictitious transfers of land and resuming lands for personal cultivation by evicting small landholders who could be intimidated or who—lacking either land records or the financial means with which to protest effectively—could not contest eviction in a civil court. The act thus contributed to agrarian unrest.

Even in 1976, the traditional agrarian structure of Bihar remains substantially unchanged as a result of legislation. But the attitudes of the have-nots are different. Expectations of change have been generated and demands for action in behalf of the rural poor have become more persistent. Tensions result.

REDISTRIBUTION BY CONSCIENCE

The Bhoodan movement, initiated by Gandhian Vinoba Bhave in 1951, tried to accomplish through moral persuasion, rather than legislation, a transformation of the agrarian system throughout India. In particular, the movement's leaders wanted to address and resolve the problem of landlessness. This simple definition of purpose was replaced by more complex and ambitious goals as the movement evolved. The amorphous "total revolution" articulated in 1974 and 1975 by Jayaprakash Narayan as a leader of the anti-Congress Janata Front[27] was one descendant of the movement.

Vinoba Bhave made Bihar a nationwide testing ground for his Bhoodan campaign. His associate Jayaprakash set out to build a network of volunteers in his home state to manage the effort. Bhoodan's record of accomplishment in Bihar, as in the rest of India, is dismal.[28] Of 3,200,000 acres targeted to meet the needs of the state's landless, only 311,000 were actually distributed by 1966, more than a decade after the campaign was supposed to end. The movement built expectations among segments of the rural poor and then dashed them. The movement did not alter the agrarian system of Bihar; it did not even spread spontaneously as a concept in the countryside. Jayaprakash Narayan's perceptions of the failure of Bhoodan in Bihar and in India to address the needs of the rural poor foreshadowed his return to more traditional forms of political action in opposition to established authority in 1974-75.

THE CYCLE OF INACTION

The Growth of Agrarian Unrest

In the early 1950s, the traditional structure of relationships of men to the land in Bihar seemed immutable. Power was concentrated in the hands of landholders, particularly those classified under law as *zamindars* and tenure holders. The rural poor had neither the capacity nor the vision required to challenge those above them in the rural hierarchy. Landless laborers, sharecroppers, and small farmers could not conceptualize a process of social and economic change that would affect them positively.

The years since the 1950s have been ones in which various programs initiated by government—even programs judged to be failures—have threatened the traditional system of relationships among haves and have-nots in rural Bihar. Attempts by government to transform rural society by means of community development and *panchayati raj* have been largely unsuccessful, but have awakened new segments of the peasantry to the possibility of change in the traditional agrarian system. Attempts by government to legislate agrarian reforms, as outlined previously, have produced direct and indirect changes in the agrarian system and have contributed to the growth of tension between rural haves and have-nots. Attempts by government to introduce Green Revolution technology in agriculture, to initiate major and minor irrigation works, to strengthen the cooperative credit system, and to promote rural electrification have produced new sets of relationships between the peasantry and established authority. While the new relationships have been both positive and negative from the perspective of segments of the rural poor, the general effect of this unprecedented penetration of rural areas by outsiders has been to weaken further the traditional fabric of rural relationships among haves and have-nots.

Similarly, the programs of nongovernmental institutions, including Bhoohan and foreign agencies associated with famine relief in the late 1960s, have threatened the traditional agrarian system. This is not to suggest that such programs have been successful when judged even by their own standards of achievement. They have, however, caused an indeterminate but clearly growing number of Bihar's peasantry to embrace the notion that change in the traditional mode of life may be possible. This notion has been endorsed and cultivated by politicians of all persuasions, by government servants performing new functions in rural areas, and by the gradual penetration of rural society by mass communication systems.

The ruling elite began to get the message during the general elections of 1967 when the traditional dominance of the Congress party was shattered. The results of that election confirmed that the rural masses would no longer deliver votes automatically. Even the lowest in the traditional agrarian hierarchy seemed prepared to challenge those above them.

The 1967 expression of anger by the rural poor was, however, inchoate. Soon there were poorly documented reports of roving bands of peasants forcibly harvesting the standing crops of landholders in Purnea, Bhagalpur, Santhal Parganas, and Darbhanga districts. During January-February of 1968, peasants of Champaran district encroached on government lands, and landless laborers demanded land from government officials in the districts of Bhagalpur, Monghyr, Gaya, and Chapra. Meanwhile, in neighboring West Bengal, there were frequent and violent outbreaks of agrarian unrest in the region of Naxalbari and elsewhere in the state. By August of 1969, 346 separate incidents of forcible occupation of land had been reported from West Bengal, and similar incidents occurring with increasing frequency were reported not only in Bihar but also in Assam, Andhra Pradesh, Gujarat, Kerala, Manipur, Orissa, Punjab, Rajasthan, Tamil Nadu, Tripura, and Uttar Pradesh.[29]

The Central Government's Response

In the period 1966-69, the central government demonstrated growing awareness and concern about agrarian unrest in Bihar and elsewhere in India. A unit within the Home Ministry associated this unrest with the persistence of serious social and economic inequalities and the failure of various programs to meet the needs of the rural poor. The ministry argued that a continuing failure to meet such needs would leave the field to "certain political parties," who had already demonstrated some success in various regions, to organize dissident groups of peasants by appealing to their hunger for land and their awakened interest in improved standards of living. The Home Ministry doubtless meant the CPM and CPML. Such parties, though not judged capable of widespread sustained agitation, were considered capable of exploiting existing tensions produced by a "widening gap between the relatively few affluent farmers and the large body of small landholders and landless agricultural workers."[30] The ministry stated that after twenty-two years of planned rural development the traditional landholders remained powerful and "the programmes so far implemented are still more favourable to the larger owner-farmer than to the smaller tenant-farmer. As for the sharecropper and the landless labourer, they have been more often than not left out in the cold. In consequence . . . disparities have widened, accentuating social tensions" and producing problems requiring urgent action by appropriate authorities.[31]

Following selective dissemination of the Home Ministry's report, Indira Gandhi called for a new agricultural development strategy which would require "not only organization and inputs but also the removal of existing institutional and social impediments to production."[32] Among measures to forestall further growth of agrarian tensions, she specifically insisted that ceilings on landholdings be implemented on a priority basis so that surplus land could be distributed to the landless.[33] By November of 1969 the central government was exhorting the states to fulfill earlier promises to transform the agrarian structure through speedy, efficient, and effective programs of agrarian reforms.

The Bihar Government's Response

With a sense of urgency, the government of Bihar took steps during the last weeks of 1969 and the first months of 1970 to implement existing programs for agrarian reforms and to initiate legislation for new programs. The flurry of activity in Bihar in this period was not only in response to the center's renewed exhortations, but also a reflection of heightened recognition among Bihar's ruling elite that conditions existed in rural areas that might be exploited by dissident politicians to produce radical change in the structure of power in the state. Bihar's ruling elite tried to take preemptive action by adopting their own radical slogans and passing a spate of new legislation for land reform.[34]

Unrest into Violence

The new legislation did not defuse agrarian tensions. By the summer of 1970, a number of political parties had called for a land-grab movement involving a mobilization of sections of the peasantry to effect permanent changes in the agrarian structure. In 1970, as in June of 1975 preceding the declaration of a nationwide state of emergency, there was widespread fear of extensive violence. In Bihar, government spokesmen pleaded for more time to implement the newly legislated reforms and declared that measures would be taken within three months (1) to effect ceilings on landholdings, (2) to distribute surplus lands among the landless, (3) to issue *parchas* (legal certificates) to the landless guaranteeing them a permanent right of occupancy to the scraps of land on which their huts stood, and (4) to inhibit the eviction of sharecroppers from lands tilled by them. On July 1, 1970, the government of Bihar ordered the speedy implementation of land reforms, noting as it did so that the failure to implement past legislation had contributed directly to the agrarian unrest.[35]

Tensions continued to mount. Rumors flourished. Newspapers carried reports that Communist-inspired mobs of peasants were taking possession of land in northern Bihar.[36] In immediate reaction a *kisan sabha* (a farmers' organization, comprised of large landholders in this instance) was formed to resist the demands of the peasants for land. Meanwhile, the government published the names of 125 of the largest landholders in the state and announced that the ceilings act of 1961 would be brought into force against them and their cases disposed of summarily.[37] Major landholders converged on Patna to hold lengthy strategy sessions and to lobby against the precipitate implementation of reforms that would impinge on their rights. Armed men, said to be Naxalites, attacked the holdings of a landlord in Bhagalpur district and forcibly harvested standing crops. Three days later, a Jan Sangh party worker was assassinated in Musahari development area in Muzaffarpur district in northern Bihar. This murder was widely considered to be part of the Naxalite strategy of mobilizing sections of the peasantry in violent revolt against landholders. Police were rushed to Musahari to forestall further violence.

Police and Quiet

Reaction came. Anti-Maoist processions were sponsored by the Jan Sangh in various regions of the state, and one such procession ended in violence on August 7 when a homemade bomb thrown into the midst of it severely wounded a bystander. Tension mounted to new heights. A government curfew was imposed in the Patna municipal area, and new voices were raised against the climate of violence. Jayaprakash Narayan was among those who then argued that Bihar's land problem should be settled by peaceful persuasion rather than by violent action, but he also warned that time was running out for those who would substitute token reforms for fundamental efforts aimed at a redistribution of land resources and income. Apparently fearing the worst, the Bihar government issued new directives to its district officers on August 8, 1970, stressing the need to use police power against all those who would lead sections of the peasantry in attempts to harvest standing crops, to occupy land illegally, and to engage in mob violence in any way associated with such activities.

Within a few days, the level of government concern diminished. Violence on a significant scale was averted. Hundreds of political workers were detained by the police. Sustained agitation in the countryside ceased. Some questioned whether any of the leftist parties had the capacity to mobilize the peasantry in a movement having meaningful scale.

The Cycle Repeated

In the following years up to June of 1975, agrarian unrest persisted in Bihar in the form of sporadic and apparently uncoordinated outbursts. Musahari continued to be a trouble spot. Jayaprakash Narayan remained in Musahari until 1971 trying to resolve disputes peacefully and to lead a nonviolent struggle for social and economic justice. But, Narayan and his associates were no more successful in this effort than they and Vinoba Bhave had been in the Bhoodan campaigns. According to Pradhan Prasad, a classic pattern emerged in which the rural poor did not benefit substantially from the efforts of J. P. and his workers.[38] Instead, landholders whom Prasad calls the "rural rich" were the prime beneficiaries of inputs provided by J. P. in association with international agencies and development units of the state and central governments. Moreover, according to Prasad, sections of the rural poor who continued to challenge local landholders were subjected to the "massive repression" of the paramilitary forces of the state government.

By June of 1975, there were ominous reports of continuing agrarian unrest and government repression of segments of the rural poor of Bihar in the name of anti-Naxalite activity. Just a few days before the declaration of the nationwide state of emergency, Arvind Narayan Das reported that a reign of terror had been let loose in rural Bihar by large landholders, their *goondas*, ("thugs"), and police functionaries.[39] According to Das, the objects of repression were landless laborers who had been given land by the government in 1970 only to have their lands repossessed by more powerful landholders. He cited other instances in which armed police in Punpun development area of Patna district joined with landholders of the region in abusing landless or poor peasants who were either *Harijans* (ex-untouchables) or belonged to other backward castes. Das concluded that the government had been indiscriminate in treating as Naxalites weaker sections of the peasantry whose only crime seemed to be one of pressing for their rights in unequal competition with the landholding elite. And he expressed despair that the protests of distinguished Biharis (including the vice-president of the Bihar Congress Committee and Jayaprakash Narayan) went unheeded.[40] The recurring pattern of nominal reform, unrest, renewed paper commitment to reform, sporadic violence, police repression, and quiescence had run its course once again.

FUTURE PROSPECTS FOR PEASANT MOBILIZATION

Five days after the declaration of a state of emergency in India, Prime Minister Indira Gandhi announced a twenty-point program of economic reform measures.[41] The program was interpreted variously. Some suggested that the twenty-point program was no more than a political gambit to deflect criticism of the emergency—a reiteration of earlier tactics when the ruling elite employed radical language for symbolic effects.[42] Others argued with equal force, ignoring the more cynical interpretations of the prime minister's motivations, that the twenty-point program was possibly more significant than the sum of its parts and reflected the prime minister's growing recognition that the maintenance of her power and the legitimacy of her regime would require the implementation of economic programs that addressed the needs of have-not communities in rural areas. The assumption here was that such communities (though still amorphous and regionally differentiated) could be perceived by the ruling elite not only as potential threats to the stability of the Indian political system, but also as a potential source of political support—if they could be mobilized or stabilized by a group capable of interpreting their needs and interests. From this perspective, the twenty-point program could be conceptualized as the leading edge of a more sophisticated set of economic reforms that would buy time for the ruling elite and give them yet another opportunity to transform slogans into meaningful action.

The program is a patchwork of measures that have been propounded many times previously, some of them of little lasting significance. Nevertheless, there is a cluster of measures which, if implemented, would provide economic benefits to neglected elements of the rural poor.[43] The thrust of these measures gives credence to the proposition that the ruling elite do believe in the political salience of the rural poor in contemporary India. There would be no need to address them, even symbolically, if there were no concern at the highest levels of government that the rural poor might, in due course, be mobilized for political action in support of their own interests.

In the following paragraphs, we try to specify the necessary implications, as they can be extrapolated from past experience, both of the government's actual implementation of Indira Gandhi's reforms that relate especially to sections of the peasantry and of the government's once more doing nothing but going through the motions. Again, the state of Bihar is the illustrative unit.

Scenario 1: Nonimplementation

The evidence of twenty-five years of nonimplementation of agrarian reforms in the state of Bihar reinforces the judgment that reform measures applicable to the needs of the rural poor will *not* be implemented. Specifically, there is no reason to believe that the state government will have significantly increased capacity within the terms of the emergency to compile the necessary land records. A central minister proposed the gap be filled by putting all the students of Bihar onto the job.[44] Consider what a threat this would pose to the district Congress officers and representatives, who have their share of *benami* lands, as well as to the local revenue officials and village accountants who have for years avoided keeping records of tenants' occupancy rights as well as of landholdings above the legal maximum. Consider also the likelihood that the incumbent Bihar government would put into contact with discontented peasants throughout the state the very students who provided the troops for J. P. Narayan's antigovernment demonstrations only a year or two ago. Here is a measure both of the kind of problem that must be solved to secure implementation of agrarian reforms and the unlikelihood of solution.

If precise records of holdings and tenancies could be obtained, however, the struggle would merely shift to the local courts. New records would certainly be impugned there. The whole program would wait upon an impossible backlog of lawsuits. And, should a determined government try to cut that Gordian knot by making specific reforms nonjusticiable, it would take on the whole legal profession scattered among the small towns. Again, this is a considerable sector of the existing political network.

We could make similar projections about the tasks of distributing surplus land, once taken by the state, about enforcing a debt moratorium benefitting only certain weaker strata and disadvantaging the private creditors who are also the politically powerful landowners in the villages, or about enforcing in remote villages a minimum wage for laborers who lack economic bargaining power because they lack alternative sources of employment.[45]

In short, it is likely that the projected reforms will be resisted, circumvented, diluted, and denied by persisting coalitions of landholding interests comprised of former intermediaries and others having superior rights in land. Landlord associations, assisted by local *goondas* in their employ, will continue to carry out acts of local repression if and when attempts are made to implement specific reforms. Local judges will grant stays of enforcement and enter cases on dockets already years long. Local elected governments, in which landed power remains strong, will continue to support bureaucratic procedures of the nineteenth century favorable to property owners.

There will continue to be agrarian unrest and a climate of uncertainty and fear in the countryside. Sporadic outbursts of violence can be expected following a pattern well delineated in the early 1970s. Local police (bolstered by central authority, including well-equipped paramilitary forces) will engage in increasingly repressive and violent counteraction. Without much evidence, those in power will suggest that rural lawlessness is fostered by the outlawed Naxalites. While the conditions of the state of emergency may be ameliorated and numbers of opposition leaders released from detention, it is unlikely that attempts by opposition groups to organize constituencies of the rural poor against established authority will be accorded legitimacy. While leaders of the present opposition parties are thereby likely to be neutralized, new leadership (more capable of violent action) will gradually supplant the old.

In sum, with the anticipated failure of the emergency-associated economic reforms, the likely scenario is one in which the central government will remain in an increasingly uncomfortable alliance with shifting coalitions of Bihar's ruling elite, remnants of the Brahman, Bhumihar, Rajput, and Kayastha groups who were so successful in the 1950s and '60s in thwarting the introduction of agrarian reforms that might have benefited segments of the generally lower-caste rural poor. Such a scenario involves a linear projection of preemergency elite attitudes toward demands for economic reform and social justice emanating from Bihar's have-nots, or their self-appointed spokesmen. It is a scenario of failure in which the slogans of stability through law and order supplant the call for fundamental changes in the agrarian system that might benefit the poor. The predictable result over time would be the escalation of demands for change from below. The polarization of interests between the landholding elite and the rural poor would become more acute, and, as tensions mount, one can predict that issues such as distributive justice and land to the tiller will become fashionable slogans for those who seek effective control over substantial segments of the peasantry.

In time, those who seek a new, direct nexus with segments of the peasantry may well include elements of the ruling elite as well as those who oppose them. The results of this competition cannot be projected with certainty, but we can be certain that the process will itself accelerate the politicization of the rural poor and increase their potential for mobilization for sustained action in their economic and political interests.

Scenario 2: Implementation

The unlikely scenario for Bihar involves the effective implementation of the emergency-linked economic reforms. It would also involve the adoption and implementation of a variety of additional reforms linked to a new rural development strategy. Such new programs will not be implemented unless the center is indeed prepared to take extreme measures, employing the coercive power of the center and the state in the promotion of agrarian reforms and economic development programs designed to benefit small farmers, sharecroppers, and landless laborers. Among other things this implies central willingness to ignore or specifically abrogate provisions in the constitution that make "agriculture" a state subject. If agriculture were to remain under state constitutional jurisdiction, the states would continue to have the power to vitiate central initiatives. Furthermore, this scenario would require central government willingness to use summary procedures (including the bypassing of civil courts with or without the assent of the judiciary) in settling rural disputes between haves and have-nots.

This unlikely scenario might become feasible if Bihar's traditional elite (including many members of the incumbent Congress) are circumvented by the central authority and partially neutralized by repressive measures directed at any who are perceived to be offering overt or covert resistance to reform measures invoked by the center.

This unlikely scenario would also involve a process by which local institutions of government (particularly those administering rural development programs and the revenue department which continues to exercise responsibility for implementing agrarian reforms) are overhauled administratively. Simultaneously, such local units of government would have to be made more responsive to central authority than to those who have worked through the years to limit the scope of agrarian reforms and to foster economic development programs that have been largely unrelated to the needs of the rural poor.

In short, the implementation of the emergency-related economic reforms in contemporary Bihar (and in many other regions of India) will require a sustained invocation of radical, coercive methods by the central government, including the abrogation or modification of provisions in the constitution, the bypassing of conventional legal processes, and an unprecedented (for India) use over time of police power in neutralizing opposition groups and in supporting the introduction and implementation of various reform measures.

The fulfillment of this scenario would not usher in an era of rural tranquility and law and order. Partial satisfaction of some needs of the rural poor may well produce increased demands as the rural poor recognize that pressuring the government gets some results. It would encourage new demands and accelerate the politicization of the rural poor, increasing their economic and political interests. The first scenario anticipates mobilization of segments of the peasantry in increasingly militant action against established authority and allies the central government (willingly or unwillingly) with a minority attempting to preserve traditional rights and prerogatives. The latter scenario offers hope to the central government that extreme measures taken in behalf of the rural have-nots will be an effective short-term means of defusing rural anger by satisfying some needs and neutralizing the appeal of opposition groups seeking to organize segments of the peasantry against established authority. From this perspective, the latter scenario is a strategy of preemptive action—one that would attempt to ensure the center its new nexus with the rural poor while denying such ties to the opposition.

The emergency imposed by Indira Gandhi may be the last opportunity for the ruling elite to establish a new nexus with constituencies of the rural poor. If new working relationships are not institutionalized between the government of India and the rural poor and if critical reforms are again not implemented, there seems little doubt but that the field will be left to those who would employ violence to promote change in the relationships of men to the land in rural India and to those who would employ violence to deny such change.

NOTES

1 For discussion of factors related to skewed distribution of the benefits of agricultural production increases in India, see Pranab Bardhan, "Trends in Land Relations, A Note," *Economic and Political Weekly* 5 (Annual Number, January 1970): 261-66; Francine Frankel, "Agricultural Modernisation and Social Change," *Mainstream* (Delhi), November 29, 1969; and F. Tomasson Jannuzi, *Agrarian Crisis in India: The Case of Bihar* (Austin: University of Texas Press, 1974).

2 Samuel P. Huntington's argument is considered to be relevant to the situation in contemporary India. "The role of the countryside is variable: it is either the source of stability or the source of the revolution. For the political system opposition within the city is disturbing but not lethal. Opposition within the countryside, however, is fatal" (Huntington, *Political Order in Changing Societies* [New Haven: Yale University Press, 1968], p. 292).

3 The word *nexus* is used here in its literal meaning: connection, tie, or link. An extractive and control nexus, exercised most often through landholding intermediaries, has long existed between those who hold power in India and the rural poor. The issue posed here is whether a new, direct nexus can be forged with the rural poor—a nexus that vitiates the power of traditional intermediaries between the rural poor and those who would control them.

4 The term "ruling elite" is used here with particular reference to those within the ruling Congress who have supported the rhetoric, if not always the programs, of Prime Minister Indira Gandhi. On the basis of my own field work in India, I suggest that the primary contemporary characteristic of this heterogeneous group (which includes British-trained intellectuals, influential landholders, elements within the administrative services, and business leaders) is growing awareness of the degree to which their remoteness—physical, intellectual, and economic—from the majority of the people of India is a threat to their own continued predominance.

5 The central Home Ministry has linked the growth of agrarian tensions with the failure of government to implement programs benefitting the weaker sections of rural society, particularly the landless, sharecroppers, and small farmers. See the widely disseminated, still unpublished report: India, Home Ministry, Research and Policy Division, "The Causes and Nature of Current Agrarian Tensions" (New Delhi, 1969).

6 The foundation was laid by V. M. Dandekar and Nilakanta Rath, "Poverty in India," *Economic and Political Weekly* 8 (Annual Number, February 1973): 245-54; and Amartya Sen, "Poverty, Inequality and Unemployment, Some Conceptual Issues in Measurement'" *Economic and Political Weekly* 9 (Special Number August 1973): 1457-66.

7 Thus in Bihar, according to Pranab Bardhan, the percentage of rural people living below a minimum level (defined by him as 15 rupees per month at 1960-61 prices) increased from 37.64 percent in 1960-1961 to 42.8 percent in 1964-65 to 80.5 percent (following severe drought and famine) in 1967-68 (Bardhan, "The So-Called Green Revolution and Agricultural Labourers," (unpublished, 1970, p. 21).

8 Again, Dandekar and Rath laid the groundwork for such a calculation. See the second part of their article, "Poverty in India," cited in note 6. The acreage of standard quality land they take to be necessary to support an average Bihar rural family at the poverty level is 2.5. Sixty-five percent of Bihar rural families in 1960-61 had no land or were below that level (ibid., pp. 115, 120). Occupancy rights are defined for Bihar in the Bihar Tenancy Act of 1885.

9 Bardhan, "On the Incidence of Poverty," p. 249, found it to be 53 percent all-India and 61 to 71 percent in Bihar (after the famine years) in 1967-68.

10 Though Bihar remains a predominantly agrarian economy, its Chota Nagpur region is rich in mineral resources (including coal, iron, mica, and uranium). Therefore, in Bihar, as in no other state of India, there exists the possibility for the development of greater balance in the economy between agriculture and industry.

11 Official statistics on poverty in Bihar tend to be inaccurate or misleading. Apart from my own field studies, my most reliable information has come from the writings of the late S. R. Bose, former director of the government of Bihar's Central Bureau of Economics and Statistics. See, for example, Bose, "Levels of Poverty in Rural Bihar," *Searchlight* (Patna), April 21, 1970.

12 The rural poor find it difficult to challenge powerful landholders in civil courts. The civil courts of Bihar have nonetheless been swamped by cases of litigation involving rights in land. In Purnea district alone, for example, I found more than 38,000 such litigations pending in 1970.

13 I have used the term "substantial" here to refer, arbitrarily, to holdings that are twenty-four acres or more in size. Though the figure is arbitrary, it is based on my intensive field investigations in Bihar over many years as well as the judgments of government officials (responsible for rural development programs in that state) that the benefits of new technology in agriculture have not "trickled down" to the majority of cultivators (62 percent of all holdings in Bihar being 9.9 acres or less). Also see Wolf Ladejinsky's article, "Green Revolution in Bihar," *Economic and Political Weekly* 2 (Sept. 27, 1969): A147-A162.

14 To secure government credit for new inputs, for example, often requires using land as surety for a loan. A landholder who enjoys secure rights in land has ready access to such credit; others who lack secure rights in land are without means, generally, of acquiring credit, except through private sources at frequently usurious rates. Thus, traditional inequalities are strengthened and the gap grows between rural haves and have-nots.

15 Land reforms in particular have been invoked as a means of providing political and economic benefits for the rural poor. In addition to documents of the government of India, including the various five-year plans, useful perspectives on this general subject are contained in Daniel Thorner, *The Agrarian Prospect in India* (Delhi: Delhi University Press, 1956); and Doreen Warriner, *Land Reform in Principle and Practice* (Oxford: Clarendon Press, 1969).

16 The election manifesto advocated "a reform of the system of land tenure and revenue and rent, and an equitable adjustment of the burden on agricultural land, giving immediate relief to the smaller peasantry by a substantial reduction of agricultural rent and revenue now paid by them and exempting uneconomic holdings from payment of rent and revenue" (Jawaharlal Nehru, as quoted by W. Norman Brown in *The United States and India and Pakistan* [Cambridge, Mass.: Harvard University Press, 1968], p. 227.

17 See H. C. L. Merillat, *Land and the Constitution in India* (New York: Columbia University Press, 1970), for specifics on the relationship between central directives, constitutional limitations, and state prerogatives.

18 For an early national government perspective, see India, Planning Commission, *Implementation of Land Reforms: A Review by the Land Reforms Implementation Committee of the National Development Council* (New Delhi: Planning Commission, 1966).

19 The complex history of these legislated reforms, together with a detailed analysis of their provisions, is contained in Jannuzi, *Agrarian Crisis in India: The Case of Bihar*.

20 The rights and prerogatives of these landholders dated from 1793 when a "Permanent settlement" was established between the East India Company and *zamindars* (landholders who had acted as "revenue farmers" for Mughal authority) of Bengal, North Madras, and Bihar. The settlement fixed in perpetuity the amount of revenue due to the company from the *zamindars* and permitted the *zamindars* to fix their own terms with tenants.

21 Those interested in the complex hierarchy of interests in land in Bihar from a legal perspective can find useful information and currently relevant definitions in the Bihar Tenancy Act of 1885 as reprinted in Government of India, Ministry of Food and Agriculture, *Agricultural Legislation in India*, vol. 6 (Delhi: Manager of Publications, 1956), pp. 34ff.

22 The legislation did not stop former intermediaries from exacting a share of the produce from dependent cultivators by claiming that such de facto tenants were really hired laborers with no permanent rights in land.

23 Sharecroppers in Bihar generally can be classified as *bataidars*, who have no right of occupancy to the lands they till, assume the full costs and risks of production, and must give up 50 percent of their produce to a landholder who has superior rights in land. There are also sharecroppers who, because they do not assume the full costs and risks of production, are required to give up two-thirds of their produce to the landholder.

24 When the legislation was enacted in 1950 there were 205,977 such intermediaries (loosely referred to as *zamindars* or "landlords") holding rights in land in Bihar. Their "estates" covered 90 percent of the total area of the state. Not more than 125 of these intermediaries could be classified as major landholders, with estates comprising hundreds, even thousands, of acres. Among the major estates were those of Kursaila in Purnea, Dumraon Raj in Shahabad, Darbhanga Raj in Darbhanga, Hathwa Raj in Saran, and Ramgarh Raj in Hazaribagh. It is emphasized here that the legislation did not abolish these estates. The lands comprising them were generally retained by the former intermediaries, employing various loopholes in the law; such large (and small) landholders simply ceased being intermediaries and became occupancy *raiyats* (rent-paying holders of land having the right of permanent occupancy on the lands held by them).

25 My field investigations in the period 1956 through 1970 enabled me to confirm holdings of 5,000 acres or more. The *Hindu*, Nov. 15, 1975, in an article entitled "Reforms in Slow Motion," suggested that the government of Bihar as of that date listed 500 landlords with holdings of between 500 and 20,000 acres. But the majority of rent-collecting intermediaries had small "estates" prior to the Act of 1950 and had small holdings thereafter.

26 The Bihar Land Reforms (Fixation of Ceiling Area and Acquisition of Surplus Land) Act, 1961, established a variable ceiling on landholdings to be based in each instance on an assessment of the quality of land in the possession of a landholder; the ceiling ranged from twenty acres of Class I (most productive) land to sixty acres of Class V land.

27 Jayaprakash Narayan is a Bihari. He has been at various times a Marxist intellectual, a leading Congress Socialist, a Gandhian Socialist, a leader of the Bhoodan movement (with Vinobha Bhave), and a militant spokesman for the rural poor of Bihar and India.

28 For details including information on village attitudes see chapter 7 of Jannuzi, *Agrarian Crisis in India.*

29 India, Home Ministry, "The Causes and Nature of Current Agrarian Tensions," Annexure I.

30 Ibid., p. 10.

31 Ibid.

32 India, Ministry of Food, Agriculture, Community Development and Co-operation, "Chief Minister's Conference on Land Reform—Notes on Agenda," (unpublished report, Department of Agriculture, New Delhi, 1969), Annexure C, p. C1.

33 Ibid., pp. C1-C2.

34 See, for example, the Bihar Tenancy (Amendment) Act of 1970, the Bihar Tenancy (Amendment) Bill, 1970, the Bihar Land Reforms (Amendment) Bill, 1970, the Bihar Public Land Encroachment (Amendment) Ordinance, 1970, the Bihar Consolidation of Holdings and Prevention of Fragmentation (Amendment) Bill, 1970, and the Bihar Privileged Persons Homestead Tenancy (Amendment) Bill, 1970.

35 Bihar, Revenue Department, "D.O. No 5LR-LA-224/70-5667-L.R." (Patna, July 1, 1970).

36 See, for example, the *Indian Nation* (Patna), July 17, 1970, p. 1.

37 The *Indian Nation*, July 19, 1970, lists the names of the major landholders who were to be brought within the purview of the 1961 ceilings act. After publishing the names, the government failed to take action to enforce ceilings on these holdings.

38 For a recent account of Jayaprakash Narayan's efforts in villages of Musahari block, see Pradhan H. Prasad, "Agrarian Unrest and Economic Change in Rural Bihar, Three Case Studies," *Economic and Political Weekly* 10 (June 14, 1975): 931-37. Also see my account of my own last meeting with J. P. in Musahari Block in chapter 7 of Jannuzi, *Agrarian Crisis in India.*

39 "Murder to Landlords' Order," *Economic and Political Weekly* 10 (June 14, 1975): 915-17.

40 Ibid.

41 The measures were reported in the press on July 2, 1975; see, for example, the *Times of India* (Bombay), July 2, 1975, p. 1.

42 I was in India when the emergency was declared and when the twenty-point program was first publicized. The perspectives in this section were shaped by my observations at the time and by my conversations then and subsequently with Indian and American scholars who have specialized in study of the political economy of India.

43 These measures included the following: (1) a pledge to complete certain agrarian reforms by updating land records, implementing ceilings on landholdings, and distributing surplus lands to weaker sections of the peasantry; (2) a pledge to provide increasing numbers of house sites for landless

laborers; (3) a pledge to end bonded labor in rural areas; (4) a plan to liquidate rural indebtedness; and (5) a pledge to review laws on minimum agricultural wages. For elaboration on these and other measures see a collection of speeches by the minister of finance, C. Subramaniam, and the minister of industry and civil supplies, T. A. Pai, in *New Programme for Economic Progress: The Turning Point* (New Delhi: Indraprastha Press, 1975).

[44] Finance Minister C. Subramanian's Lok Sabha address on August 4, 1975: "In my view whatever is necessary for other States, for Bihar there has to be ruthless implementation of land reforms. All sorts of excuses are made that there are no land records. If we have the will to do in the new atmosphere, can we not use the entire student population for the purpose of preparing land records? If six months are given for the purpose and the students are involved for the preparing the land records, I hope this thing can be achieved quickly" (*New Programme for Economic Progress*, p. 73).

[45] On this see Hiranmay Dhar, "Agricultural Labour: Implementation Still the Achilles Heel," *Economic and Political Weekly* 10 (Dec. 13, 1975): 1901-2.

8

The Military

Stephen P. Cohen

The Indian military played no direct role in the arrest of thousands of political figures, scholars, M.P.s, journalists, intellectuals, and "miscreants" on June 26, 1975. Neither were they responsible for the imposition of press censorship, the expulsion of foreign journalists, the state of emergency imposed that day, the suspension of civil liberties, nor the continuing reinterpretations of the constitution of India. Yet, the integrity of the Indian military was used as a major justification for all of these actions—and perhaps others yet to come. In her defense, Mrs. Indira Gandhi and Indian government spokesmen have repeatedly stressed that the arrests, censorship, and emergency were necessary at least in part because of appeals made to the military (and police) to revolt and mutiny.

The sole basis for this very serious charge appears to have been the statements of various opposition leaders, especially Jayaprakash Narayan; these leaders have not been accused of direct contact with uniformed forces. Narayan did raise the issue of military obedience several times before and during June 1975. For example, in a speech at Suri, West Bengal, "J. P." was reported to have appealed to the armed forces not to carry out "illegal orders."[1] A few days later, in New Delhi on the eve of a planned mass civil disobediance campaign, he repeated the appeal, calling on army, police, and government employees "not to obey any orders they considered illegal." Narayan added that "the Army act lays down that the armed forces must protect the Constitution. If the Constitution is changed legally it does not matter. But the Army must oppose any unconstitutional changes."[2] Mockingly, he dared the government to try him for treason.

While J. P. may have believed he was within both the law and the norms of Indian politics, Mrs. Gandhi thought otherwise. Even before the arrests she had responded to Narayan's suggestion that the armed forces disobey illegal orders. On the evening of the twenty-fifth, just before J. P.'s appearance at the mammoth rally in New Delhi, she claimed that "if a soldier began doubting whether his superior's order was right or wrong or started referring to the rules book then the war would be lost." After ordering the arrests of thousands of Indian politicians (including Narayan himself), she charged that "certain persons have gone to the length of inciting our armed forces to mutiny and our police to rebel."[3] Parenthetically, this is not the first time Mrs. Gandhi has made such a charge. In 1967 she accused one of the parties (CPM) that were to support Narayan in the 1975 crisis of sowing disaffection in the Indian Army.[4]

We will return to the substance and implications of Mrs. Gandhi's accusations later in this chapter, but the essential point is that the military became an *issue* in the momentous events of 1975, although there is no evidence to indicate that it ever became a *participant*. Nor is it likely to in the foreseeable future. It is the inaction of the military that will be its outstanding quality in Indira Gandhi's India, a passivity that contrasts sharply with an obvious potential for intervention. With the suspension of civil liberties and the closing of the political system, the military becomes one of the very few institutions that could—at a single stroke—terminate Mrs. Gandhi's experiment with new forms of democracy; yet, we would argue, this is not apt to happen. The soldiers are likely to continue to disappoint those who expected them to heed Narayan's call; but they are also likely to disappoint those who expect them to join Mrs. Gandhi's revolution.

To understand the basis for these conclusions it is necessary to draw back and examine the military in its larger social and political context. It relates to this context both as an institution and as an idea or model. Armies as institutions are bound in time and place, are functionally specific, and have fixed patterns of recruitment, training, and action.[5] They also share many characteristics with other armies, although no two are identical. This applies to their political as well as their military behavior. But the military as an idea is quite different.[6] It is functionally and organizationally diffuse, may take quite different forms in different societies, and—above all—can be held by civilians as part of their belief and value structure. Belief in the military as a model or ideal is voluntary, and not derived from any particular organizational format or performance standard. Those who adhere or appeal to the military virtues may do so in whole or in part, and may view the military as either an end or a means.

India has had a long and striking history of the military as an institution. The French, and then more successfully, the British, adapted Western military forms to Indian conditions as early as the eighteenth century, and these hybrid institutions have flourished in South Asia. This chapter will primarily be devoted to examining the relationship to contemporary political developments of the military as an institution.

However, we must not ignore the impact on Mrs. Gandhi's India of a different, and perhaps equally important facet of the military: glorification of military values and practices. We turn to this first.

THE MILITARY AS IDEOLOGY

Military rule, militant or aggressive foreign policies, the militarization of society, the praise or emulation of so-called military values and virtues—all of these can be called "Militarism," but they are really quite distinct phenomena.[7] They also appear as significant strands in the fabric of recent Indian history. No discussion of the military in India today would be complete without at least a brief look at these phenomena. Two areas seem to be of special importance: the military as a model for domestic politics and the martial spirit as a style in foreign policy.

Mrs. Gandhi's father, Jawaharlal Nehru, detested the military. He had no particular interest in military matters, and wrote of the profession in scathing terms.[8] He hated the automatic discipline and the mindless obedience that he associated with the military and abhorred the carnage of war. Yet, in a moment of extraordinary self-revelation, he did speculate on the relationship of war to Indian society:

> Much as I hated war, the prospect of a Japanese invasion of India had in no way frightened me. At the back of my mind I was in a sense attracted to this coming of war, horrible as it was, to India. For I wanted a tremendous shake-up, a personal experience for millions of people, which would drag them out of that peace of the grave that Britain had imposed upon us. . . . The war was not of our seeking, but since it had come, it could be made to harden the fiber of the nation. . . . Vast numbers would die, but it is better to die in war than through famine.[9]

This view reflects a subordinate but recurrent theme in Indian thought. Trial by combat might be tragic or unfortunate, but it could have beneficial consequences. Although Mahatma Gandhi rejected war in all forms (and urged nonviolence upon the British in their resistance to the Japanese), he spoke sympathetically of the military as an organization, praising its discipline and order. Gandhi advised young Indian officers to become soldiers of nonviolence, applying their (admirable) military skills to domestic problems, becoming a peace army.[10] Thus, in the attitudes of two of India's greatest leaders, there was a place for the solidarity and dedication that emerges from conflict, or for the martial virtues of discipline, obedience, and order that were thought to characterize the military.

However, the apotheosis of the martial spirit was more clearly evident in a third major Indian figure, Subhas Chandra Bose.[11] He was Nehru's major contemporary and chief political rival within Congress, styling himself *Netaji*, or leader. Bose fled India at the outbreak of World War II, eventually leading an Indian National Army (I.N.A.) against British and Indian troops. Militarily he was a failure, but politically he proved to be enormously popular. Had Bose not died in 1945 it is highly likely that he would have returned to India as Nehru's chief rival. A fine speaker, he, rather than Nehru, articulated the undercurrent of militant, aggressive nationalism that has always existed in India and that appears to have resurfaced. It is in the political philosophy and appeal of Bose that we see one historical precedent for Mrs. Gandhi's popularity.

Bose was nonsectarian and attracted a broad base of support among different regions, castes, and religions of India. He was also an extremist of the center, in Lipset's terminology.[12] He never ceased stressing discipline, order, and obedience as national virtues. Finally, Bose maintained an abiding interest in military and national security symbols, beginning with an early interest in uniforms, drills, and riflery and culminating in the leadership of the I.N.A.

Although the comparison may not be exact, some of Mrs. Gandhi's appeal would seem to be due to the similarities rather than the differences between herself and Bose. She is certainly a secularist and professes faith in democracy, although perhaps democracy of a special variety. Her speeches are dominated by references to the need for discipline and order, and she has not disowned the slogan "India is Indira, and Indira is India."[13] Finally, there is no doubt she believes that internal and external enemies require continual vigilance, militancy, and preparedness. In the face of such enemies, even the enemy poverty, civil liberties are expendable, and in fact might obstruct progress. These themes are important components in her political style, and no opposition group has yet to develop an effective reply. Although India lacks a garrison state's discipline or resources, Mrs. Gandhi is attempting to use internal and external threats and enemies to mobilize those resources and that discipline in the ultimate hope that, once India is fully mobilized, the threats can be allowed to wither away.

If this is the direction in which Mrs. Gandhi is heading, it should not come as a surprise to observers of the Indian scene; nor is there a lack of comparative data to help us define the emerging character of her regime. Analyzing predictions of the fragmentation and disintegration of India, I wrote earlier that "a profound threat to democracy in India could arise as much from too much unity as from too little; under the pretext of a national front, or as the incarnation of the national will, a movement following the Bose-I.N.A. prototype might successfully dismantle India's substantial democratic structure, in the name of the nation, and possibly in the name of democracy itself."[14] This appears to be occurring, and not without considerable support within India. For a nation beset by severe economic difficulties, political instability, and social disorder, the emergence of an all-powerful leader has come as a temporary relief. The historical precedents of a strong, dominant leader exist in Mahatma Gandhi, Nehru, and Bose (although the first two often expressed self-doubts about their unique roles). Mrs. Gandhi can claim to be heir to this tradition.

A second facet of the military as an idea in contemporary India is the role that military and security problems play in Indian politics. The most striking development here has been the importance of such issues in legitimizing an unprecedented concentration of power in Mrs. Gandhi's hands. Such issues—threats from the United States, threats from China, threats from Pakistan—have periodically become the object of publicity campaigns designed to remove an issue from the opposition parties and reemphasize Mrs. Gandhi's mastery of the situation. If poll data are any measure of success the strategy seems to work; the prime minister's popularity has consistently soared in conjunction with such events as the 1971 invasion of East Pakistan and the detonation of a "peace bomb" in 1974.[15] While we cannot attempt a full analysis of the reasons why such appeals are popular in India (and, indeed, in most other states), some elements of this appeal can be noted.

Contemporary Indian political elites grew to political maturity during a period of extraordinary foreign policy activity. India's foreign policy, created and guided by Nehru, was reasonably successful abroad, far more so at home. For years, India was the dominant nation in the Third World, was courted by both superpowers, and participated in a continuous exchange of foreign visitors and delegations. Indian intellectuals, journalists, administrators, and politicians came to believe that their nation's international role was quite special and distinct, and recognized as such by the rest of the world.

When Nehru's foreign policy was discredited by the Himalyan border fiasco in 1962 and the continued ability of Pakistan to pose a threat to India (at least as perceived by Indians), the nation turned elsewhere. If military weakness was the source of extreme shame, then India would pursue a policy of overwhelming military strength, turning to several outside sources for assistance. Defense studies burgeoned, realpolitik became the guiding star, and the military was elevated to a place of honor, despite its defeat in 1962. Indians discovered that they could have nonalignment *and* use their expanding military power to support their foreign policy; indeed, they have come to believe in recent years that military might is the basis of any sound relationship between them and the military superpowers, let alone Pakistan and China. Hence the continued development of an arms industry and an active nuclear program.

A second way in which national security issues have been utilized by Mrs. Gandhi to build political support is exemplified by her stress on the danger of penetration by foreign powers. Her argument has been that such powers (and their intelligence agencies) regard India as a threat and wish to destabilize or otherwise weaken it through cultural, political, or military action. The informed reader can independently judge the validity of such arguments, but they do have a profound political impact within India. To argue that this perception of foreign (especially American) hostility is incorrect verges on treason for an Indian citizen, since the government of India claims to have substantial evidence of foreign intervention. In fact, Mrs. Gandhi has claimed that opposition to her and to her views on Indian security problems may be taken as evidence of such foreign influence.

In an environment of fear and suspicion of foreign intentions it is easy for Mrs. Gandhi and her supporters to stress reliance upon her as an incorruptible, unassailable leader. When an insidious threat exists, democratic institutions themselves (such as opposition parties, the press, and other nongovernmental groups) become channels of foreign influence and must be limited for their own good. Only the leader and her incorruptible associates can be assumed to be free of foreign control and can defend the security of India.

We do not know how long such arguments will continue to persuade in India, nor whether they will be advanced in years to come. However, we do believe that they have been effective in mobilizing support for Mrs. Gandhi and are not likely to be relinquished soon. The crowds that applaud Mrs. Gandhi's militant style in foreign policy may not represent all of Indian opinion, or even a majority of that opinion, but they are a base on which she can build at least the appearance of mass support.

AN INSTITUTIONAL PERSPECTIVE

Any enquiry into the actual role played by the military in the Indian political system immediately encounters the problem of restricted information. Evidence about the attitudes of the military, their role in central Indian politics, and their ties with civilian elites is almost entirely indirect, and direct evidence is often unreliable or ephemeral.[16] Such matters are among the most secretive in Indian political life, though there was a temporary relaxation in this restriction on information during the years 1962-71, when India needed outside assistance to meet the Chinese challenge and to rebuild its military establishment.

However, difficulties in gathering information about the military in India are balanced in two ways. First, the Indian military as an institution has a long and important history; this institutional history can contribute to our understanding of contemporary issues and attitudes. In fact, as many Indian officers have noted, the Indian military is one of the least-changed institutions in the country, a state of affairs that they regard with mixed feelings.[17] Second, the military is a universal profession that invites comparison across national boundaries. In the case of the Indian Army we are particularly fortunate in being able to draw comparisons with the Pakistan Army (and, perhaps, the Bangladesh Army), especially in the army's relationship with political institutions and personalities, although we are not intimating that what has happened in Pakistan or Bangladesh is likely to happen in India.[18] Such comparisons are particularly easy to make in areas such as the professionalism of the military, its external defense role, and its contribution to the maintenance of internal tranquility.

The remainder of this section deals sequentially with these issues, drawing inferences, first, from the visible past of a well-established institution.

The British Legacy

In British India the role of the military in politics was a live issue for almost 150 years: it took that long for the British to conclude that civil-military relations in India were to follow the British pattern as closely as possible.[19] India had been a military preserve in many ways, and elements of this lingered on through independence. But the military no longer dominated after 1910. The turning point was the notorious Kitchener-Curzon dispute of 1905. Despite the victory of the military in this crisis (or, more accurately, because of it), civilian officials in India and Great Britain obtained effective control of Indian affairs, civil and military.

This was fortuitous because selected Indians soon joined the British Indian Army as commissioned officers. (Indians had already entered the Indian Civil Service as early as the nineteenth century, but did not appear there in substantial numbers until the 1920s and the 1930s.) As in the case of their civilian counterparts, these Indian officers were carefully chosen by the

British. However, whereas the criteria for entry into the Indian Civil Service were largely objective, those applied to Indians seeking entry into the officer corps were quite special. Not only were candidates required to pass the standard intelligence and physical examinations, they were carefully screened according to their caste and social background.[20] The British were interested in recruiting the "right type" of officer. This right type was quite conservative; he was not outspoken; he was obedient; he came from a wealthy, landed, aristocratic background, which eased his adjustment to the semifeudal Indian Army; he came from a "martial" ethnic group such as the Sikhs, Jats, Punjabi Muslims, or Rajputs; he was a "gentleman."[21] Of course, recruitment to the officer corps from such martial groups guaranteed neither martial character nor political loyalty. Many of the finest officers of the Indian Army (and its postcolonial successors) came from Bengal, Madras, or Maharashtra, or from castes not usually associated with martial prowess; conversely, many of the key officers in the I.N.A. movement were Punjabi Muslims and Sikhs.

The training given the young Indian officers reinforced their conservative social predilections. Many were initially sent to Sandhurst where they underwent the same course as the British. Later, when this became politically and administratively impractical, Indians were given an even more rigorous military education at the Indian Military Academy (I.M.A.) in Dehra Dun.[22] This education stressed loyalty to the regiment, to the officer corps, to the king, and to the viceroy. Once in their units this process of formal and informal socialization was continued. Young Indian officers were frequently reminded of their obligations and duties in various service courses and, above all, through the institution of the officers' mess. By and large this socialization process was successful. Given the hypocrisy and racism of a number of British officers, it is surprising that few Indian officers defected to the Germans and Japanese during World War II.[23]

While the substance of an officer's education specifically excluded consideration of "political" matters, it must not be thought that Indian Army officers—British or Indian—were in fact apolitical persons. It is true that they were taught to be nonpartisan, favoring neither one political group nor another. The British did not talk about Conservatives or Labor, the Indians did not talk about Gandhi, Nehru, or Bose.[24] But they were all aware that British rule ultimately rested upon the loyalty of an army almost entirely Indian in composition. Further, the Indian Army had always been used for a variety of political tasks, ranging from de facto governance of frontier regions to internal security.

The present generation of Indian military leadership was recruited, trained, and commissioned during the hectic days of World War II.[25] However, like most of their predecessors, they suppressed whatever political feelings they had and served the British well. Young political activists of that period were in the Congress or various underground and revolutionary groups, fighting the British, but Indians in the military performed no acts of revolution or insurrection (with the exception of those who had been captured by the Japanese and joined the I.N.A.). Unlike Burma, Indonesia, Algeria, and China, India achieved its freedom without an armed struggle and without the assistance of the military, factors which made it possible later to establish strong civilian control.

The Military in Independent India: Constraint and Restraint

As in other areas of public life, the leaders of an independent India sought to reshape for their own purposes what the British had left. Rejecting the model of a radical, politically attentive military on the one hand, and the Gandhian alternative on the other, the Indian leadership quietly achieved their central objective of establishing firm, effective control over the military. While Nehru and his political and administrative colleagues have been faulted for their decisions in agricultural and industrial policy or population control, they were flawless in their choice of constitutional, administrative, and political restaints on the military. In fact, no other new nation has established as effective a system of civilian control, and in many established democracies the military wield considerably more power than they do in India. Since virtually the entire network of restraints, controls, and manipulative devices remains intact today, and since the network would seem to suit the interests of both the military and Mrs. Gandhi, it is worth careful examination.

Constitutional and legal constraints. Following British practice, formal control over the military rests in the monarch-substitute, the President, although de facto control is exercised by the elected Prime Minister and cabinet.[26] Under the constitution the defense of India is reserved exclusively to the central government, and no Indian state has ever seriously contemplated the development of even a paramilitary force without union permission. There is no opportunity in the system for ambitious officers to create their own satrapy outside central government supervision. This fact alone makes meaningless any direct comparison of post-1947 India with pre-1949 China. India will not readily fall victim to warlordism or to the rivalries of competing armies, unless some unimaginable catastrophe were to destroy the cohesion of the Indian military.

To ensure dominance of civilians, steps were taken after independence to create a balance of power among the three armed services. Under the British, the Indian Army was numerically and politically more powerful than the Royal Indian Air Force and Royal Indian Navy combined. The commander-in-chief of the army had a special advisory function vis-a-vis the government of India, and was a member of the cabinet. Not only did the Indian government make the three services legally equal after independence, it has exaggerated the relative influence and power of the chiefs of the two weaker services—the air force and the navy—at the expense of the numerically dominant army. The three service heads are all designated chiefs of staff, and the Indian government abolished the position of commander-in chief, held by the senior-most Indian Army general, whose responsibilities included all three services. Further, the chairman of the Chiefs of Staff Committee is always the officer with the longest period of tenure, which has often been an air force or navy officer.[27] In brief, this has meant a partial redress of the natural imbalance between the army chief and the heads of the two other services, providing civilian leadership with substantial leverage over the army.

Structural and organizational factors. Recruitment to the officer corps in India is entirely on the basis of standardized written and oral examinations: there are no formal regional, class, or caste quotas or restrictions. However, the medium in which the recruitment and examination process takes place is the English language; and, since it is a volunteer military, the services must select from those who choose to apply. These two factors have led to an officer corps somewhat unrepresentative in terms of class and regional origins, being skewed toward an urban and northern recruitment base.[28] Officer candidates are trained via the English language, and are encouraged to adopt a life-style and professional environment closely resembling that of the Indian Army of forty years ago, complete with swagger sticks and British accents.[29] All of this, which has often been criticized in Parliament as being un-Indian, serves to encourage differences between the officer and his Indian environment, making it difficult for him to build alliances across the culture gap.

Even more surely to forestall the development of monolithic power in the army, some attention has apparently been given to ensuring that officers from "nonmartial" regions of India are overrepresented in higher commands, especially the position chief of the army staff (COAS). No caste, region, or religion, even the numerically dominant Punjabi Hindus and Sikhs, can hold a proprietary view of any position with the Indian Army.[30]

When senior positions do open up there is a natural amount of lobbying on the part of various groups within the army, but final decisions are made by civilians, although custom has usually been that the senior-most general becomes COAS. Recently, to control promotions, the tour of duty of two serving chiefs was extended. This meant that several experienced officers reached retirement age without opportunity for promotion, ultimately paving the way for the promotion of Lietuenant General T. N. Raina. The fact that Raina is a Kashmiri Brahmin (and the two superseded officers had excellent credentials) has led to some speculation about Mrs. Gandhi's motives. The episode was reminiscent, to many, of the rapid promotions given to B. N. Kaul (another Kashmiri Brahmin) by Krishna Menon and Nehru in the years and months just before the Chinese-Indian conflict of 1962. These promotions created an uproar in the Indian Army, the press, and Parliament.[31]

A structural factor that has enhanced civilian control has been the large size and moderate sophistication of the Indian military.[32] This has meant that Indian officers can be trained almost entirely within India itself, the only exceptions being routine exchange programs or training in very specialized or advanced equipment.[33] Thus, an Indian military career is highly self-contained, and most officers, whatever their service, encounter military officers from major powers. This accords with express government policy. Indian civilians did not miss the point that the ties Pakistani officers had to the American military were used as a resource in their attempt to gain control of the state. Foreign military personnel consequently find it difficult to mix with Indian officers except on the most superficial basis; this was true for Americans even during the period when the United States was providing substantial amounts of military equipment to India (1962-65).[34] There have been strong public protests over brief contacts between Indian and Pakistani generals during border demarcation talks. Indian civilian officials are very sensitive about the entire issue: they fear "informal penetration" of their own system through military links and the subsequent political contamination of their own officers.

This operational deployment also has some impact upon the military's potential for political intervention. On the crudest level the division of the Indian Army into four major regional commands, each in turn divided into areas and subareas,[35] would seem to be an obstacle to a coup. No single regional command contains a preponderance of armed forces; a coup would require collusion of all four regional commanders (officers of lieutenant-general rank). Further, there are major cities located within each command, even within the Southern Command, which is primarily a training organization. Were any one or two regional commanders to continue their support of a particular government they could serve as regional foci of resistance to the coup, and the military would immediately be confronted with a civil war. This might even occur were one or two area or subarea commanders to refuse to go along with a coup.

One additional feature of the military's structure is worth noting. Air force and navy units are controlled by their respective headquarters, and there is no unified military command structure in India. The three service heads are chiefs of their respective service staffs. As we have noted, they stand in rough equality to each other and meet together, with collective responsibility, as the Chiefs of Staff Committee. There is no substantial "Joint Chiefs" organization or staff, as in the United States, nor is there a supreme head of this committee who can act on behalf of all three services. This problem has been discussed in Indian military circles for years, although exclusively in military terms.[36] However, it might well be that the numerous proposals that have been made to streamline the command structure at the center have been sidetracked by civilians because of the political implications outlined above. The present system certainly does enable civilians to play a major role in the decision-making process, and makes it difficult for the military to act in unison against civilian authority. A comprehensive system of checks and balances, dividing power against itself horizontally and vertically, is as evident in the Indian military as in the American federal constitution. The intent was the same: to contain power deemed dangerous.

Foreign Policy and the Direction of War

India has been involved in armed conflict from the first days of independence: three wars with Pakistan, one with China, military intervention in Hyderabad and Goa. Of these conflicts, one remains of overwhelming importance for the Indian military, from the perspective of their relationship with civilian authority. The war with China still rankles: in it the Indian Army suffered a dramatic and humiliating defeat, and Indian civilians played a major—if not dominant—role in the events which led to that defeat. From the army's point of view they were betrayed by civilian leaders (and a few of their own generals who collaborated with such civilians), a betrayal that will not be forgiven save with the passage of time and the retirement of the participants who remember the events of 1959-62.[37]

From 1965 onward the Indian military have openly discussed the management of succeeding wars in comparison with the 1962 fiasco. Their overwhelming concern is twofold: that there be adequate preparation for war, and that the conduct of the war be left to the generals, subject to stated political objectives. Thus, the Indian military see the conduct of war in terms of a fairly clear-cut division of responsibility: politicians and civil servants provide the needed materials and set reasonable goals; the military are left to win the war according to their best professional judgment.[38]

The resource base of the Indian military is bifurcated: while India's own ordnance factories produce many varieties of weapons, most of these have imported components, and many vital weapons are manufactured abroad (as are all of Pakistan's advanced weapons systems).[39] This heavy reliance on foreign sources in both India and Pakistan has meant that these two states' foreign policies are oriented toward actual or potential weapons suppliers.[40] In Pakistan one important factor in domestic politics has always been the ties a particular individual or group has to a potential arms supplier; this was the case with both Ayub (the United States) and Z. A. Bhutto (the United States and China). Until now, in contrast, ties with a potential arms source have not been a major factor in Indian politics. The Indian military have not developed links to a particular arms supplier. While Indian officers were said in the 1960s to be partial to Western-manufactured aircraft and tanks, they apparently raised no objection to the creation of a heavy dependency on Soviet and Czech sources for these weapons. Nor, in fact, is there any evidence that association with Eastern European arms suppliers has made the Indian military "pro-Soviet" in any ideologically meaningful sense. It must be concluded that from a political point of view the development of an extensive arms industry within India has lessened the country's international dependency, although the quality/cost ratio of some weapons indigenously produced does not compare favorably with that of weapons imported or even indigenously manufactured under foreign license.[41]

The conflict with the Chinese represented far more than a simple defeat to the Indian Army. In the North East Frontier Agency (NEFA) whole units simply disintegrated. These units—some of brigade strength—had not been crushed by superior forces or equipment in a direct confrontation; they were psychologically disarmed before they ever saw the enemy.[42] The worst possible fate—to a military man—had overtaken the Indian Army in the NEFA. At each level there was a loss of confidence in superiors, and a sense of chaos and impending disaster swept down through the ranks.

The origins of this chaos are clear. There were important differences in strategy and tactics among Nehru, Krishna Menon, the bulk of the military leadership, civilian intelligence, and a new breed of so-called political generals.[43] An attempt to play a game of positional chess with the Chinese backfired, and yet the politicians could not bring themselves to completely hand over conduct of the war to the military (who favored large-scale retreat into India proper). The official military enquiry into the NEFA disaster concluded that there were grave mistakes made at the highest levels of the decision-making process, with civilian and military fully sharing the blame.[44]

From their perspective, the military feel that the 1965 war

with Pakistan demonstrated that they had largely overcome most of the inadequacies of 1962. The Indian Army showed little genuine military inspiration, but there were no serious lapses, and large numbers of officers died in combat (a standard measure of military machismo). From their point of view the brightest side of the 1965 war was the relative freedom of action that they were given by the prime minister, Lal Bahadur Shastri.[45] Shastri was a complete naïf in military matters, and none of his political colleagues fancied themselves as fledgling field marshals.

The army has been even more exultant over their skillfull invasion of East Pakistan in December 1971.[46] The generals who planned and led that invasion have been lionized, receiving full credit from civilian officials for their management of the war.

If there were any difficulties in the Bangladesh operation, they occurred earlier.   There is evidence to indicate that the Indian Army had been deeply involved in supporting Mukhti Bahini guerrillas for several months before the final invasion.[47] There were a number of casualties during that phase of the struggle, and before the final invasion came it appeared that the war might drag on for months or years at a low but bloody level. Would the Indian Army leadership have tolerated such losses for very much longer? Would they have agreed to keep large numbers of troops tied up on the East Pakistan border indefinitely? One suspects that their joy in victory was enhanced by relief that their involvement in a nasty and costly guerrilla struggle was over.

Aid to the Civil

Second only in importance to the external defense function, the military in India have a responsibility which is, in their argot, called "aid to the civil." Such activities as assistance during natural calamity and famine relief (including air dropping of food to isolated villages) fall in this category.[48] The Indian armed forces welcome such challenges, recognizing that they are vital and lifesaving as well as good public relations. But they do not welcome other aid-to-the-civil tasks, which are becoming increasingly burdensome. The military have been called upon to maintain essential services (telephones, roads, railways, power) during political and economic disturbances, indirectly serving as strikebreakers. Even more difficult and onerous are the requests to restore law and order. This aspect of aid to the civil has a long and inglorious history, and is worthy of detailed analysis, for it has powerful political implications.

The Indian Army still bears visible traces of its colonial heritage in the location and character of the military cantonments. These were deliberately sited on the outskirts of major population centers and insulated from local political control (they still have separate governments, statutes, and regulations).[49] The cantonment isolates the military from civilian society, but its proximity to that society permits rapid intervention.

This intervention is scrupulously controlled by statute and regulation. The military must obey any request for assistance from the highest ranking magistrate present at the scene. The commanding officer cannot refuse to give aid, "but the action he takes in pursuance of meeting this requisition is left to his sole discretion."[50] Once authority has been transferred to the military commander, a civilian magistrate cannot issue orders to the military or order that fire be opened. But the magistrate *can* make the determination when military assistance is no longer required, and the military officer in command must refrain from further action, except to protect his own troops. Such troops, when engaged in the restoration of civilian authority, are required to use the minumum necessary force.

This system has proven workable over the years, with only a few notorious exceptions such as Jallianwala Bagh. However, it was designed to handle local disturbances. In the years since independence the number of civil disturbances seems to have increased dramatically, and in the period 1961-1970 the army was called out on 476 occasions to restore order.[51] There is no data available as to the nature of these disturbances, the magnitude of the army's efforts, or the duration of what is in effect martial law. What we do know, however, is that the use of the army has expanded far beyond the historical, localized aid-to-the-civil role. Whole states have been blanketed by a variety of security forces (including the army) after the imposition of president's rule. Some states have been literally occupied by the military for two decades (Kashmir, Nagaland, Mizoram), although these are special cases, with either disputed borders or active guerrilla movements.[52]

What is startling about the army's internal security role is that it continues despite a dramatic increase in the size and quality of police and paramilitary forces. The Public Accounts Committee of Parliament noted in 1974 that expenditures on police forces had increased by fifty-two times since independence and had doubled between 1969 and 1971.[53] Most of the increase took place in such units as the Border Security Force, Indo-Tibetan Force, and Central Reserve Police, all organized along paramilitary lines, housed in barracks, subject to military discipline, and often commanded and manned by ex-army personnel.

One clear-cut lesson of Pakistan's experience was that excessive or ill-conceived aid-to-the-civil operations will be resisted by the military and may become a cause for their displacement of civilian rule.[54] This lesson was not lost upon the Indian officials most responsible for such matters.

It is certain that the expansion of the police apparatus was partly intended to lessen the need for regular Indian Army units to come to the aid of the civil, although it also gives the central government an enhanced capacity for coercion. There remain a number of points of conflict. The military are obsessed with the need to retain their own identity, separate from that of the police. This sense of separateness extends to the color of uniforms the police and the military wear, as well as to the superior armament of the military.[55] Above all, the military resist being divided into "penny-packet," police-size units; they usually insist on retaining their regular military formations.

The basis for this desire to distinguish themselves from the police forces is quite pragmatic. The military are not called in to restore order unless the police themselves have failed in this task. To increase their effectiveness, they wish to demonstrate that they are qualitatively different from the police, and that they are prepared to use more potent means. Often, the mere rumor or sight of military units is enough to restore order.

One recent and momentous incident deserves special mention. On May 21, 1973, the Indian Army was called in to disarm and relieve the Provincial Armed Constabulary (P.A.C.) in Uttar Pradesh. In the process, it suffered substantial numbers of casualties. The P.A.C. had rebelled, joining with the students that they had been sent to quell. The source of that rebellion were very poor pay and working conditions, the development of union-type organizations within the police (banned by law), and an apparent weakness on the part of the politicians.[56] Except for minor police protests in Delhi and Calcutta, this had been only the second time since 1857 that a military or police force had rebelled in India.[57] The significance of the rebellion lies not only in what it tells us about the deterioration of the morale of the police and paramilitary forces and the difficulty of maintaining large numbers of such forces, but in the fact that it occurred in the Hindi heartland area. Threats and disturbances in this area are likely to have a greater impact on the central government than similar outbreaks in states more distant from New Delhi.

A by-product of the army's periodic excursions in the law-and-order business is that regional commanders are required to develop a profound knowledge of local political, religious, and economic problems. Contacts with local adminstrators are important, but so are these with local political parties and religious leaders, the heads of National Cadet Corps units, students, and village and labor leaders.[58] Such groups are most likely to be involved in any civil disorder, and the military try to maintain their own channels of communication with them. It is not unusual to encounter an army officer who, in one breath, disclaims all knowledge of or interest in politics, but in the next, outlines with great perception the local balance of political forces and likely sources of instability.

Realization of Civilian Control

While many ex-colonial states attempted to impose civilian control over the military, few have been able to realize this objective. Such control requires, in the long run, civilian authorities who are not only determined to control the military, but are competent to do so. India has been fortunate in possessing a corps of civilian administrators and politicians who have built upon and strengthened the pattern of civilian control established during the last thirty years of British rule.

As before, fiscal responsibility is strictly within civilian hands via the Finance and Defense ministries. The military are routinely called upon to account to civilian administrators for the smallest deviation from budgetary allocations. (Perhaps apocryphally, military officers cite the example of the brigade commander who was asked why his unit exceeded its routine ammunition allocation—during the 1965 war with Pakistan.) More important, all requests for new weapons, force expansion, and structural adjustments are routinely evaluated by civilian bureaucrats from the very earliest stages of the decision-making process.[59] The general competence and intelligence of these civilians is high. While they are outnumbered by their military counterparts, they can draw upon an extraordinarily rich tradition of civilian administrative control.

This raises the fundamental question of the capacity of non-military elites to supervise and dominate in that hazy area where civilian and military interests overlap. Not only must the military be taught that civilian control is the norm, but civilians must demonstrate that they are effective. The original Clausewitzian justification of civilian control was, in fact, that political considerations were so important in war that the purely military outlook was inadequate.[60] It is never the absolute magnitude of an external or internal crisis that alone determines a realignment of political forces in a state, but the relationship of such a crisis to the will and determination of key elites. In a state with a vigorous and alert political elite—and, as in India, an attentive civilian administrative cadre—quite severe setbacks will be tolerated by the military if they have confidence in the ultimate good judgment of civilian leadership. However, quite trivial incidents can trigger off a coup in systems where such confidence and respect are lacking. Paraphrasing the aphorism, leadership must not only be competent, it must be seen to be competent.

Since the late 1950s there has been a clear-cut pattern in the appointment of the minister of defense, one of the most sensitive and important positions in the Indian government. Krishna Menon, appointed minister in 1957, was one of Nehru's most trusted associates. Menon's successors have shared this characteristic, especially under Mrs. Gandhi. Her appointees (Jagjivan Ram and Swaran Singh) have been her political supporters; and where there has been an indication that support has wavered (as in the recent case of Swaran Singh), they have been replaced. Her most recent appointee, Bansi Lal (a man of no apparent expertise or interest in defense matters), is one of Mrs. Gandhi's most fervent and useful political allies. It remains to be seen whether Lal will be trusted with such politically sensitive decisions as the promotion and assignment of senior military officers.[61] If a parallel situation is relevant, these decisions may be made by the prime minister's Secretariat (under Mrs.

Gandhi's personal control), just as decisions about the promotion and assignment of senior civil servants were shifted from the Home Ministry to the Secretariat.

Obedience and Authority

The above discussion leads us directly to what must be speculative conclusions about the relationship of the military to the momentous political changes occurring in India today. Such conclusions are based upon our knowledge of the nature of the Indian military and the character of Indian politics, and must be at a general level of analysis.

Ultimately, the question of whether or not the military will intervene in the current situation is decided inside the minds of a set of officers. It cannot be reduced to a formula. But it centers on a calculation of gains vs. losses.[62] The military compare the costs and gains of acquiescing in an ongoing system with the costs and gains of meddling in it, or even transforming it. A professional officer corps is not immune to temptation, but the kinds of issues and pressures that will lead it to intervene are different from those that tempt a politicized military establishment. We can therefore rule out a wave of sympathy with J. P. Narayan, the Jan Sangh, or the CPM propelling the Indian military to action against Mrs. Gandhi; we could probably do so even if the opposition groups were less ideologically splintered or more promilitary than they are.

There is little doubt that to the extent that they have recalculated the costs and gains associated with intervention the Indian military have at least temporarily rejected greater political involvement. They will continue to see themselves as outside of politics, neither supporting nor opposing the present government, content to carry out their assigned military tasks.

However, we do not believe that the present situation is of no interest to the military. Their concerns probably lie in three areas, each of profound importance to the professional soldier: the legitimacy of central authority, the nature of the challenge to that authority (and to the federal principles upon which India is built), and the potential for conflict between Mrs. Gandhi's rule and the values and goals of the officer corps.

The legitimacy of authority. When J. P. Narayan called upon the military to disobey "illegal" orders, he was appealing to the military to examine the nature of Mrs. Gandhi's authority—and to reject it as illegitimate. For a soldier, the accusation and its implications are profoundly disturbing. Armies function at the margin of moral behavior: they willingly perform acts that are, in any civil society, questionable, the more so if performed against one's fellow citizens. The legitimation of such behavior is therefore essential, and if the institution that performs the legitimation function for the military is itself called into doubt, the military also becomes suspect.[63] Thus when Mrs. Gandhi stresses her popular mandate, the illegitimate tactics of the opposition, and her adherence to constitutional proprieties, she has a clear purpose in mind: to persuade the military (and, of course, other bureaucracies and groups) that her rule *remains* legitimate and that their obedience to her authority is morally as well as pragmatically correct. In such circumstances, the military are told, nothing really important has changed. On their part, the military are probably eager to hear such reasurrances. Hardly devoted to civil liberties, parliamentary niceties, or a free and open press, they are undoubtedly willing to ignore Mrs. Gandhi's zestful exercise of power as long as she can make a reasonable claim to legitimacy and as long as there are no more attractive political alternatives. It is difficult to carry our analysis much further. Presumably, if the Indian constitution were rewritten to create a presidential form of government the military would acquiesce—again, not having much of a political alternative, and certainly not tempted to seize power themselves. However, if such a transformation of the constitution were perceived as having been done simply to enhance the power of a single individual, or if Mrs. Gandhi's arguments about the legitimacy of her recent actions begin to wear thin, one significant barrier to military intervention would be removed. It may have been weakened already.

The challenge to authority. The other side of the legitimacy coin is the nature of the challenge to civilian authority. The military in any state, including India, will maintain their obedience to civilian authority which lacks legitimacy if they neither wish nor are able to seize power themselves or if civilian alternatives are unpromising. The latter point is worth considerable emphasis.

The Indian military have always identified themselves with national, all-Indian perspectives and images.[64] They are, in fact, a truly national institution in India, as representative as and yet more unified than the civil services. In the military, Indians from all castes, regions, linguistic groups, and classes work in extraordinary harmony and unity. The officer corps, drawn from all over India but speaking a common language, are particularly sensitive to the difficulties and problems encountered in maintaining an all-India organization, but are not less proud to have done so since independence.

Because they and their troops are drawn from the entire nation, and because they are reliant upon that entire nation for material, transportation, funding, and moral support, the officer corps are highly sensitive to regional disputes and conflicts which threaten the integrity of the state. While they may look upon a particular regional demand as just or legitimate, they tend to support the central government in generally opposing regional pressures for autonomy or greater independence.[65] Their attitude toward caste-based or ideological demands is similar: while conceding the occasional just claim, their perspective is unshakably that of New Delhi.

Although some of the groups arrayed in opposition to Mrs. Gandhi are stridently promilitary, even these (such as the Jan Sangh) have a pronounced regional base. And Gandhian elements in the opposition are hardly regarded as promilitary. Some opposition groups favor a reconciliation with the Chinese, a position still unacceptable to many officers. Thus, from the military's point of view, the very groups that attack Mrs. Gandhi's authority lack the credentials themselves to assume power. Were a significant challenge to her authority to develop from within her own ranks, this situation might change. Both Y. B. Chavan and Jagjivan Ram, perennially mentioned as alternatives to Mrs. Gandhi, are "national" leaders in the sense that the military can understand and appreciate, but they—and others—appears to have been effectively neutralized by her.

The challenge from authority. A third area of strain in the civil-military balance might be the growth of conflict between the military and the present leadership itself. If a military organization is confronted with tension between the roles it is asked to perform or if there are discontinuities between its self-perceived status and role demands, it will seriously question civil authority regardless of the latter's legitimacy. Much of this occurred in Pakistan, and more recently, Bangladesh, when the military were in each case asked to carry out distasteful aid-to-the-civil tasks without the full authority to see them to their conclusion.[66] In Bangladesh, the military's position was further compromised by the growth of a highly politicized paramilitary force, the Rakhi Bahini.[67]

In view of the skill and intelligence with which military matters have been handled in India since independence, we would not expect such developments to occur there. Attempts to create a political youth corps were as unsuccessful as attempts to perpetuate the Indian National Army.[68] Nor is Mrs. Gandhi likely to ask the military to engage in civic action tasks, or even to subscribe to her ideological program, except in the most general way. In terms of her political interests, a neutral and politically inert military is inadequate.

However, strains might develop if the army is asked to perform quasi-military tasks without adequate resources, or without a clear termination date. It has already been engaged in a sometimes brutal campaign against Naga rebels for many years, but has been sharply restrained in the means it may employ.[69] This has been a difficult if tolerable situation because of the preponderance of Indian forces vis-a-vis the Naga rebels, but one can envision a similar situation occurring elsewhere on a much larger scale.

As I wrote several years ago, the deterioration of Bangladesh politics may force a new Indian intervention.[70] A rise in border incidents, large numbers of refugees, a stridently anti-Indian regime in Dacca, or an impending civil war are all conditions that could prompt it, especially if they were coupled with public pressure on the Indian leadership for "action."[71] Yet, as the Indian leadership knows, any intervention is likely to vastly complicate the situation and may not succeed. The burden of such intervention would fall upon the shoulders of the military, and in this case they are not likely to be equal to the task. There will be no clear-cut "enemy" forces, but only a vast, resentful, and uncooperative population. Indian military power might be sufficient to temporarily tip the balance of power in Dacca, but it can never rule Bangladesh for any length of time without deteriorating into a glorified occupation police force. Thus, unless involvement in Bangladesh were limited in time and scope, severe conflict between the military leadership and their civilian masters would be bound to arise, perhaps with momentous consequences.

If India can avoid involvement in such a Vietnam-like situation, the only likely area of disagreement between the military and Mrs. Gandhi's government will be in budgets and weapons, traditional arenas of conflict. Such disagreement will be especially likely if Mrs. Gandhi is serious about her development plans and were to seek substantial new resources. She could not then overlook the burden of defense spending that India has carried for over a dozen years.[72] But because of the rise in prices and a revision of military pay scales, the defense budget (which has grown slowly in recent years) probably cannot sustain present force levels, a problem India has in common with the United States. Additionally, pressures are mounting from the military for replacement of obsolete weapons systems and for acquisitions (such as high-performance attack planes) to fill in certain glaring gaps.[73] These are deficiencies that are obvious and clear, and cannot be balanced by continued development of the nuclear program. In fact, were India to "go nuclear" militarily, the experience of other nations seems to indicate that no less attention could be given to nonnuclear weapons systems.[74]

Clearly, the one way out of pressures for increased defense spending would be to redefine Indian foreign and security policy requirements. Some Indian observers have suggested that reconciliation with China would enable India to maintain a smaller military.[75] Here, Mrs. Gandhi and the military would seem to have a common interest in *not* making major changes in present Indian security policy: she for foreign policy and domestic political reasons (antipathy to the People's Republic of China is a precondition for the Soviet tie), the military because of their distrust of the Chinese and a desire to maintain as large and as powerful a force as possible.

THE MOST LIKELY FUTURE

Assuming the continuation of the political pattern established after June 1975, it is possible to project the likely role of the military in Indira Gandhi's India. Other scenarios could be written (some features of them have been touched on earlier in this chapter), but the following is the most likely future.[76]

1. The relative power of the military will be enhanced, if only because other centers of power and influence in Indian political life have been destroyed or reduced in stature. As we have argued, it is highly unlikely that the full potential of military

power will be exercised, but it will become more visible, and politically more sensitive. In brief, the military find themselves to be one of the few giants left and inevitably they will become more political, at least in the eyes of others.

2. The officer corps do not yet have a proper model for a coup, and any enhanced political involvement on their part is likely to be indirect or subtle. The catastrophic examples of Pakistan and Bangladesh in recent years have convinced the Indian military not only that a coup would be difficult to carry off under Indian conditions but that military rule is not likely to be successful.

3. Subversion of the military by opposition groups is not likely to be successful unless economic and security conditions deteriorate considerably.

4. The ties between the military and Mrs. Gandhi's regime will become more explicit. As it becomes clearer to everyone that the military comprise one of the few genuinely important institutions in India with some autonomy and integrity, the connection between their tacit support of Mrs. Gandhi and her continuation in power will be perceived by everyone (she has certainly made the connection, as indicated by her public remarks.) As in other aspects of her rule, this will represent a return to an arrangement once encountered in British India.

5. Greater dependence on the military, even if such dependence remains implicit, will weaken Mrs. Gandhi's bargaining position vis-a-vis requests for weapons, funds, and symbolic rewards. If India follows the pattern established in a number of other states, this will be the price to pay for military subservience, and it is likely that Mrs. Gandhi will be willing to pay it. Defense budgets are not likely to decline, and ties to foreign weapons sources will remain important.

6. The military will remain content with this arrangement. Personally and as professionals they will be well treated, and there will be no difficulty in rationalizing away any political excesses committed by the government. This situation will be stable as long as no attempt is made to interfere in what the officer corps regard as their natural sphere of responsibility, and as long as the army is not deeply involved in quelling domestic disturbances nor is bogged down in a no-win war with one of India's neighbors.

NOTES

1 *Times of India* (Bombay), June 21, 1975.

2 *Hindustan Times* (New Delhi), June 25, 1975.

3 Both quotes are from the *Hindu* (Madras), June 27, 1975. The latter statement comes from Mrs. Gandhi's broadcast to the nation on June 26. After this date press censorship was imposed throughout the country.

4 *Statesman* (New Delhi), Jan. 15, 1967.

5 For discussions of the theoretical context see Morris Janowitz, *Sociology and the Military Establishment*, rev. ed. (New York: Russell Sage Foundation, 1965); and Samuel P. Huntington, *The Soldier and the State* (Cambridge, Mass.: Harvard University Press, 1957).

6 For an elaboration of this see Alfred Vagts, *A History of Militarism: Civilian and Military*, rev. ed. (New York: Meridian, 1959).

7 For the most comprehensive analysis of the meaning of militarism see Stanislav Andreski, *Military Organization and Society* (Berkeley: University of California Press, 1968), pp. 184 ff.

8 *Toward Freedom: The Autobiography of Jawaharlal Nehru* (New York: John Day, 1941), p. 284.

9 Jawaharlal Nehru, *The Discovery of India* (London: Meridan Books, 1969), pp. 478-79.

10 For a collection of Gandhi's thoughts on the subject, including conversations he had with Indian officers, see Mohandas K. Gandhi, *My Non-Violence* (Ahmedabad: Navajivan Publishing House, 1960).

11 Bose left behind a large body of writings and speeches. For collections, see *Crossroads* (Bombay: Asia Publishing House, 1962) or *The Indian Struggle* (Bombay: Asia Publishing House, 1974), both published under the auspices of the Netaji Research Bureau of Calcutta.

12 Seymour M. Lipset, *Political Man* (New York: Doubleday, 1960), pp. 131 ff.

13 Coined by the president of her party in a speech applauding her decision not to resign upon her initial conviction for corrupt election practices. The *Hindu*, June 19, 1975.

14 "Subhas Chandra Bose and the Indian National Army," *Pacific Affairs* 36 (Winter 1963-64): 429.

15 Indian Institute of Public Opinion, *Monthly Public Opinion Surveys* 19, no. 11 (Aug. 1974): 5-6. The phrase "peace bomb" was used by one of the chief scientists in the nuclear explosive program. See N. Seshagiri, *The Bomb!* (New Delhi: Vikas, 1975).

16 A number of retired Indian generals and bureaucrats have published their memoirs or "inside" accounts. For a review of some of the literature see Stephen P. Cohen, "India's China War and After: A Review Article," *Journal of Asian Studies* 30 (Aug. 1971): 847-57.

17 The most important of the many Indian military professional journals, published by the United Services Institution of India (U.S.I.), has an article on the subject in almost every quarterly issue. These have examined such issues as cantonments, the junior commissioned officer (a unique South Asian military rank), politics in the military, and the need to reconcile military practices with ideological and social developments in India.

18 For an explicit comparison see Stephen P. Cohen, *Arms and Politics in Bangladesh, India, and Pakistan* (Buffalo, N.Y.: SUNY Council on International Studies, Special Study no. 49, 1973).

19 For a contemporary Indian study by a senior Indian Civil Service official, see Nagendra Singh, *The Theory of Force and Organization of Defense in Indian Constitutional History* (Bombay: Asia Publishing House, 1969).

20 Stephen P. Cohen, *The Indian Army* (Berkeley: University of California, 1971), chap. 5.

21 Ibid., pp. 117-18.

22 This is a judgment of a number of British and Indian Officers who had a chance to observe the products of both Sandhurst and the I.M.A., and is supported by internal studies of battle performance in World War II.

23 Cohen, *The Indian Army*, pp. 152 ff.

24 A number of retired Indian generals have discussed the moral dilemmas of serving a foreign master, most notably B. M. Kaul, *The Untold Story* (Bombay: Allied Publishers, 1967), part 1, and K. S. Thimayya. For the latter see Humphrey Evans, *Thimayya of India* (New York: Harcourt Brace, 1960), pp. 180-81.

25 The most recent head of the Indian Army (T. N. Raina) received an emergency commission in 1942 after attending college. Despite his rudimentary military training he performed with distinction in World War II and several subsequent wars.

26 The best guide to the organizational and legal frameworks in which the military function in India is A. L. Venkateshwaran, *Defense Organization in India* (New Delhi: India, Publications Division, 1967). Although ostensibly a popular history of defense issues, it is clearly designed to serve as a handbook for civilian bureaucrats who must deal with the military.

27 Ibid.; and Maharaj K. Chopra, *India: The Search for Power* (Bombay: Lalvani, 1969).

28 Exact figures for officer recruitment are unavailable. This judgment is based upon an examination of casualty figures in various wars, government statements, and visits to various Indian military establishments.

29 For a critical discussion of the incongruity of some of the Indian Army's British and authoritarian traditions, including the swagger stick, see Group Captain K. D. Singh, "Coercion to Coaction," U.S.I. *Journal* 102 (July-Sept. 1972): 236-53.

30 Of the Indian COASs since independence there have been two Coorgis (Cariappa, 1949-53, and Thimayya, 1957-61), two Tamils (Shrinagesh, 1955-57, and Kumaramangalam, 1966-69), a Rajput From Gujarat (Maharaj Rajendra Sinhji, 1953-55), a Punjabi Hindu (Thapar, 1961-62), a Bengali (Chaudhuri, 1962-66), a Parsi (Maneckshaw, 1969-73), a Maharashtrian (Bewoor, 1973-75), and a Kashmiri (Raina, 1975-present). Thus, only Thapar came from the region that supplies the most soldiers and has a historic connection with the Indian Army. There has never been a Sikh COAS.

31 For a summary of Raina's career see the article by "M.S" in *Illustrated Weekly of India* (Bombay), June 8, 1975. For details about the earlier controversies see Lorne Kavic, *India's Quest for Security* (Berkeley: University of California Press, 1967), pp. 154 ff.

32 A recent government press release boasts that India now has the world's fourth-largest army, fifth- or sixth-largest air force and eighth- or ninth-largest navy. *Hindustan Times*, Oct. 31, 1975.

33 The latter has usually been for the purpose of training in advanced or very new equipment acquired from abroad—most recently from the Soviet Union. The Indian armed forces also routinely train a large number of foreign officers and technicians, particularly from Nepal, Bangladesh, and various Middle Eastern countries.

34 Figures on foreign military assistance to India can be found in U.S. Arms Control and Disarmament Agency, *World Military Expenditures and Arms Trade, 1963-73* (Washington: U.S. Government Printing Office, 1974).

35 For a partial description, see Venkateshwaran, *Defense Organization in India*, and some of the annual *Reports* of the Ministry of Defense. A more comprehensive and technical handbook is Brig. Rajendra Singh, *Organization and Administration in the Indian Army* (New Delhi: Army Educational Stores, various editions).

36 For example, Col. R. Rama Rao (ret.), "Defense Planning and Preparations—New Imperatives," U.S.I. *Journal* 102 (Jan.-March 1972): 3-12.

37 The book that best conveys the frustration and anger of those Indian officers involved in the 1962 war is Brig. John P. Dalvi, *Himalayan Blunder*

(Bombay: Thacker, 1969). Dalvi's account is based upon his own experiences. More recently, see Brig. J. Nazareth, "If We Rest We Rust," U.S.I. *Journal* 102 (July-Sept. 1972): 231 ff.

38 This works well when, as in 1971, there is sufficient time for the military to digest what is expected of them and for political leaders to learn what is within the realm of military feasibility. It does not work well when war arises suddenly or no decisive outcome can be expected.

39 K. Subrahmanyam, until recently the director of the Institute of Defense Studies and Analyses, has written perceptively of the problem from an Indian point of view. See his *Perspectives in Defense Planning* (New Delhi: Abhinav, 1972).

40 For a recent evaluation of the militarization of Indian and Pakistan foreign policy see Stephen P. Cohen, "Security Issues in South Asia," *Asian Survey* 15 (March 1975): 203-15.

41 India has yet to produce an adequate high-performance fighter-bomber, a reliable air transport, or tanks in adequate numbers. But even some imported systems, such as the Sukhoi 7, seem to be very bad bargains. For a recent critical evaluation of the entire arms procurement problem by a former senior official in the Ministry of Defense, see V. Shankar, "Defense Needs of India," U.S.I. *Journal* 104 (Jan.-March 1974): 1-6.

42 See Dalvi, *Himalayan Blunder*, and Lt. Gen. B. M. Kaul, *The Untold Story* (New Delhi: Allied, 1967). Kaul, one of those generals most responsible for the debacle, once admitted to this writer (in 1965) that he still could not figure out why the Chinese had attacked.

43 "The manner in which the army was emasculated by furthering the cause of careers of political generals and breaking competent ones, in the years which culminated in our humiliating defeat in 1962, is a striking example" of the interference of politicians, and "is a weakness . . . apt to reoccur in a democracy such as ours." Nazareth, "If We Rest We Rust," p. 231.

44 Neville Maxwell may have had access to the Henderson-Brooks report, and it might be that document he quoted in *India's China War* (London: Jonathan Cape, 1970). For a full discussion see Cohen, "India's China War and After."

45 This separation of civil and military authority has been vigorously criticized by a former secretary in the Ministry of Defense, P. V. R. Rao. See his *Defense Without Drift* (Bombay: Popular Prakashan, 1970).

46 Exemplified by Maj. Gen. D. K. Palit (ret.), *The Lightning Campaign: The Indo-Pakistan War, 1971* (New Delhi: Thomson Press, 1972).

47 There are, of course, only oblique references to this in the Indian literature, but Pakistani authors claim that the Indian-supported guerrilla struggle was proving ineffective. For an authoritative Pakistani perspective see

Maj. Gen. Fazal Muqeem Khan (ret.), *Pakistan's Crisis in Leadership* (Islamabad: National Book Foundation, 1973). Khan is now secretary in the Pakistan Ministry of Defense. The mainstream of Indian military thought has always given guerrilla warfare a very low priority, and it would not be surprising to discover that their guerrilla campaign was ineffective.

[48] Every year the Ministry of Defense lists such activities. They are also extensively covered in the Indian press and the military's own popular weekly magazine, *Sainik Samachar*, published in a dozen languages.

[49] For a thoughtful discussion, see Brig. N. B. Grant, "London Cantonment, Dear," U.S.I. *Journal* 192 (Jan.-March 1972): 40-45.

[50] Maj. Gen. S. K. Sinha, "In Aid of the Civil Power," U.S.I. *Journal* 104 (April-June 1974): 117. This article is a typical example of discussions on aid to the civil that have appeared in Indian professional military journals for almost fifty years, as each generation passes on its knowledge and interpretation of the problem to the next.

[51] Ibid., p. 115.

[52] As any tourist can see, Srinagar resembles an armed camp. Nagaland and Mizoram are off-limits to virtually all outsiders, and the struggle still continues in the region. A recently announced "truce" in Nagaland is one of many that have been concluded in the past fifteen years.

[53] As reported in the *New York Times*, October 24, 1974.

[54] The point was made quite bluntly by G. G. Bewoor, shortly before he became COAS. Bewoor linked Pakistan's defeat in 1971 directly to the Pakistan Army's extensive involvement in "civil works" and "civil administration," warning that the same thing could happen in India if the military were diverted from its primary defense role. *Times of India*, Sept. 10, 1972.

[55] Sinha claims that the Indian Army chose to retain olive green after World War II so that they would not be mistaken for the police, who wore Khaki. "In Aid of the Civil Power," p. 116.

[56] For one brief study of the event see A. D. Pandit, "Uttar Pradesh: The Roots of the P. A. C. Mutiny," in Indian Institute of Public Opinion, *Monthly Public Opinion Survey* 18, no. 8 (May 1973): 6-8.

[57] The Garhwali Mutiny of 1930 (largely the fault of poor British leadership) was the other incident.

[58] Sinha, "In Aid of the Civil Power," p. 120.

[59] Generally, the military are content with present levels of manpower and technology; they might well be, considering the resources lavished upon them in comparison with other Indian bureaucracies and services. Indeed, much of the poor performance of lethargic sectors of India could be improved simply by an increase in resources unaccompanied by an increase in responsibility.

60 For example, Karl von Clausewitz, *On War* (New York: The Modern Library, 1943), p. 9, and a recent discussion in Bernard Brodie, *War and Politics* (New York: Macmillan, 1973), pp. 1-28.

61 Bansi Lal, appointed minister of defense in late 1975, is a man with no apparent qualifications for the post other than his very close ties to Mrs. Gandhi and her son Sanjay. However, he does come from a state with strong military interests (Haryana) where he was chief minister.

62 In the recent Bangladesh coup, for example, personal considerations interacted in the minds of the professional military with perceptions of threat. For discussion of the intervention problem see S. E. Finer, *The Man on Horseback* (London: Pall Mall Press, 1962); Edward Luttwak, *Coup D'Etat* (London: Penguin Press, 1968); Claude E. Welch, Jr., and Arthur K. Smith, eds., *Military Role and Rule* (Belmont, Calif.: Wadsworth, 1974); and Wilson C. McWilliams, ed., *Garrisons and Government* (San Francisco: Chandler, 1967).

63 In a discussion that exactly anticipates the caution exercised by the Indian military in response to Narayan's call for disobedience of illegal orders, Samuel Huntington writes that the professional soldier, when confronted with this situation, is advised to wait until a decision is reached by the judiciary, "whose function it is to decide such issues" (*The Soldier and the State*, p. 77-78). He describes other situations in which the military must consider disobedience: urgent crises when the judiciary cannot be consulted, immoral orders, militarily impossible orders by ignorant or incompetent civilians.

64 Cohen, *The Indian Army*, pp. 124 ff. The officer corps may not be convinced that *they* are a fully integrated national military. This is the same view that was held by the officer corps in Pakistan, Indonesia, Egypt, and other states that have experienced military takeovers.

65 As far as the military are concerned the politically most sensitive region encompasses the Punjab, Harayana, western Uttar Pradesh, and Delhi, which together supply a disproportionate number of *jawans* and officers. However, these regions are well represented among Mrs. Gandhi's supporters, are among the most prosperous regions in India, and would have little incentive to dream of autonomy or independence even were India to suffer massive dislocations or disruptions.

66 The first full-scale study of the Pakistan Army is Hasan Askari Rizvi, *The Military and Politics in Pakistan* (Lahore: Progressive Publishers, 1974).

67 The coup of August 15, 1975, was led by professional officers who feared that they would be balanced by the Rakhi Bahini and eventually displaced. Their image of the defense requirements of Bangladesh were largely derived from their Pakistani and American training.

68 The "National Discipline Scheme" was run by an ex-I.N.A. general for several years, but was disbanded. Plans to introduce a compulsory National Cadet Corps have not been implemented. If India were to veer toward an authoritarian or totalitarian direction one would expect the revival of such programs. The military might view them with great skepticism.

69 A new truce with the Nagas has been announced (December 1975), but this may be a temporary respite, due to the worsening situation in Bangladesh.

70 Cohen, *Arms and Politics in Bangladesh, India, and Pakistan*, p. 47.

71 Since the Indian media are entirely censored by the government of India itself, such pressure would clearly be part of an orchestrated public relations campaign, and would mean that the government had already decided to intervene.

72 In recent years the defense budget has crept over $2 billion, although on a per capita basis India ranks near the bottom of the scale of all nations. There are few serious analyses of the defense budget in the Indian literature, but see *Vikrant's Defense Diary* (New Delhi), March 1975. A major study of the defense burden of India, in comparison with other states, is Emile Benoit, *Defense and Economic Growth in Developing Countries* (Lexington, Mass.: Lexington Books, 1973).

73 For a blunt assessment see Shankar, "Defense Needs of India," pp. 5 ff.; and Rao, "Defense Planning and Preparations—New Imperatives," pp. 3-12.

74 In fact, the inclusion of nuclear weapons in India's arsenal will require a substantial improvement in conventional forces to increase their mobility and communications facilities, both very expensive items. Pressure for the development of nuclear weapons did not come from the military. For an extremely hawkish evaluation of the Indian nuclear program by a retired naval officer see Ravi Kaul, *India's Nuclear Spin-Off* (Allahabad: Chanyakya, 1974).

75 Shankar, "Defense Needs of India."

76 Speculation about Indian politics has already become closer to kremlinology or Peking-watching than anything else. Indian politics have become a variety of "palace" politics, dominated by rumor, uncertainty, surprise, and secretiveness. We have some degree of confidence in these conclusions with respect to the military as an institution, but as Mrs. Gandhi's political opponents have discovered, predicting her political behavior is infinitely more difficult.

9

Indira Gandhi:
Determined Not to Be Hurt

Henry C. Hart

This chapter opens the question of whether Mrs. Gandhi made the choices she did in June 1975 not wholly to solve her country's problems, nor the prime minister's, but in some significant measure, her own. This is an ambitious undertaking, and deserves a few words of justification.

It is true that Mrs. Gandhi's personality, so far as it has been displayed, does not exhibit those clear evidences of inner conflict that attracted Alexander and Juliette George to study the character of Woodrow Wilson,[1] nor the fleeting exposures of self-pity that raised early doubts about the stoutness of Nixon's character. Her behavior, as we know it, has been that of a person in complete control of herself. Three reasons warrant the attempt, however, to make such predictive observations as we can about her personality. The first is that Mrs. Gandhi's own explanations of her reasons for concentrating power into her hands have not thus far proved enlightening. She first said she did it to save democracy, explicitly *not* to reform the economy; six months later the economic program required it.[2] First, opposition governments in two states demonstrated she was no dictator; later, they became threats to national discipline.[3] Still later her concentration of power was necessary to thwart subversion from abroad.[4] The second consideration is that, just as James Barber gained a measure of credibility for his characterization of President Nixon because he wrote it before Watergate, so also two biographers of Mrs. Gandhi published evaluations of her character as containing dictatorial potential before June 1975.[5] The third reason prompting a character study is the personality cult centered on Mrs. Gandhi's son Sanjay. As we shall observe presently, this cannot be squared with any logic of the pursuit of power for any of Mrs. Gandhi's announced purposes.

Happily, theory in this field has matured to fit our needs in the forty-five years since Harold Lasswell initiated it with *Psychopathology and Politics*.[6] The best developed models of the relation between personality and political leadership no longer presuppose either clinical evidence nor pathological states. Fred Greenstein, starting with the sensible proposition that a political actor's behavoir is a function of his "predispositions" together with environmental influences, sorts predispositions into three categories:

1. The individual's mental and emotional set toward important forces, institutions, and problems in the political landscape—appraisals that bias or guide his more specific attitudes.
2. Patterns of self-other relations, e.g., faith in people or need to dominate.
3. Needs for "ego-defense." These are the ways, though the individual may be little aware of them, by which he manages the inner conflicts developed through the whole of his life span.[7]

These categories of psychological predispositions are, of course, capable of telling us more about the causes of some political behavior than of others. Indira Gandhi in June 1975 approached the extreme case in which psychological predispositions could have been decisive. Two aspects of her situation lead to that conclusion. First, she had by 1975 placed herself so nearly alone at the apex of the system of power that she could remake the institutional constraints ordinarily implied in the word "constitution." She had to reckon with autonomous powers (otherwise, she would not have faced a dilemma). But reckoning boldly, she could redeploy them. Ironic evidence is present in the words of her arch-opponent, Morarji Desai, who, though utterly cynical about her ruthlessness, went on record the night before the police picked him up as concluding she could never arrest him or J. P. Narayan.[8] Institutional constraints upon her, in other words, were ambiguous; her will had correspondingly greater scope. By contrast, Richard Nixon's dilemma of two years earlier was adamantine.[9]

Second, much like Nixon in 1972, Mrs. Gandhi had available to her when she learned of her high court conviction for election malpractices a least-cost solution to her problem. As we saw in the Introduction, she could at once have resigned the prime ministership, assured her eligibility to seek reelection in the forthcoming parliamentary race, and come back into office on a wave of popular support. It is difficult to explain her rejection of this option, which so many observers appraised as favorable to her interests,[10] without postulating a personal reason for her seeing it differently.

THE LONELY CHILD

Assuming the broad perspective that personality carries forward important residuals from early life experiences—reworked, to be sure, along the way—beginning an analysis of an individual's political personality with his or her early years affords the best chance to apprehend patterns of ego-defense. More specifically, in this case, Indira Gandhi stepped from a succession of family environments almost directly into the prime ministership. It is striking how strongly she herself evoked images of her childhood during her early years in office to explain her untested political characteristics.[11]

As Prime Minister Gandhi has discussed her childhood,[12] the most common adjective she has used to describe it is "insecure."[13] That is a weasel word. It may mean that the conditions in which she grew up were unstable and risky. Alternatively, it may mean psychological doubts and lack of self-confidence. We need to sort out the external conditions, which might be left behind, from any self-doubts the girl might have carried forward into womanhood. In one of her most spontaneous and intimate interviews, given in 1972—a high point of her political security—Mrs. Gandhi suggested that her childhood was insecure in both senses:

> The whole house was always in such a state of tension that nobody had a normal life. There were police raids, arrests, and so on, the physical and mental strain. And all the time it was in public.[14]

It is not easy to reconstruct the predispositions of Indira's childhood free of the coloration of high political destiny. Nevertheless it is plain that a highly idealized future role was held up to her. Aside from the usual expectations of doting grandparents

and aunts in a Hindu household, she grew up as the only successor to her grandfather and father, both of whom headed the
Congress party and captured the imagination of nationalists.
Her aunt Swarup (Vijayalakshmi Pandit) figured larger in the
Gandhi movement.[15] But Indira's ego-idealism (to use the psy-
chologists' term) must have responded to the singular impact of
her father: heroic, dedicated, romantic, articulate, startlingly
aloof. From the jail across the river from Allahabad he wrote to
her:

> For Indira Priyadarshini
> on her thirteenth birthday—*kartik sud* 5 [the date according to the
> Hindu calendar] :
>
> My dear, On your birthday you have been in the habit of receiving
> presents and good wishes . . . but what present can I give you from
> Naini Prison?
>
> In your history books you read of great periods in the life of nations.
> We read of great men and women and great deeds performed. . . .
> In India today we are making history, and you and I are fortunate to
> see this happen before our eyes and to take some part ourselves in
> the great drama. How shall we bear ourselves in this great move-
> ment . . . ? Be brave and all the rest follows.[16]

Indira very early applied her organizing ability to tending for
smaller children, for the weak and helpless. At about the time
she received the letter just quoted, the family home had been
converted into a twenty-four-bed hospital, in which her mother
was a prime mover, to care for the *satyagrahis* injured by police
beatings and firings in the 1930 mass movement. Indira took
charge of a boy so severely wounded in the stomach that the
doctor had given him up. "But he was my first patient," she
told an interviewer in 1963. "I almost staked my faith in God
on his pulling through." The boy survived.[17] Two years later, at
a boarding school attended mainly by small children, she became
known as Indira *Didi* ("Big Sister") to those she mothered.[18]

The political predispositions of her childhood—lofty expectations, patriot's conscience, sense of responsibility for depen-
dents—were acted out, and were reflected in her adoption of
Jeanne d'Arc as model.[19] Mrs. Gandhi has testified that a mar-
tyrdom like her heroine's was the end that, in childhood, she
envisioned for herself.[20]

It is possible for us to specify more exactly the sources of Indira's childhood insecurity. Henry A. Murray, who during his

career at Harvard did more than any psychologist of his generation to interpret biographical data clinically, once indexed fifty-two categories of experience that, to use his term, "press" upon the childhood self.[21] The young Indira unmistakably lived through twelve of these:

1. *Absence of parent.* Her father was in jail nine years between her fourth and twenty-eighth years.[22] Every other member of her family spent time in jail during that period.
2. *Illness of parent.* When Indira was eight, her mother, Kamala, was diagnosed as having tuberculosis; she died ten years later.[23]
3. *Aloneness.* Example: when she was thirteen, all of Indira's relatives were either jailed or away from home.[24]
4. *Unsettled home.* The family's home was occasionally occupied by police. Indira was sent to thirteen schools in eighteen years.
5. *Loss of possessions.* Gandhian discipline forbade the payment of fines imposed on *satyagrahis* by British courts; the furnishings of the home in Allahabad were therefore attached by the government in lieu of payment. Young Indira watched this several times, the first time flying at the police in anger.[25]
6. *Illness.* Indira was a sickly child.[26]
7. *Cultural discord* within the family. This is discussed below.
8. *Intrafamily conflict.* "Any live and vital family has its share of mutual friction and strife. The Nehrus seemed to have more than usual."[27] Specifics appear below.
9. *Rejection by peers.* "Vijayalakshmi regarded Indira as a gangling awkward girl and made no secret of her disdain for her."[28]
10. *Parental ego-idealism.* This was indicated earlier in this chapter.
11. *Lack of affiliation with congenial children.* Indira found friends her own age for the first time in college, at age seventeen.[29]
12. *Sense of personal inferiority.* This is discussed below.

The concurrence of so many strains warrants a conclusion of insecurity. But it is the quality of the tensions that is more significant. The first six types of strain were, at bottom, unavoidable, given the people, the times, and the politics. It is possible to imagine a family supporting a child emotionally, even in so stormy a passage. The Nehrus tried. But the last six items on the ledger suggest how little they succeeded. We can begin to see that Indira's insecurity was planted within her because it was within her most intimate family associations.

This circumstance can be detected in the item "cultural discord." The dissonance was not, for Indira, in what she learned. Her father, Jawaharlal, had received an English upbringing; as an adult he had consciously to "discover India."[30] But Indira, growing up after Gandhi made nationalism indigenous, grew up un-Anglicized. Hindustani was as much her language as English,[31] as can be seen in an exploit of her twelfth year. Barred from Congress party membership because of her age, she organized Allahabad children into an auxiliary force. She called it *Vanar Sena* (Monkey Brigade), clearly drawing on traditions of her people (of Hanuman's army in the Ramayana) and dealing in their idiom.[32] Thus she experienced a reasonable concord as to the *content* of her socialization. Not so among the exponents of culture who were closest to her. Her mother, Kamala, as an eighteen-year-old Hindu bride without English education, had entered by marriage the household of Motilal Nehru, a prominent north Indian barrister and a distinguished part of English society in Allahabad. Kamala encountered both love and (especially on the part of Jawaharlal's sister Vijayalakshmi) contempt for her lack of "culture."[33] Culture was the subject of discord among loved ones. When Indu (her childhood nickname) was six her grandfather enrolled her in a school taught by Englishwomen. This so infuriated her father that he appealed to Gandhi on nationalist principles; the argument was reported in the papers. It was ended by Indu's studying at home.[34] This was a form of cultural discord not easy for a child to cope with.

"It seemed my parents were always in jail," Mrs. Gandhi told an interviewer.[35] Surely this is an objective condition for childhood insecurity. We must remember, of course, that the whole family accepted Gandhi's moral regimen: prison was the just price for a larger freedom. Also, the mass-action campaigns were episodic, as were the punishments. Indu grew from six to thirteen in a quiet phase when Jawaharlal was not detained at all. Third, and most important, her father's creativity could discover ways, during the nine full years he spent in prison, to reach her with his love and respect through the prison walls. We have sampled one such letter already; there were more than two hundred. Largely, they made good his intent that "you shall silently come near me and then we shall talk of many things."36

The jailed political father could also, however, wall off his daughter where there were no official barriers. During her fourteenth summer, vacationing from a lonely school in Poona37 to a lonely home in Allahabad (her mother was ill in Bombay, her father jailed 200 miles away, her grandfather dead), Indu counted on the fortnightly visit prison regulations permitted with her father. At the start of the summer, however, the authorities had unjustly penalized him by banning family visits for a month. He retaliated by voluntarily foregoing visits for six more months. Indu had to return to boarding school without seeing him the rest of the summer. Likely adding to her psychological burden was her involvement in the incident that promoted the initial one-month ban; the jail authorities were, in fact, responding in a heavy-handed manner to an attempt by Indu, accompanying her mother and grandmother, to deliver a message she brought from Poona for her uncle, also a prisoner. Nehru's comment on the incident accompanying his protest to the authorities makes no mention of his daughter's involvement.38 But a lonely adolescent must have felt rejected when her father so readily denied himself her visits.39

How much of Indu's insecurity came from feelings that she had not measured up? On this point our information fails us. Sympathetic acquaintances were impressed with the sadness of the child. A schoolmate of her early teens

> remembers how often . . . Indira used to stand behind the trunk of a tree, lost in her private world of grief, and shed tears profusely, too helpless to control them and yet too proud to show them.40

But whether it was the grief of desolation or of guilt we do not know. There was one reason she might have felt guilty: she never learned the discipline of study (though once interested in a subject she pursued it voraciously). There were reasons enough for this. As we have noted, she was a nomad among schools, without benefit of consistency in either manner or content of education. Quite probably, in her earliest years she had been overindulged by doting grandparents and a widowed great-aunt. For the children before her in Motilal Nehru's Allahabad mansion, a strict English governess had compensated for this, but nationalism ruled out that antidote for Indira.[41] Kamala had not the authority in the joint family and Jawaharlal was too preoccupied with politics, too often in jail, to rectify the situation. Indu seemed at times "intractable" (her parents' word), or "obstinate" (a perceptive high school teacher's impression).[42] She excelled when skillfully taught, and at art and drama; she barely passed the academic core.[43] There must have seemed to her a growing gap between lofty aspirations and the educational means to reach them.

Kamala Nehru died of tuberculosis at the age of thirty-five. After her death, Nehru looked back with remorse at his failure to understand her, to provide "that comradeship which was her due."[44] But even then, his account of her last years reveals, to a reader of her own correspondence, how little of her potentiality and needs he perceived. Kamala had shouldered more burdens than her tubercular body could carry, managing the Allahabad household, assuming leadership of the mass demonstrations after all the male Congress leaders, including her husband, had been jailed. Her coughing and fever became chronic. Her husband was released from jail, but during the six months of his freedom he made public statements calculated to land him in prison again. On February 11, 1934, the police came for him. He greeted them casually. This is his report of the sequel:

> Kamala went up to our room to collect some clothes for me. I followed her to say good bye to her. Suddenly she clung to me and, fainting, collapsed. This was unusual for her, as we had trained ourselves to take this jail-going lightly and cheerfully and to make as little fuss about it as possible. Was it some premonition she had that this was our last more or less normal meeting?[45]

In fact, Kamala, alone and knowing that she was dying, was finding emotional solace in her spiritual initiation into the faith of the Ramakrishna mission outside Calcutta.[46] Her husband considered her, at this stage, "definitely neurotic."[47] The record, so far as we have it, can be read another way. A young woman of inner dignity came by marriage into a house where she was treated with both love and condescension. Her husband did not back her in face of the unjust criticisms of her female in-laws. Being more authentically Indian than they, and of limitless courage, she began to play a political role. For the first time, this brought her comradeship with her husband. But it also cost her her health.[48] "Possessed" by politics, as he confessed,[49] he did not succor her.

Prime Minister Gandhi leaves us in no doubt as to how she eventually resolved the conflict of loyalty and role model between father and mother. "We were very close to each other," she told her mother's biographer. "I loved [my mother] deeply and when I thought that she was being wronged I fought for her and quarrelled with people."[50] There is some evidence that by the time she was seventeen she had responded to her father's distancing of the family by putting him at a distance: he complained to his sister that Indu was no longer writing him in jail.[51] But it seems more likely that what Indu carried over from childhood into adolescence was a divided and vulnerable sense of herself. The part of her that hungered for companionship, that mothered others, that could delight in emotional expression must have seemed vitally threatened by the part that was dedicated to making history, to saving her people in the abstract, to the adventures of the intellect. Two parents, incredibly brave, intensely loving in different ways, distant and tragic enough to stand intact as models, must have ushered her into an identity crisis as profound as the gulf between them.

DIALECTIC OF IDENTITY

A person's character is discernable in the "mental or moral attitude in which, when it came upon him, he felt himself most deeply and intensely active and alive. At such moments there is a voice inside which speaks and says, 'This is the real me.'

In these words, taken from a letter of William James, Erik Erikson evokes the concept of psychosocial identity.[52] But in Indira Gandhi's case the continuities are not linear or direct. Her postadolescent discovery of herself is rather a remarkable series of pendulum-like swings in which it is her rejection of the meaning to her of one trial identity that propels her to a contrasting one. At the poles of these oscillations are the personal propensities of her mother and the career in history of her father. It is a measure of the great distance across which she struggled to reconcile these views of herself that she was unwilling to put herself forward into the world as the person she had elected to be until she was forty-two years old.[53]

Santiniketan

For Indira's transition from school to university (intermediate school, in the Indian system), the Nehrus chose well. Tagore had founded an entirely autonomous college in a rural Bengal setting. Indira found four satisfactions there. Santiniketan was discovering creative forms of Indian culture, neither emulating nor shutting out Europe. Indira found this congenial. Moreover, she could create her own expression of culture through the dance, in which she showed real promise, especially in Manipuri style. The warm human companionship, the friendship with peers that she had been denied blossomed here. Finally, she began to take delight in her femaleness. Up to then, "I had wanted to be a boy."[54]

Santiniketan was an experience that brought her close to her mother, emotionally as well as physically. This was the period of Kamala's religious refuge. "Mummy and I spent much time in the Ramakrishna Math [devotional center]. Sitting peacefully by the riverside a new world of thought and experience opened out for me."[55] But Santiniketan was an idyll unsustainable in Indira's world; in the midst of her first year she had to break away. Her dying mother needed her, first in a Himalayan sanitarium, then in Switzerland. The main yield of the brief experience may have been an awareness of a part of herself lost. In her marriage she strove to regain it. Its residue when she reached the top in politics was only a wistful interest in expressive art.

Oxford

Kamala died in 1936. Indira was eighteen. It was a time to open a new chapter. Jawaharlal was superbly restrained in telling her what to do, but clearly, this was a chapter dedicated to him, an intellectual chapter.[56]

To put it bluntly, Indira failed at the kind of education represented by Somerville College, Oxford. Alone in London in 1936 she read for the entrance examinations, and failed them. On a second try, after a visit home and preparation at an English public school, she passed. She spent one term at Somerville, apparently impressed only with the intimidating personality of the dean.[57] Nowhere have I been able to find comments by Indira on lectures, books, examinations, or discussions of ideas with those she met at Oxford. Her health would not admit of a second year there, and she returned to India. She was invited for the following summer term (1939), but she elected to spend it in Switzerland. Just before the fall term opened in 1939, she was caught in a rainstorm at a country outing, developed pleurisy, and was sent by doctors to a health resort in Switzerland. Four and a half years after starting the attempt she sailed home without a university education.

The course of studies Indira and her father had chosen must have fit her interests as well as any program at Oxford could have: social and public administration, French, and modern history.[58] It was no doubt true, as Tagore surmised, that she found herself "rather alien to the complacent English society."[59] But we get signals that deeper obstacles intervened. The lack of habits of study told upon her. She was active socially with her father's group of friends, attending concerts and the theater, part of the leftist political circles that attracted young Indian nationalists. But when called on to speak in public as "Miss Nehru," or to read out a message from her father, her voice failed her. When she found the confidence to speak in public she was twenty-four, on her way back to India having left Oxford for good. She spoke then not as Miss Nehru, but out of an inner anger at the treatment of blacks she saw in Durban.[60]

Oxford survives in Prime Minister Gandhi's character essentially as a negative identity. She did not make her own the traditions of British politics, of social amelioration, of science, that had won her father. She developed neither the intellectual skills for nor any personal attraction to ideological thinking. She entered Marxist circles among her countrymen in England—V. K. Krishna Menon's, those of her contemporaries who have since become CPI leaders—but there is not the slightest evidence that she was interested in the intellectual discipline of Marxism. A whole side of her father's eminence—the analysis of underlying social forces and basic policy responses to them, literary expression, the steady identification of an ideological position within the amorphous Congress movement—she recoiled from when she left Oxford. There is a strain of contempt in her attitude toward Indian intellectuals today that took its rise at this point.

Marriage

Resiling from Oxford, Indira fixed upon marriage to the man who most nearly, among all those whom she knew, evoked her mother's image. He was Feroze Gandhi (unrelated to the Mahatma). Feroze, who had grown up in Allahabad in constant touch with the aristocratic Nehru family, admired Jawaharlal unstintingly. But in culture (little Westernized) and temperament (emotional, decisive) he was nearer to Kamala. As Kamala became an anticolonial activist in 1930, he attached himself to her as her agent and protector.[61] It is remarkable that in her last two lonely years he shared her correspondence with the swami at the Ramakrishna mission.[62] When Indira was sixteen, Feroze asked Kamala if he might marry Indira;[63] Jawaharlal knew nothing of this for eight more years until Indira told him her decision. To the extent that Erik Erikson's proposition holds—"adolescent love is [in part] an attempt to arrive at a definition of one's identity by projecting one's diffused ego image on another"[64]—Feroze represented to Indira the Kamala part of her potential.

By the time she was twenty-four, that side of her was sufficiently central so that, when her jailed father demurred to the marriage, she was prepared to confront him with her will. For the first time in their relationship, she prevailed.[65]

The marriage, one of the most prominent of the nationalist generation, has attracted controversy, largely speculative because both husband and wife valued the privacy of their relationships. Two things are certain. Feroze and Indira remained connected to one another emotionally; but in the final years preceding his death in 1960 their lives parted. As prime minister, Indira Gandhi was prepared to say, "We were not compatible."[66] This does not explain the change in their relationship over the years. A recent, somewhat critical biographer explains Feroze's occasional bitterness during his last years as that of "a man who marries for love, only to find that his wife prefers her father."[67] True or not, it was clearly to her prime minister father that Indira made her commitment when in 1948 she became the first lady at Teen Murti (the prime minister's New Delhi residence).[68] That was a full-time role.

Having established one's identity, one also establishes its continuity with one's prior roles. What Prime Minister Gandhi has come to think about her husband provides us with a clue to her evolving image of herself. By 1960 Feroze had become the outstanding nongovernment Congress M. P., his reputation built by his successful exposure of wrongdoing between government agencies and powerful financial interests. Indira discussed with him her most difficult problems; often they disagreed. "If he had been a man of lesser calibre," said a person very close to Indira, "it would have been very smooth sailing."[69] That no doubt exaggerates the real truth that from 1955 onward Feroze had won a political position that would impose demands upon his wife: not that she "be a mere housewife,"[70] but that she not identify herself completely with her father, the prime minister. As she looks back now, she sees her husband's political career as minor and derivative. "He might not have succeeded if circumstances had thrust him further—into the Cabinet for example. Too much would have been expected of him."[71] By the time she said that Indira Gandhi had found herself needing no complementarity.

There was one price she paid, and knew it, when Feroze moved out of the prime minister's residence. Their two sons, twelve and fourteen, were at an age when they needed a father.[72]

Moratorium

For a young woman who identified herself with her mother, but who had found the roles of wife and mother unrewarding, Teen Murti house provided a setting in which these conflicting feelings could be reconciled. Indira could transfer her domesticity to the house of the prime minister she idealized and fill in his life the emptiness left by Kamala's death. "What a gentle word is domesticity," she wrote in 1957, immediately making clear that by that time her notion of it "involves my father."[73]

Biographers have treated Indira's long period in Teen Murti house as "an extraordinary apprenticeship."[74] That is to mistake a creator of roles for a learner. And she spent sixteen years in that apprentice role—she was forty-six when her father died— much too long for a self-decreed withdrawal.[75] At some point between 1948 and 1964, the prime minister's house became a prison for an individual whose full realization came in the making of decisions.

The broad sweep of political life on which the doors of Teen Murti house opened permit us to make an inventory of elements of Indira's identity, both positive and negative: we can identify possibilities she discovered she could live for, and those she determined to live down.[76] We consider the positive elements first:

1. *Relieving the misery of the helpless.* To projects involving homeless children, the crippled, uneducated women, refugee families, she brought energy and creativity parallel, for example, to that of Eleanor Roosevelt. Her concern for these disadvantaged groups often rises from sympathy for particular individuals.[77]

2. *Defense of persecuted or threatened minorities.* Gandhi had challenged her to play a part of high courage during the partition riots; she had not only risen to the challenge but had found her own way to release suppressed forces of reconciliation.[78] She incorporated this cause into her political life.

3. *Face-to-face relations with heads of foreign states.* Here her combination of urbane and gracious manners with an uncommonly reserved inner self worked to advantage. Nehru's international interests and stature gave her extraordinarily wide, but often intimate access to the leaders of the United States, the Soviet Union, European nations, and the emerging nations of Asia and Africa.[79]

4. *Organization and administration.* The remarkable aptitude she had demonstrated since childhood found application and reward in her building of a parent organization for voluntary social welfare agencies nationwide, in her management of Congress party election campaigns, and in her building of the Youth Congress and the women's wing of the Congress party.[80]

5. *Communion with great crowds of common people.* To draw together crowds of hundreds of thousands of otherwise isolated individuals, to sense their shared grievances and aspirations, to hear those sentiments resonating in their massed responses to the words spoken into a microphone—this is a capacity very different from the mediated communication of television. It is a gift at least as much of history as of one's personal powers, but Indira came to share it all across India as only Gandhi and Jawaharlal had done before her. To the young woman who lost her power

of speech when she tried to speak as Nehru's daughter,[81] it must have been the more rewarding to discover in the 1952 election campaign that she possessed this power in her own name.

6. *Subordinating her personal life to her country.* This was symbolized when she was arrested in the 1942 movement and jailed in her father's old prison for 243 days. After moving to Teen Murti house, she identified herself completely with her nation.

Indira's period of subordination to her father also developed her perceptions of roles or forces threatening her self-fulfillment:

1. *Service as an elected representative* in the state legislature or in Parliament. This role, the normal career line to the top, she rejected in every election between 1946 and 1967, even when she was intensely pressured to run. The reasons she adduced—family responsibilities, her father's need of her—would have kept her from something else that she did accept, the presidency of the Congress party. The negative meaning of a parliamentary role for her was more likely that it would have made her one of 500 critics and debaters rather than the sole confidante of the prime minister.[82]

2. *Politicians.* Indira Gandhi's contempt for politicians is surely remarkable for one who has been in politics from age twelve. But in Teen Murti house she was selectively exposed to the devious, exploitive, self-aggrandizing side of the genus. Politicians sought her out as intermediary to the man at the top precisely when they lacked the kind of case that could reach him through Parliament or the ministries. Not only did she disapprove their demands, she resented their attempts to use her. She developed a keen sense of the hidden motives of politicians of all types. She began denying that she was a politician, and she took satisfaction in the thought that her sons were not heading in that direction.[83]

3. *Constitutional niceties.* The test of Mrs. Gandhi's commitment to the spirit of the constitution came in 1959, immediately upon her taking office as the Congress party's president. For two years Kerala had been governed by an elected Communist ministry. This government had aroused resentment by a number of economic measures, and

particularly by a bill to subject parochial schools to state controls and accountability. Mass agitation was launched, precisely corresponding to that against Mrs. Gandhi in June 1975, to unseat the government. The state Congress party joined in, supported by Mrs. Gandhi. The prime minister demurred. "I am opposed to unconstitutional means at any time anyhow," he declared, "because once you adopt them they would be justified in another context." And later: "So far as I am concerned, I do not propose nor intend . . . governments falling except through democratic processes." His daughter disagreed: "The whole point is that here is an upsurge, and the Congress can't just stand by."[84]

It is important to understand the Kerala issue.[85] It is quite possible that the Communist government had lost the confidence of the voters; a special election could have tested that. It is possible, likely even, that the Communist government had employed both patronage and biased administration of justice and of election procedures to taint the electoral process. A public enquiry, e.g., by a committee of Parliament, could have ascertained that. Mrs. Gandhi wanted neither approach. She wanted the Communists out. An exchange at the height of the crisis, between a reporter for the *Hindu* and both father and daughter, is telling:

> Reporter: Are you going to fight the communists or throw them out?
> Nehru: Throw them out? How? What do you mean? They have also been elected.
> Indira Gandhi: Papu, what are you telling them? You're talking as prime minister. As Congress president I intend to fight them and throw them out.[86]

The Communist government of Kerala was, in the event, deposed by president's rule from Delhi. Rejection by the national CPI of the option of a special election, apparently offered by Nehru, provided partial, not full, justification. But the episode remains to cloud the legitimacy of duly elected governments encountering bitter, but perhaps temporary, unpopularity. It was precisely this legitimacy, of course, that Mrs. Gandhi asserted she had to defend by imposing the 1975 emergency. At the personal level, she had clashed with her father and won, but only because, as prime minister, he had come reluctantly to her position.

Rejection of Jawaharlal's Model of Leadership

Manipulating her public image, Prime Minister Gandhi has been at pains to profess somewhat contradictory views of her relation to her father's role. On the one hand she conserves his legacy: "Quite honestly, could anyone know my father's principles and policies better than I do?"[87] Equally persistently she asserts that she will not hesitate to change her father's policies if she deems changes are warranted, and that she would not be imposed on by him when he was alive.[88] It is not easy to get behind these different masks. We will have to make inferences from guarded statements.

Mrs. Gandhi gives us ground for concluding that she rejects her father's pattern of leadership in three respects. First, he permitted himself to be imposed on by the very kind of politician she holds in contempt. "He did allow everybody to grow," she said, apropos of the then-current metaphor of her father as "banyan tree" sheltering potential successors, "even those whom we considered to be weeds. He did allow them to grow even though they were constantly threatening him."[89]

Second, her father was less decisive, less forceful, than the leadership of Indian politics required. "My father was a saint who strayed into politics," she said after the emergency proclamation, "but I am not of the same stuff."[90]

Third, while she does not implicate her father by name with this issue, the basic institutions carried over from colonial times into independent India were unfit to meet modern problems. It would have been better had they been replaced at the start. Her repudiation is exhaustive. The Congress party is "moribund." "Sometimes I feel that even our parliamentary system is moribund. . . . The inertia of our civil service is incredible. . . . Sometimes I wish we had had a real revolution—like France or Russia—at the time of Independence."[91]

These are all assessments Mrs. Gandhi has expressed since her father's death. Suppose, however, she had arrived at them in her own mind by 1959-60 when she served her year as Congress party president. In that role, we know, she discovered her capability for taking decisive action colliding with her father's attachment to procedural niceties and consensual politics. Then might she not have perceived her loved and heroic figure blocking her realization of her own political capabilities? We have one clue. During that year Mrs. Gandhi quite precisely diagnosed the sickness of her party. It lacked a trained cadre of workers in nation, state, and district, committed workers who would act as a positive persuasive force upon, and not merely a mouthpiece of, local electorates. The Congress presidency afforded Mrs. Gandhi an opportunity to exercise the highest skill she had yet manifested—building an organization of the enthusiasms of new activists—to effect a lasting cure. She was only able, in her first year in office, to launch a pilot recruitment and training scheme of 110 workers. Then she declined reelection. Why? She was ill. She needed to spend more time with her husband and father.[92] But by now we know that she proved capable of surmounting both objections when her deepest sense of purpose was touched. A more satisfying reason is that she painfully discovered, as party president, that her father still held the real power as prime minister. She had to go to him, either to hold up the hand of a state party, as in Kerala, or to overrule a state party boss. "For a proud, self-willed person like Indira," Krishan Bhatia infers," that must have been galling."[93]

EMERGENCE OF A POLITICAL CHARACTER

At the time of her father's death, in her forty-sixth year, Indira Gandhi was fully aware of the "real me," the cutter of Gordian knots. The banyan tree was gone. But an identity is psychosocial, and the long period of latency that had brought self-awareness to Mrs. Gandhi had also led the key leaders of the Congress party to an impression of her that was 180 degrees from the truth. She had never run for office: they thought her shy, while in fact she disdained being a mere M.P. After a flurry of activity she had dropped the party presidency: they thought her influence was her father's, while she saw him as a obstacle to her influence. "This mere *chokri*" ("slip of a girl"), Morarji called her then. He has lived to revise that assessment. Welles Hangen, more detached, was almost as wrong.[94] So it came about that a role comprising her negative identities—the role of routine politician dependent upon give and take with others of that unworthy genus—was slated for her in the minds of those who had the power to make top careers. Her psychological situation had been that of Erikson's creative individual who "often cannot work, not because he is not gifted or adept, but because his standards preclude any approach that does not lead to being outstanding."[95] But her political situation was a trap; she would inevitably feel betrayed, as would the politicians who used the supposedly shy woman for her beloved name.

The trap was twice sprung, first when she was named a minister in Lal Bahadur Shastri's cabinet. She presumed Shastri would seek her guidance as to the direction Nehru's policies would be taking the country. When he did not, her contempt for consensus politicians was reinforced.[96] The trap was set again in 1966, after Shastri's unexpected death, when the wily Congress party president, Kamaraj, stage-managed her election as prime minister by the parliamentary wing of the party. Kamaraj and the party bosses were concerned with two criteria: they needed a Nehru to win a difficult election, and they wanted to head off Morarji Desai, because he had a will of his own.[97] "Supported by a group who banked on her weakness to bolster its own strength," writes a sympathetic biographer, "her attempts to reassert the position of the prime minister brought her immediately into a clash with those supporters."[98] Again the trap was sprung. Kamaraj felt betrayed by her independence and became her political enemy, while she felt betrayed by the desertion of the party bosses.

In broad terms, the incongruity between her view and the established Congress party leaders' view of her power finally brought about the crisis of her political survival in 1969.[99] The immediate issue was the nomination of a president of India by the party's Parliamentary Board. Both Mrs. Gandhi and the party bosses were determined it should be someone beholden to them. Mrs. Gandhi, precipitating a showdown that might have been deferred, lost. Her political life was at stake. Only then did she suddenly exhibit her full powers of decision. Within twenty-four hours she created an entirely new populist issue, nationalized the major banks by presidential ordinance, and summarily fired Desai on grounds that he opposed the decision. Having raised an ideological issue on which she could go to the people, she backed the opposition parties' candidate for president, narrowly won, split her party, and thus gained unquestioned domination of her majority fraction of it.

William James, in the letter Erikson quoted to introduce his concept of psychosocial identity, added the observation that the discovery of one's identity includes "an element of active tension, of holding [one's] own, as it were, and trusting outward things to perform their part so as to make it a real harmony but without any guarantee that they will."[100] Indira

Gandhi had held her own; outward things had performed their part. She had made ideology her instrument. She had dissolved the autonomous structure of the party, and of the presidency. She had asked for the support of the people, and received it. Emerging from that crisis she had grounds to be confident that her powers as she sensed them and the prime ministership as India required it had coincided.

We have used the concepts of both Fred Greenstein and Erik Erikson. Understanding Mrs. Gandhi's political potential requires that we fit them into a single perspective. Greenstein provides the framework for an inventory of predispositions; we will follow it to systematize our short-run predictive thinking. Erikson has in view the larger historical crises as they intersect with the lives of very remarkable individuals. "In history," Erikson writes, "identities are bound to shift with changing technologies, cultures and political systems. Existing or changing roles must thus be reassimilated in the psychosocial roles of the most dominant" members of a society or nation. Individuals of the historical stature of Gandhi or Luther or Hitler created the new ideologies for their emergent generations. In this sense, "identity and ideology seem to be two aspects of the same psychosocial process."[101]
We are interpreting a different kind of person than that described by Erikson; whether a person less creative, less "great" it is much too early to say, but certainly one originating a less complete solution to the problems of her generation. In this respect Mrs. Gandhi occupies a place somewhere between the great figures who make ideological breakthroughs and the politicians (who are in the center of Greenstein's focus) who merely press against the constraints of constitutional roles, legislative and executive.[102] Mrs. Gandhi is remaking roles. She is not making, or remaking, ideologies. We shall probe for the relevance to her own identity conflicts of both conflicts in the identities of her generation and her solution for these conflicts. But we shall not find the intersection of history and biography in her case ideological.

Predisposition to Attitudes

Ideology. Examination of Mrs. Gandhi's statements on the ideological directions of her leadership quickly reveals contradictions. Distinguishing tactical matters, which might be compromised, from basic principles, she said:

> The basic principle and policies are commitment and deep involvement with socialist policy, and commitment and deep involvement with the policy of secularism.[103]

Compare:

> I don't really have a political philosophy. I can't say I believe in any ism. . . . I wouldn't say I'm interested in socialism as socialism. For me it's just a tool.[104]

The contradiction is in the words. There is no inconsistency in Mrs. Gandhi's predisposition. Ideological positions to her are, as she told Welles Hangen in the last sentence quoted, instruments, not guides. She made the former statement at the time she split the Congress party, a split which gave her domination precisely because she took it to the people—via bank nationalization—as an ideological issue. But two who sided with her then, who indeed pressed her forward, based on principle alone, and who stand for precisely those principles today, are in jail: Mohan Dharia and Chandra Sekhar. Howard Erdman's account of her policy toward big industry (chapter 5, above) gives evidence that once she has full power in her hands, ideology is not a constraint. Mrs. Gandhi is a pragmatist.

We have seen fundamental reasons in her own personal development why she has come to reject ideologies. Systematic learning designed precisely to sensitize her to ideological questions did not capture her interest. Her father was a man concerned with ultimate goals, and with the large processes of history. Ideological thinking did not dictate his policies, nor his attitudes to the processes of politics, but it certainly influenced them. These constraints upon his decisions his daughter came to hold in contempt. They hampered and delayed his decisions when, as in the case of the Communist government of Kerala, swift action was required. Still more fundamentally, to accept a set of principles, however abstract, would be to accept power over her own will. She would not bind herself even to ideals, in any way she could not manipulate.

Institutions. India is not, like the tropical African nations in their new independence, uninstitutionalized. The difficulty is, rather, a form of overinstitutionalization. Each highly structured organization or profession operates formalistically either because it is of the Raj, heaven-born—the elite civil service, courts, universities, and some learned professions—or because it is an incompletely reworked set of caste norms, as one finds in the "babu" role behind the ticket window.

Every politician responsible for results in India, starting with Jawaharlal Nehru, has diagnosed this situation. Neither national integration nor economic productivity can be accomplished without utterly transforming it. But Mrs. Gandhi came to office uniquely equipped to act. Never having entered a profession, even that of party politician, she was without blinders. She saw the insolence of office whenever it appeared.[105] Moreover, she had demonstrated from girlhood an extraordinary aptitude and motivation for organizing human effort. One would have expected her to reinstitutionalize Indian politics.

That expectation reckons without her deeper personal need: to dominate. Any institutional structure creates stable expectations. It is an alternative, as Max Weber arrayed it, to domination by the personal qualities, the charisma, of the leader. We have discovered the point, in Mrs. Gandhi's long search for her full powers, her identity, at which she discovered that painstakingly rebuilding an organization yields far less immediate control than manipulating the existing apparatus of the state. That point was her presidentship of the Congress party, while her father controlled the state. Her enthusiasm, up to then unmatched, had been for putting through well-developed recommendations for restructuring not only the Congress party, but the government administrative apparatus and the educational system. She is now, instead, committed to bending institutions to the national good by sheer pressure of will applied at the top—her will.

Affinity for the people. Among Indira Gandhi's most deeply held attitudes is a perception of the whole of India, but especially the voiceless and helpless and the cultural minorities, as her charge. She perceives the poor not as a class in conflict with the propertied, but as a particular responsibility to nation builders and economic developers. She is genuinely enraged at the politics of exploiting prejudice against minorities and has demonstrated personal courage in defense of the most important and explosive minority, the Muslims.

Mrs. Gandhi feels she intuits the will of ordinary people. Her culturally hybrid childhood, her freedom from Western intellectual baggage (but not technological modernity), her extensive and continual contacts with her countrymen give her a unique capability. She says she is "committed (to the extent of merging my identity) to the welfare of India's people."106 What is the need, this confidence implies, of parties, representatives, newspapers to come between ruler and people?

There are, one suspects, in her personality, two bases for these attitudes, one positive, the other negative. The ugliness, the savagery of communal violence and of the economic oppression of the village poor appeal to her direct sympathy independent of any ideology. Hers is the emotional legacy of the Gandhi movement in this respect. She experiences the very real outpouring of the people's trust—adoration is not too strong a word—in her rural speaking tours. There is also the negative side. These are the people who cannot, precisely because they are subject people, challenge her power. One of the most telling indicators of the inner sources of her attitudes was her displacement of the DMK government of Tamil Nadu. Whatever may be said of that state regime, it was an authentic representation of a subnational cultural identity, one Mrs. Gandhi had herself championed in the past. But it was also organized, articulate, and compactly based enough to constitute an island in the current of her will. It had to go.

Domination. Power, to Mrs. Gandhi, comes very close to being controlled force. She is a very persuasive person. But she sees no superior value of persuasion over force. This view, proceeding from the inner makeup of her character, was powerfully reinforced in two dramatic crises after she took full control of Indian policy. The first was international, the outright military defeat and dismemberment of Pakistan. The peculiar condition of this war was its surgical character: quick, decisive, no immediate subsequent entanglements. A somewhat similar domestic test of her view of power was her crushing of the railway strike of 1974.

Mrs. Gandhi has, in recent years, been at pains to differentiate her thinking from Mahatma Gandhi's, even asserting what, to my knowledge, has no warrant in history: that she voiced her disagreements with Gandhi more than her father did.[107] This could be an indication of her rejection of authority, or a concomitant of her narrowing perception of power. Power, for her, does not grow out of the barrel of a gun, alone, but both guns and *lathis* (bamboo staffs carried by police) play their parts.

Interpersonal relations. Mrs Gandhi's dealing with individuals are founded on her basic feelings of mistrust. Within that general framework, people who are dependent upon her—her personal staff, young protégés without a political base of their own, members of dependent groups—find her not only considerate but imaginative in tapping their potentialities. She delegates abundantly to them.[108] People of independent political support-bases, of legally defined institutional roles, who can affect her, must fear her.[109] With those whose orbits intersect hers casually, she is often gracious.

There are many manifestations of her basic mistrust. She conveys an air of remarkable personal reserve. Her conduct of the prime ministership has been characterized by secrecy even from her cabinet. Her characteristic resort, in crisis, to preemptive strikes requires this, but also expresses her assumption that the other side always threatens. Krishan Bhatia ends his vivid biography with the conclusion that she is "a very private person."[110]

Sharpened by her sixteen years of observation of her father's visitors at Teen Murti house, her coolness toward people has given her "an uncanny sense about people's foibles and predilections and a remarkable capacity to exploit them to her advantage."[111] When she encountered another national leader not unaccomplished in this art, Lyndon Johnson, there are some opinions that she did the manipulating of the relationship.[112]

All this makes the more remarkable the Achilles' heel in Mrs. Gandhi's armor of mistrust: her own sons. The eldest, Rajiv, is an airline pilot and has not figured in Mrs. Gandhi's political life. The younger, Sanjay, is now the most evident threat to the success of her endeavors. She is unable to say no to him. Sanjay Gandhi, now twenty-nine, received under his mother's prime ministership not only the exclusive license to manufacture a small, cheap automobile, but a factory site in Haryana that required confiscation of land from peasants.[113] The then chief minister of Haryana has since become Mrs. Gandhi's defense minister. When, in 1974 and 1975, opposition parties began to achieve some success in identifying Mrs. Gandhi's administration with the covering up of corruption (not easy to do since she was never herself suspected of corruption), Sanjay's automobile project provided the ideal target. Mrs. Gandhi indignantly brushed aside the charges: "There is nothing wrong with a young man proving his capacity."[114] In spite of an official enquiry that discovered no favoritism, suspicion continued to spread. Since the emergency, Sanjay has leaped suddenly into political prominence. In December he was placed on the national council of the Youth Congress, and in that role speaks daily in all parts of India. It is evident that he lacks his mother's commitment to uplifting the poor, and to public sector industry. To many, he expresses the contempt for the organizational leaders of her party that she has been accused of harboring in private.

It is not easy to imagine that Mrs. Gandhi is unaware of the threat her son's activities pose to the longer-term purposes for which she justifies the emergency. With the Congress party totally dependent on her, Sanjay becomes a powerful candidate to succeed her. Few in India would then expect her reform program to be carried forward. Mrs. Gandhi has seen two of her antagonists, Ayub Khan of Pakistan, and Morarji Desai, wounded politically because of the credibility of scandals involving their sons. Why does she accept similar liabilities?

The likely conjecture is one premised upon her own personal development, as described in this chapter. She has made it clear that she did not want her sons to go through the lonely, insecure childhood she suffered. Did she also translate the injustice of her father's initial neglect and his later overshadowing of her into guilt for Sanjay's lack of the fathering he required?[115] Has this led to a determination not to constrain his early career?

Ego-Defense

We have observed Indira Gandhi as a sad, lonely child whose insecurity was caused even more by conflicting urges among those she loved than by the slings and arrows of the times. We have seen her powerful ambition frustrated as she began in her father's footsteps to develop her intellect, then in her mother's to develop her family. We have seen her inexplicably rejected by the father who so ardently nourished that ambition. As she became aware of her extraordinary powers to organize and lead, we saw her father's charisma spreading a ceiling over her initiatives. When after his death she gained power, we observed her political environment peopled with rivals who expected of her a dependence of which she was, in the deepest sense, incapable. We suspect, therefore, that at the core of Indira Gandhi's mature identity, after the confusions were sorted out, there would be the determination to dominate, lest she be dominated.

Is this an apt interpretation of Mrs. Gandhi's character? We get a fragment of direct confirmation from her. The circumstances are interesting. She was answering questions about her mother, beginning unreservedly with "I loved her deeply." Her mother had a very difficult time of it in the Nehru house. But her outstanding quality was "determination."[116] Indira identified herself with her mother. If she was now better fitted for the world it was because she had learned something from her mother's life. And then this remarkable sentence: "I saw her being hurt and I was determined not to be hurt."[117]

Writing "Afterthoughts" to his *Psychopathology and Politics* thirty years after he had pioneered the path of enquiry pursued here, Harold Lasswell reformulated his "most comprehensive proposition." Those politicians possessed of "power-centered personalities"—those subsuming within their drive to coerce, to impose, all other values—have developed their character "in response to deprivation received from persons who are also regarded as sources of great indulgence."[118] One sentence could hardly better encapsulate what we have discovered about Indira Gandhi's means of ego-defense. Once she had found her true self—once she had set out personally to dominate the apparatus of power in India—the manifestations of identity-confusion cleared away, as if by a miracle. Her frail health was replaced by superhuman energy and vitality. With her bold maneuvers, which gained command of the party in 1969,

> her confidence finally burst through to the public gaze, . . . free of her father's shadow, broken out from his mold. . . . Her emergence from extreme reserve and withdrawal was now complete. She was fluent and forceful in extempore Hindi at public meetings.[119]

A political identity is a "harmony" as James said, an "intersection" in the phrase of Erikson, between psychological and social development. That Indira Gandhi discovered the harmony to confirm her self-discovery is apparent. That her countrymen will find her remade role in harmony with the development of their society—the history side of the equation—is not yet settled.

NOTES

1 *Woodrow Wilson and Colonel House: A Personality Study* (New York: Dover Publications, 1964).

2 In August, to an American audience: "What has been done is not an abrogation of democracy but an effort to safeguard it. . . . We will not allow economic progress to become a reason for perpetuating the emergency" (*Saturday Review*, Aug. 9, 1975, pp. 10, 48). In December 1975, to her own party: "I don't want to go in for elections because that will put the 20-point program in jeopardy" (chap. 1, note 125, above).

3 Compare her August *Saturday Review* interview (p. 10) with her reference six months later to the two "islands" of indiscipline within India. *Indian Express* (New Delhi), Jan. 8, 1976.

4 Chap. 1, above, notes 116, 117, 118.

5 "Increased repression" was one possibility projected by Zareer Masani, *Indira Gandhi, A Biography* (London: Hamish Hamilton, 1975) pp. 309-10. Nayantara Sahgal, "The Making of Mrs. Gandhi," *South Asian Review* (London) 8 (Apr. 1975), wrote on the basis of a very precise personality study that "there was fear" that Mrs. Gandhi "would seize extra powers" (p. 299).

6 Chicago: University of Chicago Press, 1930.

7 Fred I. Greenstein, *Personality and Politics: Problems of Evidence, Inference, and Conceptualization* (New York: W. W. Norton, 1975), pp. 5-6, 26, 63.

8 Oriana Fallaci, "Mrs. Gandhi's Opposition: Morarji Desai," *The New Republic* 163, no. 5-6 (Aug. 2-9, 1975): 18.

9 Tom Wicker, "Could It Happen Here?," *New York Times*, June 29, 1975.

10 See chap. 1, note 9, above.

11 Sahgal, "Making of Mrs. Gandhi," pp. 193-94.

12 A word about sources: Interview material dates mainly from Mrs. Gandhi's years as prime minister, and thus shows us predominantly the persona she intends for India and the world to see. But depending on the context, some interviews appear on their face to have tapped both candid and spontaneous responses. There is also an extraordinarily detailed and

voluminous correspondence among relatives and political friends (produced by articulate people conscious of their places in history and often forced to communicate in writing if at all). Except for her father's collected papers, now published, this is tapped here indirectly through selections and biographies. And there are the published recollections of these same relatives and political associates, not all of whom, by any means, see Indira Gandhi's personality as she does.

13 Uma Vasudev, *Indira Gandhi, Revolution in Restraint* (Delhi: Vikas, 1974), p. 48; Krishan Bhatia, *Indira: A Biography of Prime Minister Gandhi* (New York: Praeger, 1974), p. 37; Anand Mohan, *Indira Gandhi: A Personal and Political Biography* (New York: Hawthorn, 1967), p. 91; Anne Cublier, *Indira Gandhi* (Paris: Gonthier, 1967), p. 188.

14 Promilla Kalhan, *Kamala Nehru, An Intimate Biography* (Delhi: Vikas, 1973), p. 141. The interviewer notes: "Her replies to some of my questions, which could perhaps be termed embarrassing, were remarkably frank and spontaneous" (p. 131).

15 Elizabeth G. Stern [Eleanor Morton], *The Women in Gandhi's Life* (New York: Dodd Mead, 1953).

16 Jawaharlal Nehru, *Selected Works*, ed. S. Gopal, 7 vols. (New Delhi: Orient Longmans, 1972-1974), vol. 2, pp. 418-19.

17 Welles Hangen, *After Nehru, Who?* (London: Rupert Hart-Davis, 1973), p. 166.

18 Vasudev, *Indira Gandhi*, chap. 5.

19 Nehru's younger sister reports Indira "practicing being Joan of Arc" at age nine or ten (Krishna Nehru Hutheesing, *We Nehrus* [New York: Holt, Rinehart and Winston, 1967], p. 55). Nehru recalled it to his thirteen-year-old daughter in the letter quoted above (*Selected Works*, vol. 2, p. 418).

20 Mohan, *Indira Gandhi*, p. 187.

21 Henry A. Murray, *Explorations in Personality* (New York: Oxford University Press, 1938), chap. 5, note 29.

22 For a tabulation of Nehru's time in prison see Michael Brecher, *Nehru, a Political Biography* (London: Oxford University Press, 1959), p. 81.

23 Ibid., p. 102; Kalhan, *Kamala Nehru*, p. 30, 123.

24 Vasudev, *Indira Gandhi*, pp. 66-7. Her boarding school life, also, was bitterly lonely. Mohan, *Indira Gandhi*, chap. 6.

25 Hutheesing, *We Nehrus*, p. 54.

26 Kalhan, *Kamala Nehru*, p. 141.

27 Bhatia, *Indira*, p. 43.

28 Ibid., p. 41.

29 Mohan, *Indira Gandhi,* pp. 120-22.

30 Her father's term for his reeducation. Jawaharlal Nehru, *The Discovery of India* (New York: John Day, 1946).

31 Bhatia, *Indira,* p. 34. Her father wrote her from jail both in Hindi and (later) in English. Nehru, *Selected Works,* vol. 1, p. 347; vol. 2, p. 416.

32 Vasudev, *Indira Gandhi,* pp. 60-61.

33 Bhatia, *Indira,* p. 40-41.

34 Mohan, *Indira Gandhi,* pp. 91-93.

35 Hangen, *After Nehru,* p. 165.

36 Published as *Glimpses of World History* (New York: John Day, 1942), first published Allahabad, 1934-35. Though no doubt intended for publication (Nehru needed the income), the letters were received by Indu as messages from her "dear Papu." Bhatia, *Indira,* pp. 83-84.

37 Mohan, *Indira Gandhi,* p. 108.

38 Jawaharlal Nehru, *Selected Works,* vol. 5, pp. 395-452. Characteristically, Gandhi urged Nehru to resume family interviews, and he eventually did. Equally characteristically, he again renounced them when he was jailed in the 1940s. Vasudev, *Indira Gandhi,* p. 198.

39 Of this episode, Richard Merelman commented to me: "It was surely a lesson in how distant one should stand to loved ones in the interests of politics."

40 Mohan, *Indira Gandhi,* p. 105.

41 "The rigid discipline that formerly had regulated the lives of the Nehru children yielded to a permissive freedom. Indira was growing up without orders from a governess. No fixed bedtime for her" (Krishna Nehru Hutheesing, *Dear to Behold: An Intimate Portrait of Indira Gandhi* [London: Macmillan, 1969] , p. 35).

42 Nehru, *Selected Works,* vol. 1, p. 343; Vasudev, *Indira Gandhi,* p. 76.

43 Compare the "bare pass" of her matriculation and her failure at her first attempt at the Oxford admission examination with her grade school performance in Geneva and her first year of college at Santiniketan: Bhatia, *Indira,* p. 73; Mohan, *Indira Gandhi,* chap. 6; K. A. Abbas, *Indira Gandhi, Return of the Red Rose* (Bombay: Popular Prakashan, 1966), pp. 60-69.

44 Nehru, *The Discovery of India,* p. 28.

45 Ibid., pp. 30-31.

46 Kalhan, *Kamala Nehru,* pp. 83 ff. Nehru confided to his diary the pain her decision caused him: "Apparently I was not to come in the way of God" (*Selected Works,* vol. 6, pp. 312-13).

[47] See the remarkable "medical history" he wrote in 1935 ending with this conclusion. Kalhan, *Kamala Nehru*, pp. 107-10.

[48] Vasudev, *Indira Gandhi*, p. 33.

[49] Nehru's word. *Discovery of India*, p. 28.

[50] Kalhan, *Kamala Nehru*, pp. 140-1. Other evidence abounds. She says her mother established a fund out of which she paid all her expenses, through college: "I never took money from my father" (ibid., p. 18). This is irreconcilable with Uma Vasudev's statement about the years at Oxford: "Indira could draw upon her father's account which consisted mostly of the royalties from his book and the sum that he had set apart for her" (Vasudev, *Indira Gandhi*, p. 31).

[51] Kalhan, *Kamala Nehru*, p. 68.

[52] "Identity, Psychosocial," in *International Encyclopedia of the Social Sciences*, vol. 7 (New York: Macmillan and Free Press, 1968), p. 61.

[53] The idea that the task of fitting adolescent potential and social role calls for "moratoria" of very different duration in different individuals is to be found in Erik H. Erikson, *Identity and the Life Cycle* (New York: International Universities Press, 1959), p. 11.

[54] Indira Gandhi, *Speeches and Writings* (New York, Harper and Row, 1975), p. 15.

[55] Ibid.

[56] Kamala, who had suffered from the lack of a formal education, had urged one upon her, too. Masani, *Indira Gandhi, A Biography*, p. 46.

[57] Ibid, p. 52.

[58] Vasudev, *Indira Gandhi*, p. 140. Her principal promised to try to get her exempted from Latin.

[59] Jawaharlal Nehru, *A Bunch of Old Letters* (Bombay: Asia, 1958), p. 214.

[60] Vasudev, *Indira Gandhi*, pp. 136, 146-47. Readers of Erikson will recognize the symptom of identity confusion as he accounts for similar blockages in the early adulthood of Luther and Gandhi.

[61] Kalhan, *Kamala Nehru*, p. 76.

[62] Feroze wrote Swami Abhayananda that "Kamalaji used to tell me about you," and received some of her letters from the swami while she was still alive. Kalhan, *Kamala Nehru*, pp. 92, 101.

[63] Vasudev, *Indira Gandhi*, p. 106.

[64] *Childhood and Society*, 2nd ed. (New York: W. W. Norton, 1963), p. 262.

65 Masani, *Indira Gandhi, A Biography*, pp. 60-61. See also the comment of an American reporter, Hangen, *After Nehru*, p. 167. Nayantara Sahgal, in "The Making of Mrs. Gandhi," introduces an even stronger interpretation: "She told her father that unless he agreed she would not speak to him" (p. 196).

66 Vasudev, *Indira Gandhi*, p. 172.

67 Masani, *Indira Gandhi, A Biography*, p. 95.

68 See Vasudev's perceptive accounting of the factors in her preference (*Indira Gandhi*, pp. 249-50): the weight of her role and the varied experience it provided her; the care she could bestow on her father; the increasing influence as intermediary; the enlargement of her sphere of interests and her growing political stature.

69 Ibid., p. 289. Indira had earlier left the impression that Feroze would grow into some "Colossus" (Abbas, *Indira Gandhi*, pp. 126-27).

70 Mrs. Gandhi's phrase, as to her alternatives. Vasudev, *Indira Gandhi*, p. 250.

71 Masani, *Indira Gandhi, A Biography*, p. 117.

72 She made the point in a letter expressing her deep sense of loss at Feroze's death. Vasudev, *Indira Gandhi*, p. 293.

73 Indira Gandhi, *Speeches and Writings*, p. 37.

74 The term is the title of chap. 6 of Bhatia's *Indira*.

75 For this concept of Erik Erikson, see his *Young Man Luther*, Norton Paperback Library ed., (New York: W. W. Norton, 1962), p. 44.

76 For the concept of negative identity elements, see Erikson, "Identity, Psychosocial," p. 61.

77 Mohan, *Indira Gandhi*, pp. 253-56.

78 Vasudev, *Indira Gandhi*, pp. 211-15.

79 Masani, *Indira Gandhi, A Biography*, pp. 86-89, 118-19, 134.

80 Vasudev, *Indira Gandhi*, pp. 230-40.

81 Ibid., pp. 174-75. Note, too, her Freudian slips in that early period.

82 Ibid., p. 251.

83 Arnold Michaelis, "An Interview with Indira Gandhi," *McCall's* 93 (April 1966): 188.

84 Vasudev, *Indira Gandhi*, p. 274.

85 A balanced contemporaneous account is Jitendra Singh, *Communist Rule in Kerala* (New Delhi: Diwan Chand, 1959).

86 Vasudev, *Indira Gandhi*, p. 276.

87 Interview with Ved Mehta, *Portrait of India,* 1st ed. 1967 (New York: Farrar, Straus and Giroux, 1970), p. 544. She impressed Welles Hangen as even more likely to continue on her father's course after his death. Hangen, *After Nehru,* p. 180.

88 "I don't brook any interference either" she told Uma Vasudev with regard to her term as Congress president. Vasudev, *Indira Gandhi,* p. 274.

89 Indira Gandhi, *Speeches and Writings*, p. 32. Similar criticism was elicited by Michaelis, "Interview," p. 191. This, as Richard Merelman suggested to me, is a judgment perhaps reflecting her own frustration under her father's authority.

90 Claire Sterling, "Ruler of 600 Million, and Alone," *New York Times Magazine,* August 10, 1975, p. 46.

91 Mehta, *Portrait of India,* pp. 545-46.

92 Vasudev, *Indira Gandhi,* p. 291.

93 Bhatia, *Indira,* p. 159.

94 Masani, *Indira Gandhi, A Biography,* p. 139; Hangen, *After Nehru,* p. 279: "If she did become Prime Minister, I would discount her staying power." For general doubts concerning her ability: Michael Brecher, *Succession in India* (London: Oxford University Press, 1966), pp. 47-54.

95 Erikson, *Young Man Luther,* p. 543.

96 Mehta, *Portrait of India,* p. 543.

97 Brecher observes that quite unlike the 1964 succession decision, the choice of Mrs. Gandhi was made without consideration of who could best govern. *Succession in India,* p. 239.

98 Vasudev, *Indira Gandhi,* p. 366.

99 Stanley Kochanek presents the issues of party control in chap. 4, above. The fullest account is in Basant Kumat Chatterjee, *The Congress Splits* (Delhi: S. Chand, 1970). The sense of crises is captured in Bhatia, *Indira,* pp. 220-28: "She was like a wounded tiger."

100 Erikson, "Identity, Psychosocial," p. 61.

101 Ibid., p. 62, 64.

102 For studies of this type of politician, see James David Barber, *The Lawmakers* (New Haven: Yale University Press, 1965) and *The Presidential Character: Predicting Performance in the White House* (Englewood Cliffs, N. J.: Prentice Hall, 1972).

103 Indira Gandhi, *Speeches and Writings,* p. 100.

104 Hangen, *After Nehru,* p. 181.

105 Vasudev, *Indira Gandhi,* p. 287.

106 Indira Gandhi, *Speeches and Writings,* Foreword.

107 Michaelis, "An Interview with Indira Gandhi," p. 191.

108 See, to take one instance, the attitude she evoked from the secretary of the women's section of the Congress. Vasudev, *Indira Gandhi,* pp. 236 ff. Concerning her personal staff, see ibid., p. 220. There is some unpublished counterevidence more recently, but I cannot weigh it.

109 Morarji Desai, on the eve of the emergency: "Beware of criticizing her. . . . Indira's revenge will be swift and ruthless. . . . There are few countries in the world where fear holds such sway as in Indira Gandhi's India" (Fallaci, "Mrs. Gandhi's Opposition," p. 13).

110 Bhatia, *Indira,* chap. 11, especially pp. 272-3, 282.

111 Krishan Bhatia, *The Ordeal of Nationhood* (New York: Atheneum, 1971), p. 158.

112 Kuldip Nayar, *Between the Lines* (Bombay, Allied, 1969), p. 85.

113 Short summaries of the Maruti (name of the planned automobile) affair are given by Bhatia, *Indira,* pp. 267-69; and Masani, *Indira Gandhi, A Biography,* pp. 267-69. Lewis Simon's account of it, dispatched from Bangkok after he was expelled from India, was published in the *Milwaukee Journal,* July 20, 1975.

114 Masani, *Indira Gandhi, A Biography,* p. 268.

115 Ibid., p. 91; Vasudev, *Indira Gandhi,* p. 293.

116 Verbatim interview in Kalhan, *Kamala Nehru,* p. 72.

117 Verbatim interview, ibid., pp. 130-41.

118 Harold Lasswell, *Psychopathology and Politics,* new ed. (New York: Viking, 1960), p. 300. A similar concept was developed by Alexander George, "Power as a Compensatory Value for Political Leaders," *Journal of Social Issues* 24 (1968), no. 3: p. 32.

119 Sahgal, "The Making of Mrs. Gandhi," pp. 199, 205.

10

Explanations

Henry C. Hart

Looking back over the account that has been presented here, certain anomalies are striking. There is, first, the evident gulf between Mrs. Gandhi's view of the impact of her takeover and our own. Aside from any conclusions about the integration of her personality around a need for domination, it is highly improbable that she (or any individual) could so control events unless she were wholly committed to the rightness of her course. Our curiosity draws us toward trying to identify sources of discrepancy between her view and our own.

A little reflection will show another anomaly. It lies between the urban-industrial and the rural parts of Indian society. Through Howard Erdman's eyes, we have seen the emergency policies fitting rather well into the all-India urban-industrial context, so that government aims in that area—i.e., more responsible but creative corporate business, plus constraint upon union-management conflict—have a good chance to be achieved. In rural Bihar the prospects are entirely different. In F. Tomasson Jannuzi's judgment, none of Mrs. Gandhi's redistributive measures seems likely to break through the cumulative inequalities of rural power, rooted as they are in the control of land. Why such contrasting prospects?

Finally, and a bit more theoretically, there is an apparent contrast between, on the one hand, the complexity and integrity of institutions and their elaborate differentiation of roles—

275

in these respects India seems already developed—and on the other, their relevance to the crisis of the country. Stanley Heginbotham has shown us a bureaucracy able to adapt almost instantly to vast new burdens imposed from the top, yet not prepared to proceed with the implementation of long-authorized programs inside the villages. The Congress party, likewise, mediated three potentially dangerous successions, defused explosive regional conflicts, entrusted itself boldly to rural self-government elections, but then docilely submitted to deboning from the top. India's elaborate political institutions seem attached to the country at the top, or at the bottom, but not both. The military, in Stephen Cohen's portrait, retains its full competence only because its ties, whether to the top of the polity or to the villages, are so narrowly vocational that it is irrelevant to the present transformation.

To look for answers to these puzzles we are drawn outside the scope of our observations so far. We have been concerned centrally with institutions. Clearly, we cannot understand them without examining the society upon which they seek to function and whose impulses they must accommodate. There is, in our case, another reason for casting our net a bit wider before we draw conclusions. We need all the predictive power we can gain. Mrs. Gandhi, increasingly as the repression she instituted many months ago solidifies, justifies her alteration of the operative constitution on the ground that economic productivity and justice are more important than civil liberties. Some of her most impassioned critics reverse the order of values.[1] We are not, in this book, entering that argument. We do not dismiss its significance. But we do think it premature to pose a choice between freedom and economic justice before we know whether the immediate contraction of civil liberties and suspension of elections will further economic productivity and redistribution. This is a predictive question to which social scientists have their contribution to make.

Prediction rests upon the identification of regularities observable in the past and present, thus warranting projection into the future. Our most effective strategy for discerning such regularities is to comb the literature for theoretical formulations which, drawn from the diverse experience of many nations, bear upon the puzzles we have identified in India. We need, first, to identify relevant processes of change in the Indian nation, in the political populace. Having some understanding of this broader field, we can return to our attempt to predict what institutions can do, confronted with new challenges and new constraints.

CHANGES IN THE SOCIETAL CONTEXT

If we can detect in Indira Gandhi's India—in the conflicts that made it seem necessary to concentrate power, in the alignments of support and hostility, in the economic and social transformations undertaken, in the preliminary results—the working of more than a single human will, more than a reaction to the decisions of two courts, more even than the coincidence of party gains and losses, then we have a chance of gaining predictive power beyond the reach of one career. Are there at work beneath the surface, generating the needs, the potentials, and the impossibilities upon which a realistic decision maker posits his or her strategic choices, those "semi-automatic trends" to which Karl Deutsch called attention two decades ago?[2] Clearly, some of the most acute analysts of Mrs. Gandhi's statecraft assume so; our own authors make such assumptions at particular points in their appraisals.

Class Contradictions, Class Conflict

India has proved frustrating to Marxist explanations to the degree that theorists have taken their theory seriously. At the negative task of revealing the impotence of the present pattern of rule, Marxist thought has proved percipient. It was twenty years ago that Paul Baran wrote of the Congress regime in India:

> Setting out to promote the development of industrial capitalism, it does not dare to offend the landed interests. . . . It merely reflects the stage which the class struggle has reached in Indian society. Handicapped by the heterogeneity and brittleness of its social foundations and by the ideological limitations resulting therefrom, the essentially petty-bourgeois [sic] regime is incapable of providing genuine leadership in the battle for industrialization. . . . [It] is powerless to mobilize what is most important: the enthusiasm and the creative energies of the broad popular masses.[3]

But at anticipating what may follow, the tendency to regard whole political systems as functions of society-wide class dynamics turns into a trap. We may use Baran again to illustrate. Regarding India's future, he wrote:

> Reactionary forces may be able to make use of the exasperation of the masses and of their disillusionment with the vacuous socialist phraseology to stage a fascist overturn . . . a dictatorship that would give a new lease on life to the rule of capitalism in city and village.[4]

This deserves comment since many of Mrs. Gandhi's critics call her regime fascist. The government does, to be sure, share with European fascist regimes the use of police against dissidents, the patronizing of large industry, the exhortation to discipline, and (to a limited extent) the replacement of institutional roles by personal dependence on the leader. But Mrs. Gandhi's sense of her mission as vindicating the poorest strata and cultural minorities could not be in greater contrast to Hitler's and Mussolini's appeal to racial or historical exclusiveness. Mrs. Gandhi is not, furthermore, acting to discipline her population by herding them into a party or any other network of groups designed to control the bottom of society. Her changes are at the top.

A scholar who uses class analysis to describe the shifts of power in societies over long sweeps of history, as Barrington Moore does, finds India a conundrum.[5] The rural poor are miserable to the point of threatened, episodically actual, starvation. Their numbers and their relative deprivation increase. But they do not rebel. Moore turns to the explanation that the caste basis of Indian society inhibits class formation in the countryside, and though he is not comfortable with cultural explanations he cannot rule out the dampening influence of *dharma* in the Indian case. He has gone part way along the escape route Marx himself took, that of regarding India as in a separate universe to which the general laws of class formation and conflict do not apply.[6]

It is therefore interesting to discover a sociologist of India, one thoroughly familiar with the impacts of caste and of cultural traditions in rural society, turning to class formation and class conflict for explanatory purposes. André Béteille defines class rigorously. In his concept it is shared interest, based upon differential property relations, raised to the level of consciousness and capable of organization in opposition or conflict with other classes.[7] Class formation, so defined, is not inhibited by caste. In Tanjore district, Béteille was impressed that the extreme segregation of untouchable laborers in separate hamlets only made them more accessible and more receptive to the propaganda of the Communist organizer of an agricultural laborers' union. Caste was thus translated into class.

There are two implications of Béteille's use of class conflict theory for empirical investigation of social relationships. One is that the formation of classes is local, and the incidence of such formations is regional. Even within Tajore, the old eastern delta could be understood in terms of conflicting classes; less so could the newly irrigated western half. Eastern India and the extreme south, Béteille finds, and Bhabani Sen Gupta's review of the Communist parties in India confirms, are more amenable to a class interpretation of politics than are the west or north. The second implication is that the awakening of consciousness of class interests and the fitting of a suitable organization to those interests to struggle for them are acts of political creativity, not "semi-automatic trends." Béteille's study of the Tebhaga movement in East Bengal, the classic case in India of an uprising of poor peasants, demonstrates that even the term *jotedar* for "noncultivating landowner" came into use only in the course of the movement conducted by the Krishak Sabha. And it didn't come to represent a single oppressing class until twenty years later when the Naxalite and CPM organizers led a wave of squat-ins and seizures of the paddy harvest. Even then the Bengal underclass was dependent on the backing of the administration, and vulnerable to its withdrawal.[8]

Francine Frankel's early suggestions to the contrary,[9] there is no evidence that the new agricultural technology changes the mediating role of political institutions in class conflict. The Green Revolution has overwhelmed the wheat areas of India, while making little headway in the paddy fields. But the incidence of Communist success, as Donald Zagoria shows,[10] is greater in the rice-growing deltas than in the wheatfields of Punjab, Haryana and western Uttar Pradesh.

Once we accept the premise of Béteille, and of Paul Brass,[11] that class conflict waits upon the political organization of property-related interests, the conventional Marxist class-contradiction analysis of Indira Gandhi's India must be modified in two respects. First, class conflict will not widen and deepen except as broader, more responsive, and more militant political party activity takes place. The three-way division Bhabani Sen Gupta shows us in Communist activity is, from this perspective, part of any reasonable basis for prediction. The large-scale industrial base, with its access to the national policy forums, supports the CPI, reaching out to the rural poor where they are relatively politicized. The CPM has had to become regionalized, trying to lead class conflict in remote villages. The CPML pits itself against the entire state apparatus. If the very process of mobilizing class conflict divides the mobilizers, we have reason to pursue our analysis of the societal trends at something less than the national macrolevel.

The other corollary is that contradictions in Mrs. Gandhi's support base do not a priori make it weaker than that of any alternative, certainly including that which might be generated by even a vastly enlarged, but still divided, coalition around one or more Communist parties. The question for Mrs. Gandhi's regime, or for any national regime in India that seeks to transform society, is whether it can mobilize its support base selectively, arousing consciousness of interests among the bottom strata, giving them political access, making bureaucracy responsive to their needs. These are questions of the effective linking of decision makers to constituents, key determinants of the accuracy of all party promises. Mrs. Gandhi's government will not fall apart from its class contradictions while the CPM waits. Neither will the rural poor benefit from her programs while she extends them through the existing rural power structure.

The Cities

The eighth of India that is distinctly urban[12] has, as we observed, generated all of the protest to date against Mrs. Gandhi's repression; yet, most of her programmatic accomplishments have been in the urban areas. Much of the urban economy is in modern, organized establishments. Much of labor is unionized. A government administration motivated from the top can act effectively on these large, accessible units. By the same token, unions aggrieved at government cuts in the annual bonus can manifest their grievance in strikes difficult to hide even under censorship. And, of course, the handful of unintimidated High Court judges and lawyers who hold civil liberties to be rights not at Mrs. Gandhi's disposal draw their ideas from the cosmopolitan culture of the cities and effectuate them through urban institutions.

In the broadest sense, Mrs. Gandhi is disciplining hitherto autonomous institutions to behave in the national interest, as her government defines it. She is forcing outright lawbreakers—smugglers, income tax evaders, and holders of black money—to behave within the law. Where powerful organizations have been deadlocked due to unresolved union-management conflicts, she is knocking heads together to cut the social loss. The need for disciplining may be the greater in a society whose most revered cultural traditions stress the discrete morality of each occupational group. In the words of the Gita:

> Better [to do] one's own [caste-] duty, though devoid of merit, than [to do] another's, however well performed.[13]

However that might work in simpler societies, residents of India's largest city had felt the effects for several years of each industry, union, and militant political party pursuing its own exclusive destiny, even to the extent of killing those who interfered. Historically, Mrs. Gandhi's emergency may be viewed as the answer, writ large, which she and her protégé, Siddhartha Shankar Ray, tried out in Calcutta five years earlier. Heavy-handed police action coupled with the mobilization of youth into the Congress to combat (often literally) the CPM cadres succeeded in reducing Calcutta's debilitating factionalism to order; voters seemed to prefer the new discipline.[14]

Even in Calcutta, however, the turmoil of the old order will tend to be forgotten, as may be the initial resistance to censorship and abrogation of rights. If we are to assess the viability of emergency discipline continued in India's cities for five or ten years in the future, we must balance more durable causes of unrest and stability. Samuel Huntington suggests what these are. The urban intelligentsia will be chronically committed to ideas of political rights and to visions of a radically restructured society. But the cities in developing nations rarely explode, because the intelligentsia is initially so tiny a fraction and because the bureaucrats, technicians, traders, and well-paid modern industrial workers who fill the jobs in an expanding economy are less and less revolutionary in outlook.[15]

Longer-run stability, then, will require the creation of urban jobs in the modern sector at a rate well above urban population growth. By this test, Mrs. Gandhi's prospects are gloomy. The truth is that employment in the modern sector, which increased by 6 percent each year in the five years up to 1966, has since been growing at less than the national rate of population increase, and at about half the rate of urban population increase.[16] The reason is obvious, and it is a problem to which Mrs. Gandhi is proposing no solution. Having allocated most industrialization to the public sector, the government has not raised capital to expand it. The figures are damning. Up to 1965-66, when growth stopped, more than 21 percent of government income was being plowed back into savings; five years later the rate had dropped to below 10 percent.[17] Private sector capital formation continued, sporadically, to increase, but because of the stagnation of public investment after 1966, total net domestic capital formation, which rose 58 percent in the six preceding years, actually declined, in real terms, from 1966 to 1972.[18] There are two stubborn reasons why public sector investments stagnated. Existing firms are too inefficient to produce investable surpluses, and government is not tapping with progressive taxation the new wealth produced by existing economic growth. Mrs. Gandhi's current measures may reduce the first problem, especially if labor peace continues in public industries. She is not touching the second, because the vast pool of untaxed wealth is in the hands of the surplus-producing village landowners who are the local pillars of the Congress party. Exempt from income tax, their net income is taxed directly at well under 1 percent. Where they put their own money into small enterprises, as in the Punjab, the economy booms. But the public sector, heavily dependent on taxes for investment, starves.[19] It will continue to under Mrs. Gandhi's announced program.

We can focus our predictive analysis more sharply on a particular group. "The students," Huntington writes, "are the most coherent and effective revolutionaries within the intelligentsia."[20] Mrs. Gandhi has put the striking students back into their classrooms all across India. But there is an obstinate barrier to their entry into the ranks of the complaisant middle class: many of them are not going to find jobs. There are no entirely valid measures of unemployment among the educated in India. But we can be clear about the magnitude of the problem. In 1971 there were about 10 million male high school or college graduates in urban India, and in that year, judging from the number of job seekers registered with the employment exchanges, 1.8 million of them were out of work. By October 1975 registered job seekers among the educated had climbed to

4.1 million.[21] In between those two dates, a sample of literate youth, ages eighteen to twenty-four, revealed 24 percent of the urban sample unemployed. This survey also showed that five-sixths of these unemployed youth had been job hunting more than six months.[22]

This is not a problem to be cured merely by stepping up job formation in organized industry and services. The educational system is, at a steadily accelerating rate, turning out youth mis-educated for the technical jobs that will open up. Over two-thirds of all degree holders, and an even higher percentage of the high school graduates, have nontechnical skills; many of these will never find work.[23] Like other threats to the stability of the political order, this one has been diagnosed for some time. Ten years ago, indeed, R. A. Gopalaswami, as a member of the prestigious Education Commission, pinpointed the problem, looking ahead to 1975-76. By that time, he said, if all job-creating programs succeed, but the educational output is not shifted to agriculture and technical skills, the average time a high school or college graduate will have to wait before finding employment will have stretched from 92 to 137 weeks.[24] Nothing has been done to implement the Education Commission's sound proposals in the intervening decade, nor has Mrs. Gandhi come to grips with the problem. It is still possible that she will. However, the vested interests in India's ubiquitous high schools and arts colleges are enormous, not only in terms of students and faculty, but also politically potent boards of supervision. Starting a home-town college—and winning a government subsidy for it—or launching a cooperative society: these are the commonest ways for prospective political candidates to accumulate resources for the next campaign.[25]

Mrs. Gandhi's programs, then, cut nowhere near deep enough to solve the manifest problems of the urban society. In Huntington's view, however, the disaffection of the intelligentsia and the students in particular will ferment regardless of programmatic success.[26] What will be the effects of Mrs. Gandhi's political changes on this unrest? First, she weakens the already flabby Congress organizations at city and state levels just when they need fresh initiative and determination to recruit and socialize into the party aggrieved trade unionists and youth: she identifies the party with the bureaucracy and with policies that may be the objects of popular protest; she confuses it with the CPI; and she systematically undermines the support base of strong, independent party leaders. We will come back to this problem.

The other grave political consequence of her repression is that she undercuts the legitimacy of two-party competition in city politics. Unlike the villages, Indian cities have enough varied organizations, enough informed citizens, and enough large-scale cultural and economic interests to sustain stable party competition. The Congress has regularly faced serious threats from the Jan Sangh in the Hindi states, and from the Communists or a party of subnational cultural identity elsewhere. Up to 1975, this competition had generated a magnetic field, drawing opposition politicians toward trying to form governments, city or state, and thus mobilizing the disaffections of the urban middle classes and students into elective politics. Bhabani Sen Gupta shows the moderating pull this magnetic field has exerted upon revolutionary parties; only the Naxalites resisted it, but they set out to incite the countryside, not the cities. Mrs. Gandhi now declares the Jan Sangh illegitimate because it is communal and harbors a quasi-military cadre, the RSS, which she outlawed. The CPM continues on a kind of probation, with tactics paralleling those of the Naxalites now a real option for it. While elections were still held, the vote—a modest 10 to 15 percent for the Jan Sangh, and a like proportion for both Communist parties, across all cities—measured the weakness of the disaffection among the electorate.[27] With the polls closed, some of this disaffection is converted into resistance, and the resistance of even 10 percent of an urban population, peaking in large cities, may be a serious threat.

Subsistence Villages

All Indian society is, in the broadest sense, involved in a very slow and incomplete transition from rural to urban (our dichotomy is, of course, an artificial one, designed to bring out elements of the change). So, also, the presently larger rural portion of Indian society is in transition from subsistence to interdependence (again we simplify the transition into a dichotomy). By subsistence villages we mean what the anthropologist Davydd Greenwood defines as peasant society:

> Peasant family farming emerges as a social type where (1) agriculture is practiced within domestic groups . . ., (2) where subsistence is supplied by the domestic group's own production or by the local

community, and (3) where some part of the family's product is appropriated by the local community and by the state for their activities.[28]

The only term of this definition we need to interpret is "domestic groups." In India they include the low-caste client families attached traditionally to farm families as laborers and domestic servants. Assuming some reasonable cutoff points as to percentage of wage labor in agriculture, percentage of produce marketed, and degree of penetration of rural society by communications, it should be possible to use the definition to sort Indian rural districts into those of predominantly subsistence character and those now commercialized.[29] The districts of eastern Uttar Pradesh and northern Bihar, of eastern and southern Rajasthan, of Madhya Pradesh, and of the nonindustrialized interior of the Deccan would emerge in the subsistence category; much of Punjab and Haryana, western Uttar Pradesh, Kaira in Gujarat, the irrigated areas of Maharashtra, Tanjore and Coimbatore in Tamil Nadu, and the rural hinterland of the metropolitan cities would fall in our commercialized category. Subsistence villages would, according to this categorization, make up about as much of rural India in 1975 as would commercialized villages.

The context subsistence villages present for Indira Gandhi's political and economic changes is described by F. Tomasson Jannuzi in chapter 7. By comparing this context with the urban one and that of commercialized villages, we can gain further insights into the likely future of India, and relate India to some of the generalizations that have been made about developing nations as a group.

Much of what Jannuzi describes and predicts is understandable if we think of the subsistence village in terms of Robert Redfield's concept, presented twenty years ago in *Peasant Society and Culture*:[30]

> A peasant society is two connecting halves. We may be able to see a sort of link or hinge between the local life of a peasant community and the state or feudal system of which it is a part.[31]

Neither Mrs. Gandhi's administrative hierarchy nor her political party penetrates the village half of a divided society; both are linked to it but feebly by brokers—Redfield's "hinge" is a better word because it connotes the possibility of a change in direction in the transmission of a force—who cannot secure compliance in the village. For this simple but fundamental reason, neither land, nor credit, nor wages—none of the essential values of agrarian life—will, in fact, be redistributed under Mrs. Gandhi's announced reforms.[32]

Redfield's concept is useful to free our thinking from the dominant stereotype of American social science—the nation as a single social system—but it does not do justice to the interlocking relationship between status inside the village and linkage to the state. Greenwood, concerned with the political economy of peasant life, corrects the emphasis: the state everywhere extracts revenue from the peasant community, giving, in return, the expectation of civil peace. The institutionalization of this link was very plain in British India, for the state reached the village almost exclusively through revenue administration: thus the earlier Mughal practice was systematized, and it lives on in the rigidities of contemporary Indian rural administration. Jannuzi calls this "an extractive and control nexus" between "those who hold power in India" and "landholding intermediaries" in the village.[33] The question posed by Mrs. Gandhi's redistributive programs, if they be taken as more than rhetoric, is "whether a new, direct nexus can be forged with the rural poor."

In various forms, this has been the question in Indian rural policy for a quarter-century, and the cumulative answer is no. The abolition of *zamindars* tended, save in the most backward pockets, e.g., in Bihar, to confirm landlords holding land within villages, though it bought off the still larger estate holders. Cooperative societies subsidized credits to larger landowners.[34] Community development programs in the 1950s put demonstrations on the larger farms, whose owners could afford experiments. This was even more true of the Intensive Agricultural Districts and the new seed-fertilizer-irrigation technology of the Green Revolution. Whether delivering water by canal or by tube well, irrigation goes first to the largest landowners in the village. Legislation nominally giving tenure to tenants on the land and regulating their rents had the practical effect, at best, of establishing the tenants of absentee landlords; those landlords who lived in the villages downgraded their tenants to the status of laborers, and were thereby able to keep possession of the land. The whole record is as the Reserve Bank enquiry found it to be twenty-five years ago:

> The *status quo* and the non-compliance are often achieved conjointly and at great effort by the leading elements in the village and the subordinate agencies of the government. . . . The persons who suffer

in the process are the weaker and disadvantaged elements of the village for whose benefit the directives and policies are conceived.[35]

The consistency of failure poses two questions. Why has it been so? Why has it not been perceived to be so? The answer to the first question is the homely truth conveniently forgotten by reformers: the administrative hierarchies of the state do not reach inside the village. The end of the modern bureaucratic chain of command is in the *taluq*, or at best the *thana*, head-quarters. The state's agents in the village are (under various names and with some variations in assignment) the *patel*, who holds revenue and police power, and the *patwari*, who maintains records of title to land. Both are within the village social struc-ture—not that of the modern state—the *patel* by being of a prominent landowning lineage in the village, the *patwari* often of a Brahmin village family. If a state law confers ownership upon a tenant who has tilled a field for a certain number of years, the *patwari* can be counted on to have no record of that occupancy on his register: to be sure he is routinely bribed, but more basic is his need to survive in the village, where power rests on land.[36] If laborers strike for the minimum wage guar-anteed by the new laws and are beaten up by the *lathials* ("hired thugs") of the landowners, the *patel* may be counted on not to have witnessed the assault, or to have seen the sticks in the hands of the laborers. It is not, thus, that the village is iso-lated, tenuously connected to the state; it is, rather, that the state institutionalizes in the village the power on which its origi-nal source of revenue was founded, land ownership. The misap-prehension of outside observers would be cleared if they recog-nized that India administers its villages by a miniaturized ver-sion of what was called in the language of colonialism "indirect rule."

Why, then, are reforms debated so seriously without regard for this fact of life? At the state level, cynicism is often the rea-son. But in Delhi some interesting stereotypes have intervened between the thinking of reformers and the control of produc-tion in the villages. The older stereotype was of the village as a consensual community, overlaid to be sure by landlord power established by the British,[37] but ready to cooperate to define and meet needs as envisioned by American rural sociologists, or to give land to the landless as envisioned by the Bhoodan pro-gram. The field work of anthropologists, many of them Ameri-cans, shattered this communitarian image in the 1950s.[38]

Village power came to be seen as divided among factions. The new perception coincided with and was the most illuminating explanation brought to bear upon the working of *panchayati raj*—the indirectly elected system of rural self-governing institutions extended to rural India beginning in 1959. The stereotype of the village split over the allocation of values supplanted the stereotype of village consensus, but the new stereotype, too, neglected the domination of village society by land ownership. Factions commonly contested individual rights to land; they never disagreed that land bestowed the right to village power or to favored access to government. That these were among the unchallengeable ground rules of factional contests was easily lost to sight as attention focused on division.[39]

When *panchayat* institutions were first given control over the development budget in the countryside, beginning in 1959, those with economic power could keep their control because they had simple procedural advantages. For example, voting for *panchayat* members was by show of hands, permitting the landed, dominant-caste farmer to watch his untouchable laborers vote. These advantages have generally been eliminated. But there are subtler ones built into the system. *Panchayats* may cover more than one village (two, on the average), and election to the higher bodies that control the budget is indirect: these features favor the candidate with wider contacts. Moreover, since *panchayat* programs are funded by state money, not self-taxation by the village bodies, access to higher administrators and politicians is of great advantage in producing results within the village. We conclude that the net effect of *panchayati raj* is, again, to reinforce existing rural power.

Yet, elections in India, including *panchayat* elections, are clearly evoking the participation of the lower strata, including the landless and the "unclean" castes. Many case studies agree on this point. How can this be squared with the reinforcement of existing power? The subsistence village has, in fact, triple linkage to the state and national political systems. The first, most firmly institutionalized, is the old link of land and revenue. It ties the propertied (in rough proportion to their size of holding) to the state via the *patwari*, the *patel*, and the irrigation staff. Second is the *panchayat* and state election system, which links the heads of village factions to the state legislature and the development staff of state governments via the local Congress party leader and the state legislator. The third, hardly

institutionalized at all, is the tie the villagers feel to Indira
Gandhi, or perhaps to members of Parliament or state ministers
as they make speeches about redistribution of rural wealth and
power. What villagers get for their votes, delivered through this
connection, is symbolic redistribution of land and productive
resources. It must remain symbolic, however, because these assets, in short supply, are controlled by the first set of links.
Links of the second type—through *panchayat* representatives
and state legislators—control real, not symbolic values. They
spend state money to distribute boons to the villages: roads,
wells, subsidized fertilizer, school buildings. They do not dis-
turb the property-revenue link, but rather involve it in the
newer forms of creating wealth—new crops, agricultural processing and marketing, credit, and transport. How important this
new economic game may be we shall see in a moment.

In the meantime we should note that our conclusion on the
relation of the control of the means of production to village
political power is exactly what Marxist theory would predicate.
Our reasoning, however, is different. We do not assume that
political power is but the superstructure of control of the means
of production. What we conclude in this instance, rather, is
that, as new forms of political power are introduced by the
state into a relatively closed system of village power through
links institutionalized to control land, the new forms tend to
reinforce the existing control. They are certainly not available
to upset it, contrary to the assumptions implicit in Indira
Gandhi's twenty-point program.

Paths to Mobilization

Even the most superficial examination of the political context in Ludhiana district of the Punjab, Kaira in Gujarat, Shola-
pur in Maharashtra, or Guntur in Andhra convinces one that
these areas are not like Bihar, as Tomasson Jannuzi has portrayed that state for us. There is no satisfactory word or concept for what has happened in these profoundly changing rural
districts; their change is multidimensional. For want of a better
term, we can consider them well along in a process of mobilization[40] into the larger state and national society.

In such parts of India, even prior to the Green Revolution, a
great economic change has been going on. Crops are grown for

the market, and new profits are being taken from the fields by the application of purchased fertilizer, new seeds, pesticides, implements, and especially irrigation water. Information penetrates, partly via the technology of the transistor radio (from which the five-acre irrigated cultivator learns daily market prices and makes his decision to transport his harvest beyond the nearest market town to fetch a higher price), partly by increased contacts with town, and in the new generation through general literacy (in these areas there is a primary school in each sizable village).

Interdependencies with the government intensify and spread. Most of this commercial cropping is irrigated; the government supplies water from the canal network or electricity to run the tube wells. A large share of credit is from the government. If new seed varieties are used, the harvest depends absolutely upon quick diagnosis and chemical treatment of exotic plant diseases and insect attacks; two weeks without government help and the crop fails. No longer can the headman, the three or four big landlords, or even the heads of the village factions, broker these connections. All commercial farm operators are drawn into contact with government agencies.

No longer traditional, the new farming puts a premium upon owner-operation of farms, and handsomely rewards skilled manipulation of new technology. Tenancy-reform laws genuinely worked in two ways to institutionalize the high returns to farm management: they dispossessed absentee landlords; and, as we saw, by permitting farming landlords to retain title to their land, they reduced tenants on these farms to laborers. Thus the characteristic demographic shift: a complex, multilevel tenurial situation is reduced to two producing classes—owner-operators and wage laborers. Rice farming differs from the rest. In the paddies the hired workers continue to be a majority. In northern and western India, on the other hand, owner-cultivators have become a majority of all rural workers. The laborers lose their traditional patron-client securities. They tend also to be untouchables, still suffering caste as well as economic disabilities. But they gain bargaining power, for intensive cultivation increases the need for their work, and a labor market develops. There are the seeds here either for class conflict or for rural collective bargaining.[41]

Within the broad trend to commercialization are several patterns. Wheat farmers in Punjab and the environs of Delhi are putting their profits into small industries. In Ludhiana district 65 percent of all work is outside agriculture.[42] Implement, transistor, and bicycle factories provide a safety valve for Chamar and Mazbi laborers. The state government buys all of the marketable wheat and most of the rice; it has its nexus, thus, with the majority of all the rural population who are owner-cultivators. In Maharashtra it is a web of credit cooperatives, cooperative sugar factories, and extension services that has permitted the small owner to make it and to join in the rewarding patronage of the elective district boards.[43]

In all of these areas, agriculture has ceased to be a zero-sum game. When the Green Revolution had caught hold in Ludhiana, the landowners forced down the laborers' share from one shock of wheat in twenty to one in thirty; but because the yield had almost doubled, the laborers took home one-fourth more wheat than before. The Chamar and Mazbi laborers lost their traditional clients' rights to grazing and to loans, but they organized, looked Sikh and Jat landowners in the eye, and by threat of a strike prevented a real wage cut. Both sides knew the laborers could find other jobs.

This path into economic and political mobilization has implications for Indira Gandhi's program. Redistribution of wealth and power will not be achieved in these areas by state governments, for those governments rest upon the owner-cultivators, who constitute the rural majority and who are tied to government directly. The growing sense of exploitation on the part of untouchable laborers will not necessarily polarize into class struggle as long as their bargaining power is maintained economically by the labor demand of a growing economy, or politically by available alliances with the large urban labor force. Predictions that the Green Revolution carries red revolution in its train have not been borne out. They might be if economic growth halts after patron-client bonds have been cut, or if the organization and politicization of laborer grievances is repressed.

A few districts in India demonstrate a different path by which the little societies of the villages can enter the larger fabric of state and national life. Oversimply, we might refer to this as the path of political mobilization to distinguish it from the essentially economic routes we have been examining. The Malabar area of Kerala approximates the ideal type. The eastern *tàluks* of Tanjore district, where class conflict is more acute than in the newly irrigated parts, provide other cases. The conditions appear to be three: slow industrial growth, so that the proportion of laborers, undertenants and smaller-than-subsistence farms remains large after agriculture is commercialized; enlistment of these strata into a political party dedicated to class struggle; and availability of urban support for redistributionist movements. Under such conditions, two lines of development seem possible. In Kerala, because the politicization of the rural have-nots took place as a part of the nationalist movement, led among others by E. M. S. Namboordiripad and A. K. Gopalan, it was possible step-by-step to orient the party system of the communally fragmented state on the basis of cleavages of rural classes.[44] In other parts of India, where the rural class struggle has cut across party alignments already solidified around other cleavages, it has remained local, episodic, and consequently more vulnerable both to abortive Maoist leadership and to economic and political repression.

It is in this very special case of rural class struggle, mobilized by parties at the state level, that redistribution of economic and political power by state action has happened. Kerala shows the only substantial success of the measures Mrs. Gandhi advocates; there it was the firm ties of the CPM with the rural have-nots that energized redistribution that the CPI-Congress coalition merely consummated. There are two significant corollaries. First, despite the most severe overcrowding on agricultural land and the highest rate of educated unemployment in all of India, Kerala has won, not lost, political stability since 1967. Class struggle was at once legitimized and harnessed in the state party system. Only the extraordinary liberality of Indian politics—pre-1975—and the room in the federal system for one small state to develop its own party alignment permitted that remarkable development. The other corollary is that mobilization of rural society into the larger state fabric has been distinctive in many ways that complement the party alignment. The whole complex of national programs premised on village solidarity has remained quiescent in the state; to this day there is no significant establishment of *panchayati raj*. Libraries and schools came ahead of the new technology, newspapers ahead of railroads. Of course, it would be naive to take Kerala as a model for what any immediate set of party initiatives or government policies could make of any other state.

POLITICAL CULTURES AS EXPLANATIONS

Westernized vs. Indigenous Politics

Mrs. Gandhi's critics have been editors, lawyers, judges, opposition party leaders and M.P.s, a few Socialist trade union leaders, students at the most prestigious universities, and young Indians living abroad. Not only do these people communicate their criticisms in English, but the criteria they apply—government bound by law, civil liberties, individual rights—are ideas Indians made their own through English. It becomes an attractive thesis, from this viewpoint, that in taking over control at the expense of these ideas Mrs. Gandhi has shifted the basis of legitimacy from English to indigenous values and expectations, that she rests her case with the hundreds of millions who expect authoritarian and personal rule to produce results. To be sure, we have noted that corporate entrepreneurs and executives, and probably many top civil servants, welcome her disciplining of society. The cultural explanation could accordingly be modified to propose that Mrs. Gandhi has confronted one Westernized cultural tradition—the liberal tradition in politics—with another—productive efficiency in economics—to meet the expectations of some hundreds of millions of people of indigenous traditions.

It is true that scholarly interpretations of India's political cultures have distinguished what the British political scientist W. H. Morris-Jones called the "Western idiom"[45] and the American political scientist Myron Weiner called "elite culture"[46] from indigenous traditions. The cultural thesis thus seems to gain authenticity. But if we probe further into the scholarly interpretations of the *relation* of Westernized to other political cultures in India, the picture changes. In Weiner's view, politicians of the "elite culture" withhold full participation from the emerging leaders, seeing them as parochial in political loyalty, unwilling to sacrifice for the nation, unable to implement Delhi's plans, and inclined to contest what should be national consensus policies. These are just the criticisms Mrs. Gandhi has made in displacing the "old-style politicians." Far from casting off the elite blinders, she is, according to this theory, fully acting out the elitist premise.

Morris-Jones carried his cultural analysis farther. Failures of legitimacy occur in Indian politics, he wrote, because actors whose roles are of one political culture are suspected of conforming to norms of another. Thus the chronic mistrust of leaders in Westernized roles, always suspect of favoring caste or kin or linguistic subculture. Most suspicious are the educated middle class, because of the culture-conflict in which they themselves are caught. Morris-Jones called them "the really threatening force in Indian political life."[47]

Mrs. Gandhi, we can observe from this vantage point, was trusted precisely because she came to the top clean of these traditional ties. Will she some day be seen as having betrayed that trust by creating the conditions, when she gained full control, for the access to power of her son Sanjay?

Our knowledge of the complex effects of culture on politics warns us not to derive from them direct explanations of the conduct either of those who rule or those who follow. We have observed of Mrs. Gandhi that she will not be guided by any ideology that we might trace to a cultural source. If we reflect on Jannuzi's picture of rural Bihar, we must admit the ambiguity of traditional cultural expectations to predict the behavior of people no longer controlled and protected by their traditional patrons. Hierarchical authority is an accepted part of their non-Western cultural inheritance,[48] built into the foundations of caste and the Hindu concept of *karma*. Does it sanction the sharecropper's obeying his newly capitalist landlord, obeying Mrs. Gandhi, or obeying a resident Communist cadreman? It will be the role models supplied by modern politics that translate the norms supplied by culture into specific patterns of action.

Likewise, if we seek to specify from assumptions about culture the norms that may guide and the perceptions that may inform Indian elites, we are compelled to drop the simple paradigm of cultural duality, of a Westernized elite misunderstanding and being misunderstood by people unshaped by English. Ashis Nandy has shown how long English and indigenous conceptions of authority have interpenetrated in Indian politics.[49] Much of the acceptance of Mrs. Gandhi's regime, thus, might come from its fulfillment of the Hindu yearning for consensus, valued at the philosophical level as monism, and translated into contemporary politics as a deep skepticism about party competition, or, indeed, the institutionalization of opposition in any form. If so, Mrs. Gandhi's acceptance comes from the same cultural source as that for Jayaprakash Narayan's "partyless democracy." The fundamental point is that Indian political leaders do not operate in a cultural milieu sufficiently unambiguous to exclude a wide variety of options. Neither do the people in the villages. In this respect India is not unlike the United States at the stage when parties were forming: a careful scholar has called the American political culture of that time "deferential-participant."[50] Such cultures give hostages to heroic leaders.

Center vs. Periphery

There is, of course, one other salient fact about the indigenous cultures of India: they are not one. Mrs. Gandhi has justified some of her police actions, censorship, and specifically the ejection of the elected DMK government of Tamil Nadu on grounds that the unity of India would be otherwise menaced. The DMK she specifically accuses of supporting secession, the Jan Sangh of religious divisiveness. It has long been evident that political identities are divided in India, that the nation shares loyalties with linguistic and religious communities.[51] It is not so obvious that concentration of political legitimacy in New Delhi is the answer. Indeed, for the five years up to 1975, just such a centralizing policy was generally seen to have cost Pakistan Bangladesh, whereas the Indian policy of plural federated cultural communities had defused an equally dangerous Tamil separatist movement.

There is, to be sure, an important strand of political analysis which holds that parties competing for the votes of a new and culturally divided electorate will deepen communal divisions.[52] This is the initial impact. Further competition may subdivide linguistic, religious, or ethnic populations along geographic or factional lines, and eventually communal loyalties, redefined and broadened, may be fixed upon economic or other policy demands.[53] Only two points need be made about the divisive potential of subnational loyalties in the Indian case. The first is that the peripheral culture that Mrs. Gandhi has treated as most threatening have progressed some distance, already, beyond the politics of separatism. Cultural mobilization against the center climaxed twenty to twenty-five years ago in the demand for states redesigned along language lines. Nehru began by resisting that demand stoutly in the name of national unity. He gave in because, if he hadn't, his party faced certain defeat at the polls, and because his police power was insufficient to suppress the agitations. It is, of course, these vulnerabilities of the central power to unforeseen subnationalist demands that Nehru's daughter has now sought to eliminate. Paradoxically, however, Nehru's ultimate softness toward subnationalist demands defused and divided them. The DMK itself split into personal factions; the Communist parties mobilized genuine class grievances locally within the Tamil region. The DMK had gradually since 1965 overlaid its crusade against Brahmin-Hindi cultural imperialism from the north with negotiable issues of budget allocations and the constitution of administrative services. Some of its leaders experienced the rewards of a balance of power role in Parliament. Most important, it had succeeded in bending national language policy to accommodate its most serious concerns. The system had, by avoiding rigid specifications of allegiance, gained working legitimacy among those most inclined to disaffection.[54]

Another aspect of the center-periphery cultural situation is less evident. It might be called the danger of a Hindi backlash. Quite in contrast to the integration of English- and regional-language cultural development in the peripheral states (West Bengal, Tamil Nadu, Kerala, Karnataka, Maharashtra, and Gujarat), Hindi culture has been emerging against English. This is true in a sense much deeper than party cleavages, though the Jan Sangh does exploit this cleavage against the Congress, as does the Socialist party. While the Hindi areas around Delhi prosper, most of the Hindi heartland is backward. Developing late, these areas are ripe for the appeal that has been successfully in Bombay and Hyderabad: that jobs be reserved for "sons of the soil." As peripheral states claim a larger share of development investment from the central budget (and Mrs. Gandhi's administration of Tamil Nadu will no doubt be especially generous in this respect), a large potential grievance will rise in the much poorer Hindi states—Bihar, Madhya Pradesh, Rajasthan, and the eastern portion of Uttar Pradesh. Since 1967, the Jan Sangh has been restrained from raising these regional claims because it has had national ambitions. As Mrs. Gandhi frustrates those ambitions, designating the Jan Sangh a party of communal division, its restraint will correspondingly decline.[55]

INCOMPLETE LINKS

Neither semiautomatic trends, nor class conflict, nor emerging cultures will, we have concluded, determine India's future political direction. All these processes create sectoral potentials. The question is whether these potentials are harnessed and channeled into progress, or explode into chaos. Linkage is crucial. Mrs. Gandhi has seriously weakened three vital links. The CPM is no longer energized (as Bhabani Sen Gupta has shown) to collect the grievances of the rural poor into votes for the party state legislators or demonstrations demanding implementation of land reforms. Nor are other opposition parties energized to harness regional cultural allegiance (Tamil, Sikh, tribal, Muslim, Hindu-Hindi) toward state legislative majorities. Second, newspapers are no longer energized to ferret out discrepancies between official programs and the actual conduct of politicians or bureaucrats. Third, there is little reason for legislators to dramatize popular grievances to ministers sitting across the parliamentary aisle, since both now know that the government will censor the newspaper reports of critical speeches.

A double overload is thus placed from 1975 onward upon the two existing institutional links: the Congress party and the bureaucracy. Mrs. Gandhi must call upon them alone to transform power in the least accessible part of the country, the subsistence villages, since she has cut the auxiliary links between government and people. Stanley Kochanek has shown quite clearly that the structure of the Congress could not, even before 1975, carry that load, and that Mrs. Gandhi has weakened it further. Mrs. Gandhi herself made the same diagnosis in 1972: "The party continues to function in a rather flabby way. . . . It lacks the apparatus which could enable it to do systematic work amongst the young and rural people."[56] But toward correcting institutional structure she has done nothing. She has, therefore, no instrument for reaching inside the subsistence village, enlisting for the party a stable membership of the poor, who now vote for her, but depend for all other access to government on the present links through the landowners, who are also the local stalwarts of the Congress.

Analogous structural failings remain in the bureaucracy. It has no field men who can penetrate the power structure of the subsistence village while retaining their effectiveness in the chain of command.[57] The bureaucracy cannot thus redistribute rural power. There are two other structural weaknesses. Indian bureaucracy is essentially a translated caste system entered not by birth but by written examination. Each closed career follows its own *dharma*, with the writing caste, the Indian Administrative Service (IAS), at the top in status and access to policy. There are two things such a bureaucracy cannot do. One is to manage an ever-changing technology. The other is effectively to challenge citizens to participate in social transformation.

Both structurally inadequate link institutions have taken shape over generations: the bureaucracy for more than a century and the Congress party since Gandhi give it its present structure in 1920. Changing them will be enormously difficult, not only because of overpowering inertia,[58] but because it is not possible to be sure what reforms will work better. A *sine qua non* is that these two institutions remain autonomous, each capable of criticizing the linkage function of the other. They were, unfortunately, fused at the bottom by *panchayati raj.* Unless the Congress can get a base in the villages from which it can criticize the present control of that enormous patronage process, nothing will change. What Mrs. Gandhi has done is to fuse party and administration also at the top; she has supplanted the institutional loyalties of both with personal dependence upon her. It is a process of political fusion exhibited in extreme form in the second decade of some African nations.[59]

THE MEANING OF THE TRENDS

In its broadest outline, the future of India is surprisingly clear for five or ten years ahead. We know the semiautomatic trends. We know they will not be channeled into the social transformations Mrs. Gandhi envisions, for the linking apparatus does not exist. She has deinstitutionalized, not reinstitutionalized. Lives of leaders will alter the broad outline little: we know the range of variation of the monsoon, though not the year in which the drought will come. Only war can upset the chain of probabilities.

Uprooted and Unmobilized

Subsistence agriculture will continue to be commercialized. Minifarm owners and laborers and village artisans will be displaced by the millions. Mrs. Gandhi's programs accelerate this both by making traditional patron-client relations risky to landlords and by opening the eyes of tenants and laborers to the injustice of their situations. It is unlikely that these millions will be drawn into small factories as in Ludhiana, or into a network of government and cooperative services as in Maharashtra, because it is the industrially and administratively backward states whose villages will now be commercializing. Jobs will depend on central investment. The central budget will not have funds to invest because it is not taxing the net incomes of commercial farmers, on whom the Congress party depends. Unemployed in the countryside, then, and on the pavements of the cities, will be rural poor, awakened to their own distress by Mrs. Gandhi.

In the cities the graduates of academic high schools and of colleges of arts and commerce, who are not only unemployed but in tragic measure unemployable, will continue to register at the employment exchanges. Their numbers are growing by about 1 million per year. It would be naive to assume that these two explosive forces would at some point combine. Nothing is more difficult than for disaffected urban middle-class youth to enlist followings among the rural dispossessed. We saw that it did not happen in Bihar under the relatively auspicious efforts of Jayaprakash Narayan. However, there is one set of conditions that could make it possible.

Subnationalisms

Some of the locally prospering regions of India will continue, based on the above projections, to advance relative to the rest. The lagging regions will come more keenly to feel their disadvantage as a grievance against the government of India, because Mrs. Gandhi has taken responsibility into her own hands; no state Congress leader can challenge her to meet his state's problems on the base of his own state support—she has systematically undermined it. Nor can he demonstrate that unless state grievances be met the Congress will lose to an opposition coalition in the next election. That threat is weak now; elections can be put off.

In the states where subnational identities were felt so sharply as to form the basis for parties, economic grievances will be translated into perceived subjugation. Delhi's rule will be considered colonialism in the Tamil country. If, as in Kashmir, central domination attempts to deal with subnationalism by largesse, then the backlash of the Hindi heartland, itself containing some of the most desperate areas of impoverished subsistence villages, will become a real possibility. Subnationalism, no less than nationalism, provides the atmosphere in which the disaffected students and the desperate rural poor can unite in rebellion. We can foresee the principal triggering event. Whenever, after four or five years, the monsoon fails over great reaches of the subcontinent, driving the starving into the cities and simultaneously closing the factories for want of electric power, agricultural raw materials, and rations for mill workers at prices they can pay, then the brittle system will fail.

A national leader, however powerful, can be judged fairly only upon his or her exercise of options actually opened to him by history. The dual nature of the Indian constitution did afford Mrs. Gandhi a choice in 1975. She could have continued to govern through institutions of defined powers testable in the courts. She bears responsibility for choosing the constitutional alternative, to rule by executive decree and unilateral punishment.

In this chapter's longer perspective, however, no prime minister could have continued long under the democratic rules of the constitution without rebuilding incompetent and overloaded institutions. Mrs. Gandhi's graver responsibility in history is thus her neglect of structural reforms, at least to her party and her bureaucracy, in the years 1971 and '72 when she had full control of the course of Indian politics. The task was extraordinarily difficult (perhaps greater than M.K. Gandhi's reorganization of the Indian National Congress in

1920), but she had herself diagnosed the problem. Her appeal to the country might have been: "We will get rid of poverty *if* we all work productively, and *if* we rebuild our national institutions." Invoking the authoritarian provisions of the constitution cannot spare her the consequences of that nondecision. Those provisions were suitable to hold an empire, not to govern several hundreds of millions who have been taught that their poverty is unjust.

Now that Mrs. Gandhi no longer shares power, thus responsibility, with anyone, it seems likely that another failure to deliver results will discredit entirely civil rule from Delhi. A breakdown of domestic order, moves toward secession, military rule—one perhaps creating the occasion for another—may result. That is speculation. The observable fact is that the constitution no longer constrains Indian politics with the firmness emerging forces require. The firmness that came from the conviction that the nation guided itself on right principles is no more. Now it is Indira Gandhi's India.

Political indeterminacy is of uncommon significance in the case of India because of the indeterminacy we have noted in this chapter of social forces and cultural norms. Democracies have been established, hitherto, by men who held "these truths to be self-evident" or shared so closely the experienced abuses of authority that they were prepared, step by step, to eliminate them. Communist systems differ profoundly one from the other, but their strength and creativity appears, analogously, to vary with the national commonness of the oppression they set out to fight and the authenticity in the national culture of the principles on which that oppression is challenged. In all these cases shared beliefs concerning society-wide changes shaped political systems.

In India, even in the Gandhian phase of the nationalist movement, politics held a greater share of the initiatives. Whether we consider the territorial extent of the national community or the drawing of villages into the large-scale web of interdependence, it is politics that has been guiding society. The same is true of the cultural basis of authority. For more than a generation, leaders have attained respect upon the spreading popular belief, "We chose him; he has to obey the same rules that bind us." But Indira Gandhi saw deeply enough into the hearts of her countrymen to perceive there, still, the old contrary sentiment, "Who is invulnerable must be obeyed." Because the state was the nursery of an emergent society, dissolving the certainties of the constitution unsettles the existence of the nation. Because the experiences of politics, agreed upon by a tiny band of nationalist leaders, were teaching the people which, among unreconciled views toward authority, was right, inconstancy in the use of the constitutional alternatives threatens legitimacy itself.

Of course, Indian society may, by 1975, have attained more coherence than it manifested. The principles of government by consent may have captured the minds of humble people to a degree they have not shown—the minds, for instance, of the nearly 3 million men and women who now hold elective office in the *panchayat* bodies of village India. Alternatively, it may be that the rural poor, betrayed again by promises from Delhi, will take the enormous risks of determining their own political futures as a class. If either of these potentials exists the fate of the country might be taken from the hands of one prime minister by the people, or most of them. But if either potential exists it is out of sight beyond a dusty horizon.

NOTES

[1] An eloquent example is an address by M. C. Chagla, once chief justice of the High Court of Bombay, then successively foreign minister and education minister in the cabinets of Nehru, Shastri, and Indira Gandhi, opening the All-India Civil Liberties Conference in Ahmedabad, October 12, 1975 (printed in India by Citizens for Democracy, no place or date indicated).

[2] *Nationalism and Social Communications*, 2nd ed. (Cambridge, Mass.: M.I.T. Press, 1966), p. 164.

[3] *The Political Economy of Growth* (New York: Monthly Review Press, 1957), p. 222.

[4] Ibid., p. 226.

[5] Barrington Moore, Jr., *Social Origins of Dictatorship and Democracy* (Boston: Beacon Press, 1966), chap. 6.

[6] Marx wrote on "the stationary character of this part of Asia," June 14, 1853, in Karl Marx and Frederick Engels, *Selected Correspondence* (Moscow: Foreign Language Publishing House, 1956), p. 102. See also K. Marx, *Capital*, ed. F. Engels (New York: International Publishers, 1967), vol. 1, pp. 216, 332-34.

7 André Béteille, *Studies in Agrarian Social Structure* (Delhi: Oxford University Press, 1974), pp. 169-70, 189.

8 Ibid., pp. 138-9, 174-86.

9 *India's Green Revolution: Economic Gains and Political Costs* (Princeton, N. J.: Princeton University Press, 1971).

10 "The Ecology of Peasant Communism in India," *American Political Science Review* 65 (March 1971): 145-49.

11 "Political Parties of the Radical Left in South Asian Politics," in *Radical Politics in South Asia,* ed. Paul Brass and Marcus F. Franda (Cambridge, Mass.: M.I.T. Press, 1973), pp. 95-97.

12 We follow Myron Weiner's classification, considering urban places of 50,000 or more people as unmistakably urban in political behavior. Myron Weiner and John Osgood Field, "India's Urban Constituencies," *Comparative Politics* 8 (Jan. 1976): 185.

13 *The Bhagavad-Gita,* ed. R. C. Zaehner (London: Oxford University Press, 1969), p. 394. The prescription here (in chap. 18, verse 47), is substantially repeated from chap. 3, verse 35. Interpolations are Zaehner's.

14 Here I follow the account, somewhat different in tone from Bhabani Sen Gupta's in chap. 6 above, given by Marcus Franda, "Radical Politics in West Bengal," in *Radical Politics in South Asia,* pp. 207-16.

15 Samuel Huntington, *Political Order in Changing Societies* (New Haven: Yale University Press, 1968), pp. 298-302.

16 Editorial, *Economic and Political Weekly* 10 (Oct. 25, 1975): 1671; confirmed in India, Planning Commission, *The Fourth Five Year Plan Mid-Term Appraisal,* vol. 1, (New Delhi: The Commission, 1971), p. 51. Updating through 1974-75 is from *Economic Times,* Feb. 11, 1976.

17 India, Planning Commission, *Fourth Five Year Plan*, p. 38.

18 Editorial, *Economic and Political Weekly* 10 (Nov. 22, 1975): 1794.

19 A sound overview of the situation is George Rosen, *Peasant Society in a Changing Economy: Comparative Development in Southeast Asia and India* (Urbana: University of Illinois, 1975), chap. 6. Untaxed, the rural surplus goes partly into holding grain off the market, thus doubly burdening the economy. The need to tax agricultural surplus has been pointed out for decades; it is reiterated in India, Planning Commission, *Draft Fifth Five Year Plan, 1974-79,* vol. 1. (New Delhi: The Commission, 1973), p. 59, which is the source of the 1 percent figure. The want, however, is of control of the party at the grass roots.

20 Huntington, *Political Order,* p. 290.

21 Figure of high school graduates and matriculates from Census of India,

1971, series I, part II, *All India Census Tables Estimated from a One Per Cent Sample* (Delhi: Manager of Publications, 1972), table IIIA. Unemployed from *Economic Times,* Feb. 10, 1976. A reliable sample survey of urban unemployment is, unfortunately, nine years old: National Sample Survey, *Twenty First Round, July 1966 to June 1967, Number 181, Urban Labour Force* (Delhi: Manager of Publications, 1971).

22 Indian Institute of Public Opinion, *Monthly Public Opinion Surveys,* 13 (Nov. 1972), tables following p. 14. The projection from this survey to the whole urban population gives us 2.8 million unemployed among literate youth. This could be reconciled with the figure derived from employment exchanges.

23 Census of India, 1971, Series I, India, Part VII (i), *Degree Holders and Technical Personnel* (Delhi: Controller of Publications, 1974); and *All India Census Tables Estimated from a One Per Cent Sample,* table IIIA.

24 India, Education Commission, *Report, 1964-66: Education and National Development* (Delhi: Manager of Publications, 1966), p. 537. This entire "Minute of Supplementation" is remarkable for its foresight.

25 Robert G. Wirsing, "Associational 'Microarenas' in Indian Urban Politics," *Asian Survey* 13 (April 1973): 408-20.

26 Huntington, *Political Order,* pp. 369-71.

27 Weiner and Field, "India's Urban Constituencies." The CPML did not contest elections.

28 Davydd J. Greenwood, *The Political Economy of Peasant Family Farming,* Rural Development Occasional Paper no. 2 (Ithaca, N.Y.: Cornell University, Center for International Studies, 1973), p. 6.

29 This is parallel to, but unfortunately requires slightly different criteria than, the classification of districts based on development criteria by the 1961 Census Commissioner, Ashok Mitra. Census of India, 1961, vol. I, part I-A (i, ii), *India: Levels of Regional Development in India* (Delhi: Manager of Publications, 1965, 1966).

30 Chicago: University of Chicago Press, 1956. The edition cited here was republished, 1960, together with *The Little Community.*

31 Redfield, *Peasant Society and Culture,* p. 27.

32 I elaborated this explanation to show why the much less radical transformations assumed by the community development programs of South Asia in the 1950s were not producing the predicted effects in the villages. See "The Village and Development Administration," in *Spatial Dimensions of Development Administration,* ed. James J. Heaphey (Durham, N. C.: Duke University Press, 1971), chap. 2.

33 See note 3 of his chapter.

34 A penetrating survey of the sources of credit available to Indian farmers in the early 1950s showed that the average loan from cooperatives per large landholding family (cultivating an average of twenty-six acres) was twenty-one rupees. For the three-acre farmers (who perhaps needed low-interest loans more desperately), the average loan from cooperatives was less than two rupees. Reserve Bank of India, All-India Rural Credit Survey, Committee of Direction, *The General Report,* vol. 2 (Bombay: Reserve Bank, 1954), p. 234.

35 Reserve Bank, *General Report,* vol. 2, p. 278. For a more recent confirming assessment, see "Tale of Three Surveys" (editorial), *Economic and Political Weekly* 10 (special no., Aug. 1975): 1227.

36 The best picture of the *patwari* and his records is in Oscar Lewis, *Village Life in Northern India* (Urbana: University of Illinois Press, 1958), Appendix. The effect on land-ceilings legislation of reliance on the *patwari* for records of rights in land was neatly put by the economist Raj Krishna of Jaipur University five years ago: "There will be no *recorded* surplus to redistribute" (lecture at H. C. Mathur Institute of Public Administration, Jaipur, 1970).

37 A brief, but incisive, essay on the sociology of knowledge of the Indian peasant village is Bernard S. Cohn's "Notes on the History of the Study of Indian Society and Culture," in *Structure and Change in Indian Society,* ed. Milton Singer and Bernard S. Cohn (Chicago: Aldine, 1968), pp. 18-25.

38 Oscar Lewis, *Village Life in Northern India,* struck the hardest blow. As optimism about community development projects waned, many government policy makers accepted the concept of the village as dividing into factions under the stress of development programs. First was the Reserve Bank, *General Report,* vol. 2, chap. 5, incorporating the anthropologists' findings into its report.

39 In what seems to me the most illuminating piece of social science writing on factions in village politics, Ralph W. Nicholas suggests that institutions of land tenure—*zamindari, ryotwari, mahalwari*—predispose villages to horizontal or vertical lines of cleavage. Yet, in keeping with his definition of politics as "organized conflict over public power," and not also authority constraining conflict, he does not introduce the undisputed system of control over land among the "rules of politics" that define "the extent of political activity." See his "Structures of Politics in the Villages of Southern Asia," in *Structure and Change in Indian Society,* ed. Singer and Cohn, chap. 11, especially pp. 245-56. On the other hand, at a more modest level of generalization, Ralph H. Retzlaff concluded his study of *panchayat* elections in an Uttar Pradesh village north of Delhi with the

realistic observation that redistributive decisions of land tenure were beyond the powers with which villagers were prepared to entrust *panchayats.* Retzlaff, *Village Government in India: A Case Study* (Bombay: Asia Publishing House, 1962), pp. 119-20, 124.

[40] Combining the extension of interdependencies, in Karl W. Deutsch, "Social Mobilization and Political Development," *American Political Science Review* 55 (Sept. 1961): 494, with the concept of becoming participant, in J. P. Nettl, *Political Mobilization: A Sociological Analysis of Methods and Concepts* (London: Faber, 1967).

[41] Interaction of individual participants in this struggle is dramatically portrayed for a Ludhiana village by Richard Critchfield, *The Golden Bowl Be Broken, Peasant Life in Four Cultures* (Bloomington: Indiana University Press, 1973), chap. 3.

[42] Rosen, *Peasant Society,* p. 183.

[43] Donald B. Rosenthal, "From Reformist Princes to Cooperative Kings," *Economic and Political Weekly* 8 (May 19): 903-10; ibid. (May 26): 951-56; ibid. (June 2): 995-1000.

[44] Ron Herring and I develop this view of Kerala in "The Political Conditions of Land Reform: Kerala and Maharashtra," in *Peasants and Land Reform in South Asia*, ed. Robert E. Frykenberg (New Delhi: Orient Longmans, forthcoming).

[45] In two landmark articles: "India's Political Idioms," in *Politics and Society in India*, ed. Cyril H. Philips (London: George Allen and Unwin, 1963), pp. 133-54; and "Behaviour and Ideas in Political India," in *Constitutionalism in Asia*, ed. Richard N. Spann (Bombay: Asia, 1963), pp. 74-91.

[46] "India: Two Political Cultures," in *Political Culture and Political Development,* ed. Lucian W. Pye and Sidney Verba (Princeton, N. J.: Princeton University Press, 1965), chap. 6.

[47] Morris-Jones, "Behaviour and Ideas," pp. 88-89.

[48] Ashis Nandy, "The Culture of Indian Politics: A Stock Taking," *Journal of Asian Studies* 30 (Nov. 1970): 69.

[49] Ibid., especially pp. 64-66. The whole essay is must reading for one questioning the earlier "two cultures" thesis. For somewhat startling evidence of the acceptance of one-party rule (51 percent of a Punjab college sample agreed or strongly agreed to it as against 27 percent who disagreed more or less strongly), see Yogendra K. Malik and Jesse F. Marquette, "Democracy and Alienation in North India," *Journal of Politics* 37 (Feb. 1975): 44.

50 Ronald P. Formisano, "Deferential-Participant Politics: The Early Republic's Political Culture, 1789-1840," *American Political Science Review* 68 (June 1974): 473-87.

51 Selig Harrison, *India: The Most Dangerous Decades* (Princeton, N. J.: Princeton University Press, 1960).

52 Robert Melson and Howard Wolpe, "Modernization and the Politics of Communalism: A Theoretical Perspective," *American Political Science Review* 64 (Dec. 1970): 1122.

53 Ibid., 1123-38.

54 This is the thesis of Thomas E. Hendrick, discussing in part the language crisis. "Crises and Continuity: India in the Mid-1960's," in *Crisis, Choice and Change, Historical Studies of Political Development,* ed. Gabriel A. Almond, Scott C. Flanagan, and Robert J. Mundt (Boston: Little, Brown, 1973), chap. 9.

55 A quite different case might be made against the semisecret, semimilitary organization within the Jan Sangh, the Rashtriya Swayamsevak Sangh (RSS). A protracted parliamentary or judicial investigation of the charges that the RSS incites anti-Muslim violence would have served to differentiate the mixed tendencies within the Jan Sangh. Blanket condemnation of what is, in part, a championship of Hindi-language cultural aspirations merely deepens the slowly accumulating sense of grievance.

56 Uma Vasudev, *Indira Gandhi, Revolution in Restraint* (Delhi: Vikas, 1974), pp. 534-35.

57 Village level workers are told, not asked, what their villagers can do. See the diary of one V. L. W., in S. C. Dube, *India's Changing Villages* (London: Routledge and Kegan Paul, 1958), Appendix.

58 Comprehensive recommendations for restructuring the civil service were made at the start of Mrs. Gandhi's prime ministership. Resisted by the IAS, they have been shelved. Among many reports, see India, Administrative Reforms Commission, *Report of the Study Team on Personnel Administration;* and, by the same commission, *Report on Personnel Administration.* Both were published in Delhi: Manager of Publications, 1969.

59 Aristide R. Zolberg, *Creating Political Order: The Party States of West Africa* (Chicago: Rand McNally, 1966).

Index

Akali Dal, 6, 157
Ali, Sadiq, 43
Allahabad, home in, 247
Ambedkar, 40, 43, 62
Amery, Leo S., secretary of state, 45, 47, 51, 53, 59, 61
Ananda Marg, 21
Andhra Pradesh, 106, 109, 112, 155, 156, 173, 190
Assam, 107

Bahuguna, 173
Bangladesh, 18, 29, 106, 113, 178, 214, 222, 229-30
Bansi Lal, 226
Barooah, D. K., 96, 102, 104, 142, 172
BBC, 45, 64
Bharatiya Lok Dal (BLD), 5, 10, 13
Bhave, Vinoba, 188
Bhoodan (land gift) movement, 9, 187-89, 287
Bhushan, Shashi, 104
Bhutto, Z. A., 221
Bihar agitation, 1974-75, 8-11, 51, 84, 104, 107, 109, 112, 155-56, 172-73, 184-99, 289, 294
Birla, K. K., 125
Black money, 24, 85, 130, 139
Bonus of Industrial Workers, 171
Bose, Subhas Chandra, 63, 210-11

Brezhnev, Leonid, 166, 167
Bureaucracy, 67-89, 287
  resignation in protest, 74
  and village society, 287-89

Cabinet, 217
Chagla, M. C., 302
Chandra Sekhar, 32-33, 260
Chaudhury, Mohinder Mohan, 110
Chavan, Y. B., 104, 116, 172, 229
China, relations with, 231
Civil service. See Bureaucracy
Civilian control over the military, 216-20, 225-31
Class conflict, 277-78
Communist Party of India (CPI), 11, 21, 103, 136, 153-75, 280, 283
  All-India Trade Union Congress (AITUC), 157
  naxalite, 21
  New Age, 174
Communist Party of India (Marxist) (CPM), 6, 10, 13, 34, 81, 153-75, 157, 182, 208, 227, 292, 297
  Center of Indian Trade Unions (CITU), 157
Communist Party of India (Marxist-Leninist) (CPML), 153-55, 158-59, 163-64, 175, 190-91, 279-80

309

Company Law (1956), 129
Congress Forum for Socialist Action, 103-4, 172
Congress party, 11, 38, 42, 46, 48, 55, 78, 89, 95, 98, 106-8, 110-11, 114, 132, 157, 168-69, 173, 254, 257, 259, 265, 300
  All-India Congress Committee (A.I.C.C.), 38, 48
  candidate selection, 106
  Central Election Committee, 95, 97, 99
  district congress committees, 98
  grass roots, 89
  Indian National Trade Union Congress (INTUC), 38, 157
  members, 107-8
  organization of, 258
  in Parliament, 111, 114
  Parliamentary Board, 95, 97, 98, 100, 259
  Pradesh congress committees, 98
  president of, 255-58
  relations with CPI, 168-69
  state leaders, 300
  Syndicate (bosses), 110
  Working Committee, 42, 46-47, 55, 95, 97
  Youth Congress, 173, 254, 265
Congress party (Old), 5, 10, 11, 13, 134, 153, 171
Constitution of India, 13, 15, 16, 33, 198, 208, 216-17, 255
  article 352, 16, 33
  federal allocations in, 198
  president's rule in Kerala, 255-56
  provisions for military, 216-17
  Thirty-ninth Amendment, 15
Corruption, 24-25, 80
Courts, local, 201
Cripps Mission, 39, 43, 45, 51

Dandekar, V. M., 183
Dange, S. A., 157, 171
Defense of India Act and rules, 18, 42, 46, 54, 56
Desai, Hitendra, 117

Desai, Morarji, 5, 10, 13, 38, 242, 258, 259, 265
Dhan, Ram, 103
Dharia, Mohan, 7, 12, 18, 33, 103, 261
Dharma, 75-77, 278-79
Dikshit, Uma Shankar, 104, 116, 172
Dravida Munnetra Kazhagam (DMK), 6, 13, 22, 157, 295

East Bengal, 279
Economic program (twenty points), 22-27, 83-88, 138, 143, 199
  ceilings on land holdings, 25
  moratorium on debts and small farmers, 25
Education Commission, 1966, 283
Emergency, proclamation of, 12, 17, 82
  bureaucracies in, 82
  jailing of politicians, 12
  jailing without trial, 17
Erikson, Erik, 249, 252, 259, 260

Federation of Indian Chambers of Commerce and Industry (FICCI), 131. 132, 140

Gandhi, Feroze, 20, 252-53
Gandhi, Indira, 1, 3, 6, 11, 19, 27, 28, 81, 94, 114, 132, 153, 167, 207, 228, 241
  appeal of conviction, 3
  control of the Congress party, 98-100, 110-15
  control of executive offices, 100-102
  corrupt election practices, 1-4, 114
  deinstitutionalization of politics by, 117-20, 298, 300-301
  executive dominance, concept of, 81
  industry, policies toward, 138-45
  and the military, 207-8, 227-32

personal character of, 241-67
preliminary Supreme Court order,
    6
rationale for emergency, 27-30
retention of prime ministership, 4,
    12, 116
socialism, 28
Gandhi, M. K., 27, 40, 43, 49, 54,
    56, 58, 135, 210, 300
Gandhi, Rajiv, 264
Gandhi, Sanjay, 86, 102, 141, 242,
    253, 264, 265, 294
Ganesh, K. R., 103
Garibi hatao, 1971 election issue,
    25, 86, 134
Giri, V. V., 101
Gopalan, A. K., 179, 292
Goray, N. G., 15
Green Revolution, 131, 159, 279,
    286, 291
Greenstein, Fred, 260
Gujarat, state election in, 5-6, 8,
    26, 84, 89, 107, 109, 111, 113,
    129, 173, 190

Harayana, 104, 117
Harijan, 42-43, 44, 49, 63
Himalayan border war, 1962, 221
Hutchins, Francis G., 65

India, constitution of, 300
India, government of (British),
    37-66
Indian Administrative Service (IAS),
    70, 74, 75, 298
Indian Army, British, 214
Indian Civil Service (ICS), 70, 75,
    214
Indian Foreign Service, 74
Indian Military Academy, 215
Indian National Army (I.N.A.) of
    World War II, 210
Industry, private sector, 85, 125-46
Inflation, 23

Jamaat-i-Islami, 21

Jammu and Kashmir, 106, 107
Jan Sangh, 5, 8, 10, 11, 13, 21,
    153, 164, 171, 192, 227, 229,
    284, 295
Janata (People's) Front, 5-6, 26
Jinnah, Mohammad Ali, 39, 40, 62

Kamaraj, K., 96, 117
Kamaramangalam, Mohan, 103
Kant, Krishan, 103
Kanthamma, Lakshmi, 33
Kapoor, Yashpal, 3
Kaul, B. N., 218
Kerala, 104, 109, 118, 155, 159,
    160, 165, 170, 173, 174, 190,
    256, 291
Kerala Congress, 160
Khan, Ayub, 265
Khanna, B. S., 74
Khilafat movement, 63
Khosla, G. D., 72
Kidwai, Rafi Ahmad, 44
Kisan sabhas (peasant organiza-
    tions), 158-59, 192
Konar, Harekrishna, 158, 160
Krishna Iyer, Justice V. R., 2-5, 30
Krishna Menon, V. K., 218, 226,
    251

Labor disputes, 24
Lal, Bansi, 117
Land reforms, 181, 185-87
  Bihar ceilings legislation, 187
  Bihar Land Reforms Act, 1950,
    185-86
Lasswell, Harold, 242, 266
Linguistic states, 295-96
Linlithgow, Lord, viceroy, 45, 51,
    53, 54, 59, 61
Litigation involving rights in land,
    201

Madhya Pradesh, 104, 107, 117
Maharashtra, 107
Maintenance of Internal Security
    Act (M.I.S.A.), 18, 34

Malaviaya, K. D., 103
Manipur, 190
Maoism. *See* Communist Party of India (Marxist-Leninist), 158
Marxist theory, 277-78
Mazumdar, Charu, 158-59
Military ideas, 209-13
Military institutions, 213-51
  aid to the civil, 222-25
  army, 219
  chief of the army staff (COAS), 218
  Chiefs of Staff Committee, 219
  National Cadet Corps, 225
  officer corps, 217
  ordinance factories, 220
  regional commands, 219
Monopoly and Restrictive Trade Practices (MRTP) Act (1969), 133, 141
Morrison, Herbert, 73
Muslims, 39
Mysore, 106

Naga rebels, 230
Naik, V. P., 110
Namboordiripad, E. M. S., 292
Narora, 22
National Herald of Lucknow, 42, 44
Nationalization, 133
Narayan, Jayaprakash, 7-13, 37-38, 50, 113-14, 153, 164, 188, 193-94, 203, 207-8, 227, 242, 295, 299
Naxalite movement. *See* Communist Party of India (Marxist-Leninist), 155, 192
Nayar, Kuldip, 19
Nehru Forum, 104, 172
Nehru, Jawaharlal, 8, 43, 54, 80, 101, 155, 209, 244, 246, 256-57, 262, 296
Nehru, Motilal, 247, 248-49, 250, 252
Nijalingappa, S., 96

Nixon, Richard, M., 241-243
North East Frontier Agency (NEFA), 221
Nuclear test, 212

Orissa, 104, 173, 190
Oxford University, 250-51

Pai, T. A., 104-41, 142
Pakistan, 18, 39, 214, 218, 222, 224, 229, 263
Panchayati raj, 9, 79, 118, 288-89, 292, 298
Pandit, Vijayalakshmi, 244, 246
Parliament of India, 4-7, 14, 17, 19, 20-21, 102, 117, 154, 171, 224
  communist parties in, 154
  Congress party in, 7, 102
  Lok Sabha, 6, 14, 21
  monsoon session, 1975, 7, 14
  Public Accounts Committee, 224
  Rajya Sabha, 14, 20
  Supreme Court, 14
Patel, Sardar, 127
Patna, 11, 51
Peasantry. *See* Rural poor, 182
Pillai, N. Raghavan, 71
Police, 11, 17, 197, 224
  Border Security Force, 11, 224
  central forces, 17, 18
  central reserve, 11, 224
  Indo-Tibetan Force, 224
  local, 197
Praja Socialist Party (PSP), 103
Prasad, Rajendra, 43
President of India, 14, 16, 100
  Fakhruddin Ali Ahmed, 14
Press censorship, 20
  preindependence, 41-44
Preventive Detention Act, 72
Prime minister, 217, 226, 253
Provincial Armed Constabulary, 224
Punjab, 72, 107, 190

Quit India Resolution, 49-50, 58, 61

Rae Bareli, 3
Raina, T. N., lieutenant general, 218
Raj Narain, 3
Rajagopalacharia, C., 40, 43
Rajah, 40
Rajasthan, 104, 107, 111, 190
Ram Dhan, 7, 32-33
Ram, Jagjivan, 96, 101, 104, 116, 172, 226, 229
Ramaswamy Aiyar, Sir C. P., 52, 62
Rao, Rajeshwara, 172
Rashtriya Swayam Sevak Sangh (RSS), 21, 284
Ravi, Vayalar, 103
Ray, Siddartha Shankar, 102, 281
Reddy, K. Brahmananda, 110
Roosevelt, Eleanor, 254
Roy, M. N., 43, 44, 62
Rural class conflict, 181-99
Rural class struggle, 160, 162-63
Rural poor, 181-99
Rural society, 284-92

Saksena, M. L., 52
Samyukta Socialist Party (SSP), 13
Sanjivayya, D., 96
Santiniketan, 250
Sarvodaya movement, 8
Satpathy, Nandini, 104, 172
Satyagraha, 7, 29, 244
Sekhar, Chandra, 103
Sharma, Dr. Shankar Dayal, 96
Shastri, Lal Bahadur, 81, 94, 132, 259
Shukla, S. C., 110, 117
Singh, Dinesh, 102
Singh, Swaran, 116-226
Singh, Tara, 62
Singh, Zail, 104
Socialism, 103, 127, 251, 261
Socialist Forum. See Congress Forum for Socialist Action
Socialist party, 5, 8, 11, 171
Soviet Union, 165-67
  relations with, 165-67, 254

State governments, 77
Strike, 1974 railway, 137
Student uprisings, 8-9
Subramaniam, C., finance minister, 96, 104, 141, 143
Sukhadia, Mohanlal, 110
Supreme Court, 1, 6, 15, 17, 19, 22, 115
  decision on Mrs. Gandhi's appeal, 16

Tamil Nadu, 18, 22, 84, 89, 117-18, 165, 172, 190, 263, 295, 300
Tata, J. R. D., 126, 127, 136
Tebhaga movement, 279
Tenants, 10
Tripathi, Kamlapati, 104
Tripura, 34, 190

Unemployment, educated, 281-83
Underground opposition, 84
United States, relations with, 219, 254
Uttar Pradesh, 42, 104, 117, 173, 224

Wars, 220
West Bengal, 18, 104, 107, 109, 155, 159, 160, 170, 173
Wilson, Woodrow, 241

Yadav, Chandrajit, 103